Meaning and the English Verb

Hituzi's Linguistics Textbook Series 1

Geoffrey Leech

Japanese Notes by
Harumi Sawada

Meaning and the English Verb

Third Edition

HITUZI SYOBO

MEANING AND THE ENGLISH VERB 03 Edition
by Geoffrey Leech
Copyright ©Pearson Education Limited 1971, 1987, 2004

Published in Japan by Hituzi Syobo Publishing
Japanese notes are written by ©Harumi Sawada

Reprint rights in the English and all rights in Japanese notes in this book are reserved; no part of this publication may be reproduced, stored in a retrieval system, or transmitted in any form or by any means, electronic, mechanical, photocopying, recording, or otherwise without the prior written permission of the publisher.

This edition of MEANING AND THE ENGLISH VERB 03 Edition is published by arrangement with Pearson Education Limited through The English Agency (Japan) Ltd.

Hituzi Syobo Publishing
Yamato bldg. 2F, 2-1-2 Sengoku Bunkyo-ku Tokyo, Japan
112-0011

phone +81-3-5319-4916 fax +81-3-5319-4917
e-mail: toiawase@hituzi.co.jp
http://www.hituzi.co.jp/
postal transfer 00120-8-142852

ISBN978-4-89476-562-7
Printed in Japan

はしがき

　本書は Geoffrey Leech 著 *Meaning and the English Verb*（第 3 版）(Pearson, 2004) の本文と「研究課題」から成っている。Leech は、この第 3 版への序文 (Preface to Third Edition) の中で英語法助動詞の変化に触れ、その変化の様相を示すために各種のコーパスからの用例を挙げたと述べている。挙げられている用例はどれもわかりやすく的を射たものであり、ゆきとどいた説明は、目から鱗が落ちる思いがする。本書を読みながら、読者はあらためてことばの精妙さに気づかされるであろう。筆者の知る限り、本書は言語学(特に、意味論)のテキストとして最も優れたものの 1 つである。

　本書で論じられているテーマに関して、プレゼンテーションをしたり、レポートを提出したり、さらには卒業論文を書いたりする際の参考になるように、先行研究を挙げたり、突っ込んで議論をしたり、専門書や文学テクストからの用例を詳しく分析したりした。本書を理解することはもとより大切であるが、それだけでは創造的営みとは言えないからである。

　英語であれ、日本語であれ、文の意味は話し手の心的態度と深く結び付いている。このことは、テンス、アスペクト、あるいはモダリティにおいて特に著しい。例えば、次の例はどのように異なるのであろうか。

(1) a.　Here comes the bus!
　　 b.　The bus comes here.
　　 c.　The bus is coming here.

(1a)はバスが来るのを目撃して話し手が瞬間的に発する文である。(1b)では、話し手は、バスの路線地図や時刻表など見ながら、バスがここを通ることを確認しているのかもしれない。(1c)の場合、バスは今やって来る途中だという意味のほかに、(場所の副詞 here があるために)このバスは、正規のバスではなく、今回だけ特別にチャーターされたバスの可能性もある。

　こうした意味の違いは、ややもすれば、軽視して気にとめないことが多い。しかし、たとえ、(1a)は(1b)の倒置形であることがわかっていても、両者の意味や使用文脈がどう違うのか、すなわち(1a)はなぜ倒置されなければならなかったのかという理由がわからなければ、英語の「心」が理解できたとは言えないであろう。

　本書で、Leech は次の文の違いに触れている。両者ともに、「ゴーギャン展に行きま

v

したか？」を意味している。

  （2）a. Have you visited the Gauguin exhibition?
    b. Did you visit the Gauguin exhibition?   （Leech（2004³: 38））

本書では、前者はまだ展覧会は開催されていることを、後者はそれがもう終わっていることを含意するとされている。日本語で説明するとすれば、「ゴーギャン展をやっているけど、もう行きましたか？」、「ゴーギャン展をやっていたけど、（開催期間中に）行きましたか？」となるであろう。こうした違いはどこから出てくるのであろうか。
 ある人がメガネを探しているとする。彼が次のようにつぶやいたとしよう。

  （3）a. Where did I put my glasses?
    b. Where have I put my glasses?   （Leech（2004³: 43））

この2つの文の意味の違いは話し手の視点とどのように関係しているのであろうか。Leechによれば、(3a)の場合、話し手の視点は自分がメガネを置いた時（＝過去）に置かれているという。その時を思い出そうとしているのである。一方、(3b)の場合には、置いた結果（＝完了）に視点があり、それが今どこにあるのかが重要だという。
 次のような文の意味の違いも興味深い。

  （4）a. I'm surprised that your wife objects.
    b. I'm surprised that your wife should object.   （Leech（2004³: 117））

(4a)のthat節の内容が「あなたの奥さんが反対していること」といった具合に「事実的」と捉えられているのに対し、法助動詞shouldを含む(4b)のthat節の内容は「あなたの奥さんが反対しているなんて」といった具合に「感情的」に捉えられている。助動詞は「助」ということばからもうかがえるように、ある意味では動詞という「主役」に対する「脇役」である。しかし、これは「名脇役」というべきであろう。なぜなら、助動詞1つで文のニュアンスが大きく違ってしまうからである。
 ことばの研究のおもしろさは、普段何げなく使っている表現を不思議だと感じることから生まれる。
 研究とは何であろうか。このことについて、すぐれた言語学者・国語学者、藤原与一氏は次のように述べている。

  （5） 研究の具体的方法を、ひとことで言えと言われたら、私はつぎのように答えます。
    研究は、分析することです。

はしがき

(藤原与一『言語研究—方法と方法論』三弥井書店(1988)p.31)

　ことばを分析する時、人はことばという対象に主体的、能動的にかかわっている。研究のゆくてには発見がある。発見は喜びであり、感動である。
　英語について考えることは、日本語への新たな興味につながっていく。例えば、(1a)に対して、日本語では、次のような「瞬間的な」表現がある。

　　（６）a.　あ、バスが来る！
　　　　　b.　あ、バスが来た！

両方とも、バス停でバスを待っていて、向こうにバスが見えた瞬間に使うことができる。(6a)の「る形」と(6b)の「た形」とはどのように違うのであろうか。(3)と比較して、次の例を見られたい。

　　（７）　夫：俺のメガネどこ？
　　　　　　妻：何言ってんの。そこにあるじゃない。
　　　　　　夫：なんだ、ここにあったのか。

物理的な状況から言えば、メガネは今その場所に存在している。それゆえ、メガネの存在を「ある」と表現するのか、「あった」と表現するのかは、話し手の視点の違いによるであろう。「あった」と表現するためには、通例、メガネを以前から探していたという意識がなければならない。
　(4)と比較して、次の例を見てみよう。

　　（８）　道理で妾が話したら変な顔をしていましたよ。貴方もよくないじゃありませんか。<u>平生あんなに親しくしている間柄なのに、黙って知らん顔をしているのは</u>。
　　　　　　　　　　　　　　　　　　　　（夏目漱石『こゝろ』）（下線筆者）

この文章中の

　　（９）　平生あんなに親しくしている間柄なのに、黙って知らん顔をしている<u>のは</u>。

という部分は次のように言い換えられる。

　　（10）　平生あんなに親しくしている間柄なのに、黙って知らん顔をしている<u>なんて</u>。

vii

(9)が「事実的」に響くのに対し、(10)は「感情的」に響く。それゆえ、(9)と(10)の関係は、(4a)と(4b)の関係と平行している。「研究課題」にことさら日本語への言及が多いのは、英語について考えることは、日本語の再発見につながっていくという思いからである。

　前書(第2版)の「注・研究課題」を執筆した際に数々の貴重な示唆をいただいた高司正夫、久島茂、新井永修、中安美奈子、岡田聡宏の各氏、そして、本書(第3版)の「研究課題」を執筆する際に多くの有益な助言をいただいた久保進、山田陽子、岡本芳和、長友俊一郎、澤田治、堀内夕子、内田真弓、澤田淳、片岡宏仁の各氏をはじめとするモダリティ研究会のメンバーの方々、ならびに、熊谷滋子、大村光弘、中村愛理、海野弘芳、原口教次、安本真由美、澤田奈央の各氏をはじめとする静岡言語学談話会のメンバーの方々と関西外国語大学 Richard Cleveland 准教授に感謝したい。なお、本書の第3版への序文の中で Leech 自身が述べているように、本書には、第2版にはなかった、英語の変化に伴う新しい言語事実が数多く付け加えられている。よって、本書の「研究課題」にも興味深い最新の研究成果をできるだけ多く盛り込むように努めた。

　前書(第2版)に注釈を付けて刊行したのが1994年であった。それから17年たち、第3版についても刊行することができたことをうれしく思う。

　末筆ながら、本書の企画を立て、絶えず励まし、援助していただいたひつじ書房社長松本功氏、専務松本久美子氏、編集部の細間理美氏のご厚意に対し心から感謝を申し上げたい。

2011年4月

澤田治美

Contents

Acknowledgements	vi
Key to Symbols	vii
Preface to Third Edition	viii
Introduction	1
1 Simple Present and Past Tenses	5
2 Progressive Aspect	18
3 The Expression of Past Time	35
4 The Expression of Future Time	55
5 The Primary Modal Auxiliaries	72
6 Modality Continued	90
7 Indirect Speech	107
8 Mood: Theoretical and Hypothetical Meaning	114
Further Reading	133
Index	138

Acknowledgements

I am very grateful

- to Valerie Adams for reading through and commenting on the earlier chapters of this book
- to the late Sidney Greenbaum for chapter-by-chapter comments, and for kindly undertaking some research on American English
- to R.A. Close, for a careful reading of the manuscript with a particular eye to the needs of the foreign learner
- to Paul James Portland for detailed observations from the point of view of the speaker of American English
- to Julia Youst and Susan Conrad for kindly helping me in advising on American English for the third edition
- to Nicholas I. Smith for reading and commenting on the third edition of this book, and in advising on the compilation of the Further Reading section. I am also grateful for the help Nicholas Smith has given me during 1999–2004, in researching recent grammatical change in English, concentrating on the verb
- the Arts and Humanities Research Board and the British Academy, for the funding of the research just mentioned

GNL
Lancaster University, 2004

Key to Symbols

'*will*:
: The bar ' indicates that the following syllable is stressed.

**It has rained tomorrow*:
: The asterisk * indicates an unacceptable or 'non-English' piece of language.

?*He is being ill:
: The *?** indicates that an utterance is marginally unacceptable.

(*have*) *got to*:
: The brackets are sometimes used to mark elements that can be omitted.

Simple Present:
: The initial capitals indicate a grammatical category.

'possibility':
: The quotation marks indicate a semantic category or explanation of meaning.

AmE: American English

BrE: British English

Preface to Third Edition

It is now over thirty years since the first edition of this book was published in 1971. Like the second edition (1987), this new edition has been thoroughly revised and updated to take account of relevant new research, which has been plentiful in recent years. The book has been thoroughly revised, but those who are familiar with the second or even the first edition will find little difficulty, I believe, in adapting to the changes made in the third edition.

Another kind of updating needed is that of keeping up with a language undergoing change. It is easy to assume that major grammatical areas of the language such as tense, aspect and modality remain the same from one generation to another, or at least change only very slowly. In part, the contrary seems to be the case. In the period 1961 to 1991, from corpus studies undertaken by Nicholas Smith and myself as well as others,[1] it appears that modal auxiliaries and some other constructions have been gradually changing. The modals, except for *will* and *would*, decreased significantly in frequency between the 1960s and the 1990s – and part of this was apparently due to the decline or obsolescence of certain uses of modals – for example, the *must* of obligation and the *may* of permission. Conversely 'semi-modals' such as *be going to* and *need to* have been increasing in frequency. In spite of evolving usage, there are of course many aspects of the grammar and semantics of the verb which show little or no change since 1971.

It seems strange, but perhaps not unsurprising in view of the above paragraph, that the major changes in this edition are similar in scope and grouping to changes made for the second edition in 1987: they stem particularly from what has been newly learned about modal auxiliaries and comparable constructions. Thus Chapters 1–4 of the book are comparatively unchanged: there are hundreds of minor changes and additions,

---

[1] See, for example, Leech (2003), Mair and Hundt (1995) and Smith (2001, 2003) in the Further Reading section at the end of the book.

Preface to Third Edition

but very few major ones. Chapter 5, on the other hand, has been more extensively rewritten, taking account of new work on the modal auxiliaries, as well as corpus findings. Incidentally, this chapter, which was twice as long as the average chapter in the earlier editions, has now been subdivided into two separate chapters, to make this part of the book more manageable for the user. Chapter 7 (previously numbered 6) is, like Chapters 1–4, relatively unchanged, but in Chapter 8 there have been many small revisions and some substantial revisions consequential on the new look at the modals. Exemplification has been improved. Hundreds of examples have been replaced or added, many new examples coming from electronic corpora such as the Freiburg-Lancaster-Oslo/Bergen Corpus of written English (1991), the Freiburg-Brown Corpus of written American English (1992), the Longman Corpus of American Conversation (early 1990s) and the British National Corpus (mainly 1991 ± 3 years), as well as more recent Internet sources. (The dates refer to the years when the corpus data was produced.) Usually the examples from corpus data have been adapted to make them simpler and more suitable for illustrative purposes.

As for section numbering, the first half of the book (up to §90) has section numbers corresponding to those of the second edition. With the addition of new material, however, the section numbering has been augmented slightly from here on, so that by the end of the book, we have reached §186, as compared with §177 in the previous edition. The Further Reading section (pp. 133–7) has been thoroughly updated and expanded.

Re-reading the book after thirty years with a new critical awareness, I noticed a stodgy, overly academic flavour in many of its sentences, and have taken this opportunity to make the style simpler and more congenial. These stylistic adjustments reflect another way in which the English language has been changing over the generation's time-span since this book's original publication.

GNL
Lancaster University,
March 2004

Introduction

1 Every language has its peculiar problems of meaning for the foreign learner. Many people would agree that in the English language, some of the most troublesome yet fascinating problems are concentrated in the area of the finite verb phrase, including, in particular, tense, aspect, mood and modality. The goal of this book is to describe these fields of usage systematically and in some detail for teachers and advanced students of English as a foreign or second language.

Much has already been written over the years on the semantics of tense, aspect, mood and modality in modern English. But experience has suggested that there is still a need for a book like this, which co-ordinates and makes more accessible what can be learned about these crucial areas of meaning. My aim is to explain systematically the semantics of the English finite verb phrase, without invoking discussions of syntax and morphology, and without assuming any specialist interest in linguistics. For this purpose, I have tried to rethink the subject in the light of recent research. In this third edition, I have also made use not only of recent advances in English language description, but of the resources of corpus linguistics, a field which involves analysis of computer databases of textual material, and which has grown in significance enormously over the past 20 years.

While stressing what is new in this book, I should also acknowledge what is old – that is, the extent to which I have drawn (as anyone writing in this field cannot fail to draw) on the extensive literature on tense, aspect and modality in English. I have avoided placing bibliographical references in the chapters of description: they would merely distract attention from the task in hand. But this obliges me here to make clear my general indebtedness to others, and to point out that the guide to Further Reading (pp. 133–7) gives a more precise indication of how this study has drawn on the work of previous writers.

2 As this book is essentially concerned with a set of grammatical forms in relation to a set of meanings, a reader might expect a presentation which works from the forms to the meanings like this:

1

INTRODUCTION

> CHAPTER 1 Meanings of the Present Tense
> CHAPTER 2 Meanings of the Past Tense
> CHAPTER 3 Meanings of the Perfect Aspect...

or else one that works from the meanings to the forms, like this:

> CHAPTER 1 Ways of expressing past time
> CHAPTER 2 Ways of expressing present time
> CHAPTER 3 Ways of expressing future time...

In fact, I have found it best (since in any case there is continuing need for reference back and forward from one section to another) to adopt a combination of these two approaches, grouping topics now according to form and now according to meaning. For example, Chapter 1 'Simple Present and Past Tenses' takes grammatical forms as its point of departure, while Chapter 4 'The Expression of Future Time', starts from meaning. What is lost in consistency here is, I feel, redeemed by the flexibility which makes it possible to bring together contrasts and similarities in whatever seems to be the most illuminating way. At the same time, for convenience of reference, there are summaries at the beginning of all chapters, and a full index at the end of the book.

3 In discussing the relation between grammar and meaning, we are faced with problems of terminology. Most of the grammatical categories that have to be discussed (Present Tense, Perfect Aspect, etc.) have labels which are derived from a characteristic feature of meaning, but which can be very misleading if they are used both as semantic and as grammatical labels. It is a well known fact, for instance, that the English Present Tense, although it refers mainly to the present time zone (see §5 below), can also refer to past and future time as well. To overcome this difficulty, I have made use of a typographical convention whereby formal grammatical categories are marked by initial capitals (Present Tense, etc.) to distinguish them from corresponding categories of meaning or reference (present time, etc.). Where necessary, single quotation marks are used to indicate that I am talking about meaning rather than form. Thus the following arrangement:

> Lightning can be dangerous. ('It is possible for lightning to be dangerous.')

shows a sentence together with its semantic gloss.

Grammatical terminology has been chosen with the goal of immediate intelligibility in mind. The term 'Tense' is used not only for the primary distinction of Present Tense and Past Tense, but also for the sub-categories Present Perfect Tense, Past Progressive Tense, etc. The term 'Aspect' is reserved for the primary categories of Perfect (*has eaten*) and Progressive (*is eating*) modification. In case terms are not found to be self-evident, the following table can be used as a guide to the grammatical terms of tense and aspect in the first three chapters. As the table shows, the expressions 'non-perfect', 'non-progressive' and 'ordinary' are used (wherever necessary) to denote forms unmarked for one aspect or the other. 'Simple' is used of forms unmarked for both aspects.

	(non-progressive)	Progressive Aspect
(non-perfect)	Simple Present Tense *they speak*	(ordinary) Present Progressive Tense *they are speaking*
	Simple Past Tense *they spoke*	(ordinary) Past Progressive Tense *they were speaking*
Perfect Aspect	(ordinary) Present Perfect Tense *they have spoken*	Present Perfect Progressive Tense *they have been speaking*
	(ordinary) Past Perfect Tense *they had spoken*	Past Perfect Progressive Tense *they had been speaking*

4 The type of English I will be describing can be called 'contemporary standard English'. But discrepancies between the most influential regional varieties – American and British English – as well as variations of style, are noted where they are important. Dialect variation in verb usage has not been widely investigated, but it appears that there are considerable differences, at least in terms of frequency, within the British Isles and the USA, and even between different age groups. This book therefore necessarily simplifies a rather more complex picture, and the labels 'BrE' (British English) and 'AmE' (American English) can at best be regarded as showing *typical* standard usage in their respective countries. For information about the English language, I have relied to a considerable extent on my own interpretations of examples as observed in recent and current language use. At the same time, I have referred to many recent studies, and have also made my own analyses of corpus data. Some of the examples I use are invented rather than borrowed from texts and dialogues, as it is of great value in this kind of study to have simple, self-explanatory, economical illustrations. However, I have also made wide use of corpus examples, that is, real examples from spoken and written discourse. These have often been simplified, to avoid creating unnecessary difficulties. The fact that this study has been read in manuscript by other native speakers of English, and has made use of research carried out on real language data, has provided a check on my own observations.

INTRODUCTION

5 In talking about time, tense and aspect it is often useful to use **time line** diagrams, showing progress in time as an arrow chain going from the left-hand side towards the right-hand side of the page:

→→→→→→→→→→→→→→→→→→→→→→→→→→→→→→
earlier   later

Events, states and habits (i.e. states consisting of a sequence of events) are shown as follows:

•   event
———— state
• • • • • • • • • • habit

A happening or situation in progress, as signalled by the Progressive Aspect (e.g. *is waiting*), is shown by a wavy line as follows:

∿∿∿∿

The present moment of time or a past moment of time as a point of reference is shown as a vertical line intersecting the time line as follows:

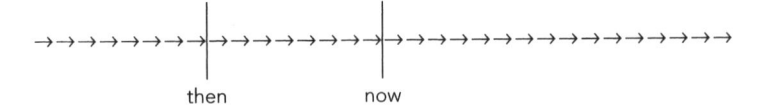

→→→→→→→→→|→→→→→→→→|→→→→→→→→→→→→→→→
              then   now

When thinking about 'present time' we can think of a period including the present time and extending indefinitely into the past and into the future. In this sense, 'present time' is potentially all-inclusive. On the other hand, 'past time' is limited by the fact that it cannot extend up to the present moment. Similarly, 'future time' is limited by the fact that it cannot extend back as far as the present moment:

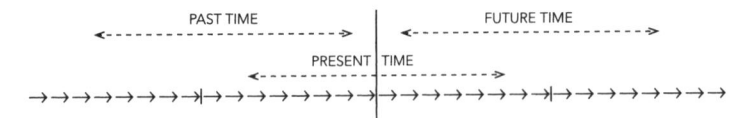

                    PAST TIME   FUTURE TIME
            ←---------------------→   ←---------------------→
                                 PRESENT | TIME
                                 ←-----------------→
→→→→→→→→→|→→→→→→→→→→→|→→→→→→→→→→→|→→→→→→→

However, in English the major formal distinction of Present and Past Tenses can be associated with two major TIME ZONES, 'past' and 'non-past', so that future time is subsumed under 'non-past'. This helps to explain why English, which does not have a Future Tense as such, uses Present Tense (or Present Tense auxiliaries such as *will* and *is going to*) to express future time (see further §§113, 139c, 150, 174).

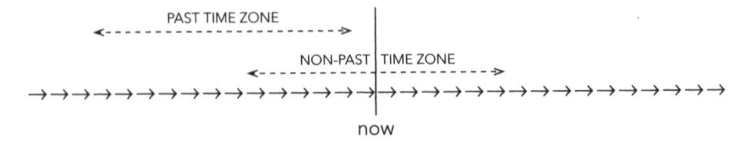

                    PAST TIME ZONE |
            ←-------------------------→
                                 NON-PAST | TIME ZONE
                                 ←-------------------------→
→→→→→→→→→→→→→→→→→→|→→→→→→→→→→→→→→→→→→
                                      now

CHAPTER 1

Simple Present and Past Tenses

6 introduction. SIMPLE PRESENT – STATE USE: *7* state present; *8* 'eternal truths'. SIMPLE PRESENT – EVENT USE: *9* event present; *10* comparison between event present and Progressive Present; *11* performatives. STATES AND EVENTS: *12* 'state verbs' and 'event verbs'. SIMPLE PRESENT – HABITUAL USE: *13* habitual or iterative present. SIMPLE PRESENT REFERRING TO PAST AND FUTURE: *14* referring to future; *15–17* historic present. SIMPLE PAST – NORMAL USE IN REFERENCE TO PAST TIME: *18* the happening takes place before the present moment, the speaker has a definite time in mind; *19* there is no clear 'state'/'event' contrast in the past; *20* simultaneous and sequential use of Past. OTHER USES OF THE SIMPLE PAST: *21* hypothetical use; *22* narrative past; *23* Past Tense referring to present. SIMPLE PRESENT – IMAGINARY USES: *24* imaginary present; *25* fictional use; *26* travelogues and instructions.

6 The distinction between the Present Tense and Past Tense in English is a prime example of how grammatical labels can both help and mislead us. It is true that there is a rough and partial correspondence between 'Present Tense' and present time, and between 'Past Tense' and past time. But the ways in which these labels fail to correspond with reality are also notable, as this chapter aims to show. In many ways, it would be better to call the Present Tense the 'Non-past Tense', as it can be used for future as well as present time (this will become clearer in Chapters 4 and 5). The parallelisms between what can be expressed by the Present Tense and by the Past Tense divide the sphere of temporal reference into two broad semantic time zones – the past and the non-past, as already suggested in our discussion in the Introduction. But in exploring the relation between grammar and meaning, as in other areas of specialist knowledge, it is generally better to stick with the familiar terms – knowing their deficiencies – rather than to seek out unfamiliar ones. This means sticking with Present and Past, rather than the less familiar terms such as 'non-past' and 'preterite'.

In all uses of the Present Tense, after all, there is a basic association with the present moment of time (the moment of speech). This association can be expressed as follows: 'The state or event has *psychological* being at the present moment'. It does not (as we see in §§14–17) exclude the possibility of the Present Tense having *actual* reference to a time other than the present. The Present Tense in special circumstances can refer to past and to future time exclusive of present time. In the 'historic present', it represents past events *as if* they were happening now. In the 'futurate present', it refers to future events regarded as *already planned or predetermined*.

We can start, however, with the more usual application of the Present Tense to present time – limiting discussion in this chapter to the Simple Present and Past Tenses.

Simple Present: 'state' use

7 The 'STATE' use of the Simple Present is found with verbs expressing a temporally stable state of affairs. It is also called 'unrestrictive' because it places no limitation on the extension of the state into past and future time:

> Honesty *is* the best policy. | War *solves* no problems. | How many languages *does* he *know*? | They *live* in Washington. | I *don't have* a TV.

However, limits to the duration of the state may be implied by an adverbial expression which underlines the 'presentness' of the period in question, so indicating a contrast with some other period:

> Crime is the best policy *these days*. | War *no longer* solves any problems. | *At present* they live in Washington. | *Just now* I don't have a TV.

The limits of the duration can also be implied by other factors, such as common sense or practical knowledge. For example, the length of time applicable to *Bambi* SUFFERS FROM *shortness of breath* is bound to be restricted to Bambi's life-span, and probably to a shorter period than that.

> a. **I have these shoes since I was in eighth grade* and **I have these shoes for years* are unacceptable because these expressions beginning with *since* and *for* identify a period of time leading up to the present moment. The Present Perfect tense is used in these cases: *I've had these shoes for years* (see §55).

8 The Simple Present is suitable for use in expressing 'eternal truths', and so is found in scientific, mathematical and other statements made 'for all time':

> Hydrogen *is* the lightest element. | Two and three *make* five. | Basmati rice *has* a sweet flavour.

Not surprisingly, it is also characteristic of proverbs:

> It *takes* two to tango. | No news *is* good news. | Time *flies*.

Geographical statements are likewise, for practical purposes, without time limit:

Rome *stands* on the River Tiber. | The Atlantic Ocean *separates* the New World from the Old.

These usages all follow from the definition of the state use of the Present in §7.

Simple Present: 'event' use

9 The EVENT use of the Simple Present contrasts with the STATE use in that it occurs with verbs expressing events, not states. It signifies an event REFERRED TO AS A WHOLE and viewed as simultaneous with the present act of speaking. Thus it typically refers to something which happens over a very short time: another name for it is the 'instantaneous present'. It normally occurs only in a few easily definable contexts – for example:

In sports commentaries: Larry O'Connell *calls* them together. The first bell *goes*... and they *get* into an untidy maul straight away. (Boxing) | Adams *intercepts, plays* it up-field. (Football)

In the patter or 'running commentary' of conjurors and demonstrators: Look, I *take* this card from the pack and *place* it under the handkerchief – like this. | Now I *put* the cake-mixture into this bowl and *add* a drop of vanilla essence.

The event present is particularly suitable for commentaries in real time, as there is a tendency for references to events to form part of a sequence: Event 1, then Event 2, then Event 3, etc. In most cases, the event probably does not take place *exactly* at the instant when it is mentioned: it is a question of subjective rather than objective simultaneity.

10 When there is no event sequence, the event present generally sounds inappropriately 'stagey' or theatrical. We can compare the following as two ways of describing the same action:

I *open* the cage. | I *am opening* the cage.

The second sentence, which contains a Progressive verb form, is a natural description in answer to the question *What are you doing?* But the first sentence is rather dramatic, because it implies the total enactment of the event just at the moment of speaking. If spoken, one would expect it to be accompanied by a gesture or flourish; in writing, it seems incomplete without an exclamation mark. The event use of the Present is generally the 'marked' or abnormal alternative to the Progressive Present, because there are few circumstances in which it is reasonable to regard an action as begun and completed at the very moment of speech.

a. However, the event present does occur exceptionally in ordinary speech in exclamations such as *Here* COMES *my bus!* and *Up we* GO!

MEANING AND THE ENGLISH VERB

b. The stagey quality of the event present is evident in its employment in old-fashioned theatrical language (not used in present-day English except in fun): *The bell tolls! He yields! The spectre vanishes!* etc.

c. It is significant that there is no event present question form *What do you do?* compared with the frequently heard question *What are you doing?* This is perhaps because by the time an instantaneous action has been observed and queried it is already in the past, whereas the Progressive allows for a time lag. (However, *What do you do?* can be used in a habitual sense, meaning 'What is your job?' – see §13 below.)

11 Another special use of the event present is in PERFORMATIVE utterances, normally with *I* or *we* as subject: e.g. *I beg your pardon*. Here the present event and the act of speech are simultaneous simply because they are identical; that is, the thing announced and the act of announcement are the same. Other examples are:

We *accept* your offer. | I *dare* you to say it! | I *deny* your charge. | I *say* the whole thing was kind of weird. | I *give* you my word. | I *refuse* to pay for that meal.

These PERFORMATIVE speech-act VERBS often express formal acts of declaration, in contrast to the Progressive forms *We are accepting your offer*, etc., which may merely report the speaker's present activity or future intentions. Performative verbs are also characteristic of more ceremonial contexts, such as

ship-launching: 'I *name* this ship Aurora.'

judge passing sentence: 'I *sentence* you to . . .'

card and board games: 'I *bid* two clubs.' | 'I *resign*.' | 'I *pass*.'

wills: 'I *revoke* all former wills . . .' | 'I *give* to Warwick College all my books . . .'

In these examples the word *hereby* could be inserted before the verb, to emphasise that the verb refers to the current act of speech or writing.

a. The performative acts discussed here can be extended to include expressions of wishes and condolences such as *We wish you every success* and *I send you my deepest sympathy*. Also, in very formal letters the verb *write* is sometimes used as a performative: *I write to inform you that* . . . (But in a more informal style *I am writing* . . . is preferred.).

b. Performatives rarely occur in the passive, but one example is *You're fired!* (used by a boss to dismiss an employee from his/her job): an utterance more likely to be found in comic-strip dialogue than in real life.

States and events

12 The contrast between STATES and EVENTS has already appeared in the distinction between the state and event uses of the Simple Present. It is time now to consider this contrast more carefully.

SIMPLE PRESENT AND PAST TENSES

The choice between 'state' and 'event' is inherent in all verbal usage in English. A state is undifferentiated and lacking in defined limits. An event, on the other hand, has a beginning and an end; it can be viewed as a whole entity. It can also make up one member of a sequence or plurality of happenings: a HABIT.

The difference between events and states is parallel to that between countable nouns and mass or uncountable nouns. Countable nouns can be made plural, as in *house/houses,* while mass nouns, such as *milk,* cannot. The distinction in nouns, however, is more clear-cut, because it is grammatically indicated by the plural ending. There are no such indicators of 'event' status in the verbal phrase. What is more, nouns (with the exception of words like *cake*) must normally be placed in one class or the other; whereas verbs are often neutral, and capable of switching from 'state' to 'event' or vice versa.

Putting it more plainly, 'state' and 'event' are semantic rather than grammatical terms. Strictly, we should not talk of 'state verbs' and 'event verbs', but rather of 'state' and 'event' meanings or uses of verbs. It would be inconvenient, however, to avoid the expressions 'state verb' and 'event verb' altogether. These useful labels are retained here, but it must always be remembered that they are *convenient labels*, for what would be more precisely designated 'verb being used to refer to an event' and 'verb being used to refer to a state'. Take the verb *remember* as an example:

> I suddenly *remembered* her name was Jane. | Oh, I *remember* the good old days.

In the first sentence *remember*, because it refers to the act of recall, is an 'event verb'; in the second it is a 'state verb', representing the notion of having something in one's memory. (Quotation marks will always be used with these two labels, as a reminder of their provisional status.)

The following are among the most frequent verbs typically used as 'STATE VERBS', listed in order of frequency:

> *be, have, know, want, mean, need, seem, like, include, believe, live, stand, consider, expect, require, continue, remain, understand, involve, hope, support, stay, contain.*

The following are among the most frequent verbs typically acting as 'EVENT VERBS', again listed in order of frequency:

> *do, say, get, make, go, take, come, give, find, tell, put, become, leave, ask, show, call, provide, turn, begin, bring, start, write, set, pay, meet, happen, offer, lose, open, reach, build, return.*

Verbs such as *keep, hold, think* and *feel* do not fit easily into either category, as they can easily switch between 'event' and 'state' according to the context. Also, it should not be supposed that these are the only two categories: 'event verb' and 'state verb' are the most general categories,

Simple Present: habitual use

13 A third use of the Simple Present, that of the HABITUAL (or ITERATIVE) USE, typically occurs with 'event verbs'. In fact, its relation to the event present is analogous to the relation of a plural to a singular noun. The habitual present represents a series of individual *events* which as a whole make up a *state* stretching back into the past and forward into the future. It thus combines aspects of the event and state uses:

```
An event: •      A state: ──────────      A habit: • • • • • • • • • •
TIME: →→→→→→→→→→→→→→→→→→→→→→→→→→→→→→→→→→→→→→→
```

We *don't go* out much (in the evenings). | I *buy* everything I *wear* from Marks & Spencer. | There's a lady down the road who *walks* with a stick. | I *take* lessons in self-defence. | Actions *speak* louder than words (a proverb). | If the temperature *falls* below 22°C, the yield of grain *decreases* sharply.

As the last two examples show, the habitual present resembles the state present in its suitability for 'eternal truths' of a scientific or proverbial nature. To emphasise the element of repetition and universality in the last two examples, we can paraphrase them: *Every time someone performs an action, it speaks louder than words do* and *On every occasion the temperature falls . . . the yield of grain decreases . . .*

As a way of interpreting 'event verbs', the habitual present is more common than the event present, which, as we saw in §9, is rarely found outside a few special contexts. Many verbs more or less have to be taken in an iterative sense, because the event they describe takes far too long to be envisaged as happening singly, once-and-for-all, at the moment of speech. *She walks to work*, for example, makes us think of an established habit (a series of repeated events), not just of a single event. In fact, few sentences are ambiguous in this respect. Sometimes a plural object helps to single out the habitual meaning:

He scores *a goal*. (event use)   single event: •

He scores *goals*. (habitual use)   repeated event: • • • • • • • •

On other occasions, an adverbial expression of frequency reinforces the notion of repetition:

I *generally/often/sometimes* get to bed very late. | She lectures here *most days / twice a week / every day*.

SIMPLE PRESENT AND PAST TENSES

Hence, even when the verb permits both event and habitual interpretations, often some other linguistic indication of repetition is there.

a. Despite the close link between 'event verbs' and the habitual use of the Present, the habitual present can also occur with 'state verbs' where the states have a limited time-span: *Many women* FEEL *fitter and healthier when they* ARE *pregnant*. The verbs *feel* and *be* here are 'state verbs', but in a general statement of this kind, they refer to a multiplicity of happenings at different places and times.

Simple Present referring to past and future

14 In addition to these three uses with reference to present time (i.e. time including the present moment), the Simple Present may refer to events or states realised in future time:

> I *retire* from work next month. | The train *leaves* at eight o'clock tomorrow. | Goalkeeper Stephen Pears *goes* into hospital tomorrow. | Racing on Saturday *starts* at 11 a.m. | See you there! We *begin* at 3.30. | Athena *inherits* the fabulous riches when she *reaches* 18.

This use is called the FUTURATE PRESENT, and will be discussed in relation to other means of indicating future time in §§103–5.

15 Also the Present Tense may be used in reference to the past. The use traditionally known by the term HISTORIC PRESENT is best treated as a storyteller's licence, whereby past happenings are portrayed or imagined *as if* happening at the present time. It is most evident where the Present Tense, with apparent incongruity, goes with an expression indicating past time:

> At that moment in *comes* a message from the Head Office, telling me the boss *wants* to see me in a hurry. | She *says*, 'I'm gonna smack you, right, come here', and she *gets* him and she *whacks* him in front of everybody, didn't she Robert?

The second example is typical of a highly coloured popular style of oral narrative, a style one would be more likely to overhear in a bar or a pub than in the lounge of an expensive hotel.

There is a close similarity between the strict historic present, described here, and the use of the Present to narrate fictional events, considered later (see §25).

a. In popular conversation, the verb *say(s)* and its synonym *go(es)* are very commonly used to report dialogue in the historic present. E.g.:

> So to shut the parents up – he SAYS, 'I'm going to marry you'.
> So I told her about the party – and she GOES, 'Are you going?' And I GO, 'Yeah'. And she said, 'I'll probably come.'

The verb *goes/go* meaning 'say(s)' is particularly common in the speech of young people. The past form *went* ('said') occurs much less frequently.

16 A different kind of historic present is found with 'verbs of communication' in such sentences as:

> Francesca *tells* me you're a champion skier. | (in an academic book) In 1888 Durkheim already *writes* that . . . | The editor *says* her newspaper has undergone considerable change. | The intellectuals in the nightclubs, we *learn*, can be spotted because they don't dance. | I *hear* the highway's flooded.

The verbs *tell*, *write* and *say* here refer to a message that seems to have taken place in the past, so we have reason to expect the Past or Perfect Tenses: *Francesca has told me* . . . ; *The editor said* . . . ; etc. However, it appears that the timing has been transferred from the initiating end to the receiving end of the message. The communication is still in force for those who have received it, and so the Present Tense is allowed. In a sense, what Durkheim wrote in 1888 'speaks' at the present time: its message is still there for whoever wants to read it. The verbs *learn* and *hear*, which refer to the receiving of the message, here refer rather to the state of *having received* the message. Thus *I hear the highway's flooded* can be replaced, with little change of effect, by *I understand* (= 'I have the information') *the highway's flooded*.

17 The following sentences illustrate a similar extension of the Present Tense to cover information which in strict historical terms belongs to the past:

> In *The Brothers Karamazov*, Dostoevsky *draws* his characters from sources deep in the Russian soil, not from fashionable types of his day. | Like Rubens, Watteau *is able* to convey an impression of warm, living flesh by the merest whiff of colour.

When discussing an artist's work, we feel justified in using the Present, because the work, and through it (in a sense) the artist, are still 'alive'. The whole career of a painter, writer or musician may, in fact, be viewed as a timeless reconstruction from the works themselves. Here there is almost free variation of Past and Present Tenses. The sole difference between *Brahms* IS *the last great representative of German classicism* and *Brahms* WAS *the last great representative of German classicism* is a difference of point of view: i.e. whether we prefer to think of Brahms as a composer still living through his compositions, or as a man who died in the nineteenth century. Subject to §17c, however, we do not have this choice in dealing with the purely biographical details of an artist's life: the Present Tense cannot be substituted for the Past Tense in *Brahms* WAS BORN *in Hamburg; Brahms* COMPLETED *his first symphony in 1876; Brahms* SPENT *the last 35 years of his life in Vienna*.

a. Free variation between Past and Present Tenses occurs also in cross-references from one part of a book to another: *The problem* WAS/IS *discussed in Chapter Two above*. For cross-references to a later part of a book, a similar free variation exists between Present and Future: *Later chapters* (*will*) *explore this topic in greater detail*. The author has the choice of whether to see his/her book as a whole, existing at the present moment (so that what is written on page 2 is just as much in present time as what is written on page 300); or to see it on a shifting time-scale, from the point of view of a reader who reads page 2 before reading page 300.

b. In newspapers, especially in headlines, the Simple Present is preferred (no doubt because of its brevity and vividness) to the Past Tense or Perfect Tenses as a way of announcing recent events: *Doctor attacked as he walks dogs*. As a further example, *Ex-champ dies*, a headline reporting the death of a former boxer, contrasts with the Past Tense found in the corresponding prose account: *Bill Turton, one-time holder of the British welterweight championship,* DIED *at his home in Chesterfield yesterday*. This 'headlinese' use of the Present Tense has something of the dramatic quality of the 'event present' (see §9).

c. Two minor extensions of the 'historic present' are (1) in captions accompanying illustrations (*Father O'Brien gives his first blessing*); and (2) in historical summaries, tables of dates, etc.: *1558 – The English lose Calais. Ferdinand I assumes the title of Holy Roman Emperor. Mary, Queen of Scots, marries the Dauphin, future Francis II of France.* Once again, the effect of the Simple Present here is to present a past event as if on a stage or TV screen in front of a present audience.

Simple Past: normal use in reference to past time

18 There are two elements of meaning involved in the commonest use of the Past Tense.

One basic element of meaning is: 'the happening takes place before the present moment'. This means that the present moment is excluded: *She worked as an executive secretary for five years* makes it clear that she no longer has that job (as contrasted with the Perfect: *She has worked as an executive secretary for five years*).

Normally another element of meaning is: 'the speaker has a definite time in mind'. This definite time in the past is often made explicit by an adverbial expression accompanying the Past Tense verb:

> She won the Pulitzer Prize *in 1988*. | *Once* this town was a beauty spot – now it's an industrial wasteland. | We visited Selfridges *last week*.

Both these aspects of Past Tense meaning are more fully discussed in connection with the Perfect Tenses in §§61, 63–4.

19 With the Past Tense, the difference between 'state' and 'event' is less important than it is with the Present Tense. In fact, as the Past Tense normally applies only to completed happenings, everything it refers to is in a sense an 'event', an episode seen as a complete entity. There is nothing in the past corresponding to an indefinitely extensive present state: whole lifetimes or even whole eras of civilisation may, in historical retrospect, appear as complete, unitary happenings:

> William Barnes *was born, lived,* and *died* in his beloved county of Dorset. | The water of the Nile *sustained* the prosperity of the Pharaohs for thousands of years.

MEANING AND THE ENGLISH VERB

Thus for the Simple Past Tense, there is no clear-cut contrast between 'event' and 'state' uses, corresponding to that between the event and state presents. There is, however, a distinction to be drawn between the unitary past above and the HABITUAL PAST, describing a repeated event (or state – cf. §13); an example of this is: *In those days the ghosts enjoyed Hallowe'en, and little children stayed indoors* (= '. . . used to enjoy . . . used to stay . . .'; see §85).

20 There is also a contrast between past events happening SIMULTANEOUSLY and past events happening IN SEQUENCE.

> Her mother *loved* and *worshipped* her. | She *addressed* and *sealed* the envelope.

The first sentence does not alter its meaning if the order of verbs is reversed (*worshipped and loved* . . .). But an alteration of the order of verbs in the second sentence suggests an alteration of the order in which the actions took place: *She sealed and addressed the envelope* usually means something different from *She addressed and sealed the envelope*. Sometimes, as in *She kissed and hugged us all*, it is not clear whether the happenings are meant to be at the same time or one after the other. When the happenings each last only a short time, however, it is more natural to regard them as stages in a sequence, especially in narrative contexts.

a. Other temporal relations between two neighbouring Past Tense forms are possible. For example, the first verb can refer to a later time than the second verb, if this is overtly signalled by a conjunction or adverbial expression, or made clear by our knowledge of history: *A stranger* CAME *to the house just after our son* WAS BORN; similarly (comparing the maritime achievements of Phoenicia and Portugal) *The Portuguese* LIVED *on the fringes of Mediterranean civilisation; the Phoenicians* HAD *the advantage of being in its midst*. The English language does not forbid this arrangement, although good style more frequently dictates the opposite ordering, or the use of the Past Perfect (see §§73–4).

Other uses of the Simple Past

21 The Past Tense can be used in certain dependent or subordinate clauses to express HYPOTHETICAL meaning:

> It's time we *took* a holiday. | If I *had* children, I would teach them good manners.

Discussion of this use, which is not concerned with past time, is postponed until §§169–74.

22 Two extensions of the normal past meaning have to be mentioned. First, because the Past Tense deals with past events, it is the natural form of the verb to use in narrative, whether the events narrated are true historical

SIMPLE PRESENT AND PAST TENSES

events or the fictional events of a novel. There has grown up a convention of using the Past for narrative even when the events described are supposed to take place in the future, as in science fiction:

> In the year AD 2201, the interplanetary transit vehicle Zeno VII *made* a routine journey to the moon with thirty people on board.

We are invited, by this convention, to look at future events as if from a viewpoint even further in the future. Narrative typically assumes, in the imagination, such a retrospective view.

23 A second special extension of the normal past meaning is the use of the Past Tense, in some contexts of everyday conversation, TO REFER TO THE PRESENT; in particular, to the present feelings or thoughts of the speaker or hearer:

> A: *Did* you *want* me?
> B: Yes, I *hoped* you would give me a hand with the painting.

The subject of this exchange would probably be the *present* wishes of Speaker B, despite the use of the Past Tense. In fact the Present and Past Tenses are broadly interchangeable in this context, but there is quite a noticeable difference of tone. The effect of the Past Tense is to make the request indirect, and therefore more polite. We can explain the politer tone here as a hint that the intending or hoping were formulated in the past, and that the speaker is not necessarily committed to them in the present. The Present Tense (*I hope you will . . .*) in this situation would seem rather brusque and demanding – it would make the request difficult to refuse without impoliteness. The Past Tense, on the other hand, avoids a confrontation of wills. Politeness also extends to the original question *Did you want me?* The logically expected Present Tense (*Do you want me?*) might have peremptory overtones, and seem to say: 'Oh, it's you, is it? You always want something'.

Other verbs similarly used are *wonder* and *think*:

> I just *wondered* if you had any little pieces of furniture you'd like to sell.
> | I *thought* I might come and see you later this evening.

Notice the verb following the main verb is also often in the Past Tense (*wondered . . . had . . .*), although its meaning applies to the present. As before, the speaker seems to be testing the listener's reaction to a past attitude, whereas in reality a present attitude is implied.

a. In this kind of context, the Progressive Past is frequently preferred, as it adds a further overtone of indirectness and politeness to that of the Simple Past: *I was wondering . . .* etc. (see §43*a*).

b. The indirect and polite connotation of the Past here might suggest that the origin of the usage lies in the hypothetical use of the Past, rather than in the 'past time' use. This is unlikely, however, since hypothetical meaning is expressed by the

15

ordinary Past Tense only in dependent clauses. In main clauses, it is normally expressed by *would* + Infinitive (see §§166–9).

c. The above usage can be compared with the use of the Past to point a contrast with an unspoken present alternative: *I* THOUGHT *you were leaving* ('... but now I see you're not'). In both cases the 'non-present' element of Past Tense meaning is emphasised, and the 'definite time' element is not evident: there is nothing in such sentences to say precisely *when* the speaker had the attitude or opinion mentioned (see §64).

Simple Present: imaginary uses

24 Before closing this examination of Simple Present and Past Tenses, we have to look at one or two less important uses of the Simple Present with reference not to real time, but to IMAGINARY PRESENT time.

25 Technically, a distinction can be made between the historic use of the Present (illustrated in §15), and its FICTIONAL use. It is usual for novelists and story-writers to use the Past Tense to describe imaginary happenings (whether past, present or future with respect to real time), so that the employment of the Simple Present in fiction (except in direct speech) strikes one as a departure from normal practice. Some writers use the Present in imitation of the popular historic present of spoken narrative. For more serious writing, transposition into the fictional present is a device of dramatic heightening – it puts the reader in the place of someone actually witnessing or experiencing the events as they are described:

> Mr. Tulkinghorn *takes* out his papers, *asks* permission to place them on a golden talisman of a table at my Lady's elbow, *puts* on his spectacles, and *begins* to read by the light of a shaded lamp.
>
> (Dickens, *Bleak House*, Chapter 2)

As with the Simple Past, the above succession of Simple Present forms represents a sequence, rather than a coincidence, of events.

a. In some other narrative contexts, it is not the Past Tense, but the Present Tense that is conventional. For example, stage directions: *Petey enters from the door on the left with a paper and sits at the table* (from the beginning of Harold Pinter's play *The Birthday Party*). Whatever the imagined time of the play's action, in the make-believe of the theatre anything that happens on the stage is 'in the present' as it comes before the audience's eyes. Also in the spirit of the stage direction are narrative summaries in the popular media. For example, here is the beginning of a movie plot summary from the magazine *Radio Times* (11 January, 2004, p. 65): *Batman responds when Gotham City is threatened by the vengeful Penguin and his gang.*

b. Similar summaries of stories (whether in books, on the radio, on television or in magazines, for example recapitulations of previous instalments of the same narrative) tend to occur in the Present Tense. Here is part of a summary of Victor Hugo's *Les Misérables*: *Jean Valjean, a simple peasant,* STEALS *a loaf of bread to feed his sister's starving children. Condemned to five years of hard labour, he* TRIES *to escape,* IS *caught, and* HAS *to serve nineteen years in the galleys.* This convention dates back to the habit

SIMPLE PRESENT AND PAST TENSES

adopted by novelists such as Smollett and Dickens, of giving chapter summaries in the Present Tense in place of simple chapter titles: *Chapter XXI. Madame Mantalini* FINDS *Herself in a Situation of some Difficulty, and Miss Nickleby* FINDS *Herself in no Situation at all. (Nicholas Nickleby.)*

c. A further example of summary narrative in the Simple Present is the following example from Frank Cook, a British Member of Parliament, objecting to bed shortages in a local hospital:

> You can picture the scene: a consultant *walks* into a care unit with five or six patients struggling, fighting for their lives and *says*: 'Hands up those who have 15 breaths left in them to make it round the corner'.

26 Two special uses of the Present Tense hard to classify are (a) that of the travel itinerary:

> Across a stile *begins* the descent to the river. At first the way *is* between confining trees. Then, suddenly, they *are* behind us and we *find* ourselves held enraptured by a vista of exquisite beauty. The hillside *falls* away to a tree-lined meadow which *spreads* flatly to the River Eden. (Adapted from Charlie Emett, *The Eden Way*.)

and (b) that of the instruction manual:

> You *test* an air-leak by disconnecting the delivery pipe at the carburettor and pumping petrol into a container.

The second of these has a spoken counterpart in such verbal directions as:

> You *take* the first turning on the left past the roundabout, then you *cross* a bridge and *bear* right until you reach the public library.

In each of these cases, it is possible to interpret the sequence of events as habitual present. For instance, one could preface the set of street directions with: *Every time you want to get to the library* . . . (understanding *you* as an impersonal pronoun equivalent to *one*). On the other hand, perhaps a more plausible interpretation is that of the 'imaginary present': the person describing the set of events imagines them as happening now, before the mind's eye, at the time of utterance.

a. Notice that there is a difference between the *you* + Present Tense construction illustrated above and the *you* + Imperative construction of *You leave this to me, You mind your own business, etc. You* preceding an Imperative receives sentence stress, (*'You 'mind*) whereas normally as subject of a statement it does not.

CHAPTER 2

Progressive Aspect

27 Progressive Aspect. PROGRESSIVE ASPECT REFERRING TO TEMPORARY HAPPENINGS: *28* temporariness; *29* duration; *30* limited duration; *31* not necessarily complete; *32* 'temporal frame' effect; *33* there is not always a 'temporal frame'. CLASSES OF VERB WITH THE PROGRESSIVE ASPECT: *34*; *35* A 'Momentary Verbs', *35* B 'Transitional Event Verbs'; *36* C 'Activity Verbs', *36* D 'Process Verbs'; *37* verbs normally incompatible with the Progressive; *37* E 'Verbs of Inert Perception', *37* F 'Verbs of Inert Cognition', *37* G 'Verbs of Attitude', *37* H 'State Verbs of Having and Being'; *38* J 'Verbs of Bodily Sensation'. SPECIAL CASES: *39*; *40–1* verbs in class E; *42–3* verbs in classes F & G; *44–5* verbs in class H; *46* further exceptions. PROGRESSIVE ASPECT – OTHER USES: *47*; *48–50* habitual uses of Progressive; *51* future use; *52* 'persistent' or 'continuous' use.

27 The term PROGRESSIVE has frequently been used, and is used here, to designate those verb constructions in which the *-ing* form of the verb follows a form of the verb *to be*: *(i)s working*, *(wi)ll be working*, *(ha)s been working*, etc. The term is widely used because it suggests a happening 'in progress,' and because it avoids some misleading associations which belong to other terms commonly used by grammarians: 'durative', 'temporary', 'continuous', etc. In the most general terms, the Progressive ASPECT (as it is called) is said to give us an 'inside view' of a happening, rather than an 'outside view', seeing the happening as a single whole. Examples such as *I was spending the day at home* and *I spent the day at home* illustrate this contrast. But this description does not account for all cases of the use of the Progressive, which has been gradually extending its range of use in English for centuries. The Progressive is increasing in frequency in English, especially in the spoken language. But it is worth noting that the Progressive construction is still much less frequent than the non-progressive Simple Present and Simple Past.

This chapter complements Chapter 1: it compares the Progressive Present and Past Tenses with the Simple Present and Past. Consideration of other Progressive forms (Perfect Progressive, *will* + Progressive, etc.) will come later (see §§75–82, 106–9).

Progressive Aspect referring to temporary happenings

28 First, let's consider the most salient function of the Progressive Aspect, which is to refer to TEMPORARY situations, activities, or goings-on:

'Where's Joan?' 'She's *cooking* the dinner.'
'What on earth *are* you *doing*?' ' I'm *trying* to play the violin.'
'What's *happening*?' 'The river's *overflowing* its banks.'

These examples illustrate the Progressive Present: the temporary situation includes the present moment in its time-span, stretching for a limited period into the past and into the future. To distinguish the Progressive Present as used here from the Simple Present, we need to stress three separate aspects of meaning:

1 The Progressive Form indicates *duration* (and is thus distinguished from the non-durative 'event present').

    Event Present: •   Progressive: ∿∿∿∿

2 The Progressive Form indicates *limited duration* (and is thus distinguished from the 'state present').

    State Present: ─────────   Progressive: ∿∿∿∿

3 The Progressive Form indicates that the *happening need not be complete* (and is again thereby distinguished from the 'event present').

Points 1 and 2 show that the Progressive *stretches* the time-span of an 'event verb', but *compresses* the time-span of a 'state verb'. It should be emphasised again, though, that this is a matter of psychological rather than real time: it is possible for the same incident to be described by either the Simple or the Progressive Present, depending upon a speaker's point of view: *You look tired / You're looking tired.*

Let's now examine each of the three features of meaning separately.

29 The durative element of meaning is seen in the contrast of *I raise my arm!* or *The house falls down!* with *I am raising my arm* or *The house is falling down*. The first two sentences (which seem unusual and overdramatic – see §10) suggest a sudden movement, the second a more gradual one. With the Progressive, the event is no longer instantaneous: it stretches some way into the past and into the future.

a. Radio and TV sports commentators tend to use the Simple Present for single brief events in the progress of the game: *Seagram* WINS *the Grand National!* (horse racing); *He* LOOKS *around the field – and in* COMES *Roberts to bowl* (cricket) – see §9. The Progressive tends to be used for sports happenings which take a longer time or are more gradual – especially those that are not part of the main action: *Seagram's* CLOSING *on him* (horse racing); *And Joe Bloggs* IS *just* PACING *around in the pits waiting for Fabi to bring that car in* (car racing).

30 The difference between unlimited and LIMITED DURATION is evident from the following sentences, in which the Simple Present, in its unrestrictive state meaning, contrasts with the Progressive Present:

My watch *works* perfectly (permanent state – 'my watch is generally a reliable one').
| My watch *is working* perfectly (temporary state).
Which team *do* you *support*? (in general).
| Which team *are* you *supporting*? (at this particular match).
I *live* in Wimbledon (permanent residence).
| I *am living* in Wimbledon (temporary residence).
I *enjoy* the seaside ('I like holidays by the sea in general').
| I *am enjoying* the seaside ('I am enjoying this particular holiday').

The notion of 'limited duration', seen from a slightly different point of view, means that the situation is 'subject to change'. For example, the Present Progressive brings with it the concept that the current happening or state of affairs does not have the prospect of continuing indefinitely. This connotation is important for some extended uses of the Progressive (see §§43, 104).

a. Along with the 'temporary' meaning of the Progressive there is often a notion that the situation is 'actually in progress now'. *I am enjoying the seaside* would be spoken when the speaker is actually at the seaside; this is not necessarily true of *I enjoy the seaside*. Notice a similar difference between *This basin is leaking* (actual: even now water is escaping) and *This basin leaks* (potential: this is a permanent problem with the basin); similarly *These shirts wash nicely* and *These shirts are washing nicely*.

31 That the action expressed by the Progressive is NOT NECESSARILY COMPLETE is best illustrated in the Past Tense, by 'event verbs' which signal a transition from one state to another (e.g. *become, die, fall, get, go, stop, take off*). Using the event past, one might say *The bus stopped*, so indicating the vehicle's arrival at a state of rest. But *The bus was stopping* means only that the bus is slowing down towards a stop: cessation of movement is not described. Similarly:

The dog *was drowning* in the sea. | The dog *drowned* in the sea.

To the first sentence one could add . . . *but someone jumped into the water and saved her*; but not to the second, which implies that she actually died.

The following sentences illustrate lack of certainty about completeness in another context:

I *was reading* from 10 p.m. to 11 p.m. | I *read* from 10 p.m. to 11 p.m.

The Simple Past tells us that the speaker started to read at 10 o'clock and finished at 11 o'clock. The Progressive, however, does not specify either the time of beginning or the time of completing the activity: all we know is that reading was in progress for that hour. Hence it would be a fitting answer from a suspect being interrogated by a detective. The detective would ask *What WERE you DOING between* 10 p.m. and 11 p.m.? – being uninterested in whether the activity continued after that period or not; and the suspect would reply in a similar way.

Notice a further difference between *Meg was reading a book that evening* and *Meg read a book that evening*. The Simple Past here suggests that Meg reached the end of her book before the end of the evening, but completion in this sense is not implied by *was reading*.

a. Typically events are BOUNDED – that is, they have built into them the idea of completion. An activity verb such as *rain, read, walk* or *write*, however, is not bounded in itself: it needs some kind of following word or phrase to 'complete' it and turn it into a proper event. Compare:

1a. They *walked for* a couple of hours.   1b. ?*They *walked home for* a couple of hours.

2a. *They *walked in* a couple of hours.   2b. They *walked home in* a couple of hours.

Walked in 1a and 2a is UNBOUNDED: it is an activity that could go on and on. But *walked home* in 1b and 2b is BOUNDED: it has a built-in destination. Once you have walked home, you have completed your walk. The difference is clear from the unacceptability of 1b and 2a: an *in*-phrase of duration is acceptable only when the happening is bounded, while a *for*-phrase of duration is acceptable only when the happening is unbounded. The Progressive, because of its idea of non-completion, cannot be combined with an *in*-phrase, but only with a *for*-phrase:

3a. They *were walking for* a couple of hours.   3b. They *were walking home for* a couple of hours.

4a. *They *were walking in* a couple of hours.   (4b. ?*They *were walking home in* a couple of hours.)

The interesting thing is that both 3a and 3b are acceptable, while the non-progressive in 1b is not acceptable with *for*. The explanation is that the Progressive, with its built-in non-completion, turns the bounded happening in 1b into an unbounded one. Sentence 3b implies they had not reached the end of their journey: *They were walking home for a couple of hours, when the storm interrupted their journey.* (Example 4b is placed in parentheses for the following reason. Although it is acceptable in a future-in-the-past sense – see §83 – it cannot be interpreted in the sense relevant here, because the boundedness of the *in*-phrase conflicts with the unboundedness of the Progressive.)

b. Note this feature of Progressive meaning is termed not INCOMPLETE, but NOT NECESSARILY COMPLETE. This cautiously negative label is justified, since the Progressive allows the possibility that the activity continues up to the end of a named period, and FINISHES AT THAT POINT. For example, the above example *I was reading between ten and eleven* allows the possibility that the speaker continued reading up to the stroke of 11 o'clock, and stopped reading at that point.

32 The Progressive Aspect generally has the effect of surrounding a particular event or moment by a 'temporal frame', which can be diagrammed:

That is, within the flow of time, there is some reference point ▲ from which the temporary happening indicated by the verb can be seen as stretching into the future and into the past. With the Progressive Present, the reference point is normally identical with 'now', the present moment of time. But in the Progressive Past, some other definite reference point must be found to 'anchor' the situation. Often this point is made explicit by an adverbial phrase or clause:

> *This time last year* I was travelling round the world. | *Five minutes later* he was sleeping like a baby. | Don was looking very ill *when I last saw him.*

In both Past and Present Tense narrative, the Progressive often forms a 'temporal frame' around an action denoted by a non-progressive form. Hence, whereas the relationship of meaning between two neighbouring Simple Past forms is usually one of *time-sequence*, the relationship between a Progressive and a Simple Past form is one of *time-inclusion*. The contrast can be seen in these two sentences:

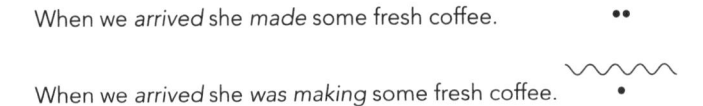

> When we *arrived* she *made* some fresh coffee.
>
> When we *arrived* she *was making* some fresh coffee.

The first example tells us that the coffee-making immediately *followed* the arrival; the second, that the arrival took place *during* the coffee-making.

a. A Simple Tense verb in a main clause is often 'framed' in this manner by a Progressive Tense verb in a subordinate clause: *I ASKED him what he WAS THINKING about* (i.e. '... at the time when I asked him').

b. Verbs referring to utterances or other meaningful acts can be 'framed' by a Progressive verb form referring to the mental attitude or communicative intention lying behind the utterance: *'Were you lying when you SAID that?' 'No, I was telling the truth.'* This is sometimes called the 'interpretive' use of the Progressive: it is as if we are seeing the speech act 'from the inside', not in a temporal sense, but in the sense of discovering its underlying interpretation. There is no temporal-frame effect here, as the 'lying' and the 'saying' are apparently coextensive in time.

33 The 'temporal frame' effect is not an independent feature of the Progressive form's meaning; it follows, rather, from the notion of 'limited duration'. Whenever a point of time or a brief event is in a contemporaneous relation with a happening that has duration, it is natural that that happening should extend beyond the event-without-duration or point-of-time in both backward and forward directions – in short, that a 'temporal frame' should be set up.

When no event or point of time is in question, however, the framing effect does not occur. For example:

> Throughout the Prime Minister's speech, the Foreign Secretary *was listening* in the gallery. | We *were watching* a football match on Saturday afternoon.

Here a temporary activity is related to a period. There is no point around which the 'listening' or 'watching' forms a frame. In the second example, we would be more inclined to say, in fact, that the afternoon forms a 'temporal frame' round the 'watching', since we know that normally football matches begin and end within the duration of an afternoon.

Another case where there is no 'frame' is that where two Progressive Past verbs are put near to one another.

> While she *was muttering* to herself, she *was throwing* things into a suitcase.

All we know here is that the two happenings were *at some time or other* simultaneous. We know nothing about the relation between their starting-points or finishing-points: whether she started muttering before or after she began throwing things is an irrelevance. The four main possibilities (excluding exact coextensivity) may therefore be diagrammed thus (where a = 'muttering to herself', and b = 'throwing things'):

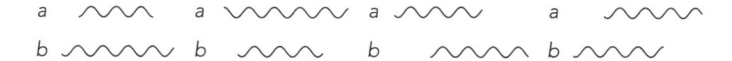

a ∧∧∧   a ∨∨∨∨   a ∧∧∧   a   ∧∧∧
b ∧∧∧∧ b ∧∧∧   b   ∧∧∧   b ∧∧∧

The framing effect is, incidentally, rarely found with the Perfect Progressive Tenses (see §§75–81).

a. The framing effect is used in a special way in fiction writing. For example, the point of time or the brief event to be 'framed' may be implied rather than stated. Consider this example:

> And then the funeral was over, and they *were coming* out into the grey, windy day.

It would be more natural to present the two events as in sequence, using the Simple Past: . . . *and they came out into the grey, windy day.* But the Progressive Present is more immediate: it seems to give us *an inside view of* a vivid experience of the mourners coming out into the open air. Even more dramatic are examples such as: *Like a dam bursting, suddenly she was diving across the room.*

Classes of verb with the Progressive Aspect

34 The Progressive Aspect varies its effect according to the type of meaning conveyed. We have already noted this with 'event verbs' and 'state verbs'; but now it is convenient to distinguish further classes of verb (or more correctly, of verbal meaning).

a. It is worth bearing in mind that in talking of states, events, activities, etc. we are really talking about the meaning of the verb with its associated complements, such as Objects and Adverbials (as in *They ran* THE MARATHON; *It lasted* FOR A MONTH. But for convenience, a 'default' classification is adopted for each verb.

35 We begin with two classes of 'event verb'.

35 A. 'MOMENTARY VERBS' (*hiccough, hit, jump, kick, knock, nod, tap, wink*, etc.). These verbs refer to happenings so momentary that it is difficult to think of them as having duration. Consequently, the Progressive form, in giving them duration, forces us to think of a series of events, rather than of a single event. Compare *He nodded* (a single movement) with *He was nodding* (a repeated movement); *He jumped up and down* with *He was jumping up and down*; *Someone fired a gun at me* with *Someone was firing a gun at me*.

35 B. 'TRANSITIONAL EVENT VERBS' (*arrive, die, fall, land, leave, lose, stop*, etc.). As exemplified earlier with *The bus was stopping* (§31), 'event verbs' denoting transition into a new state are used with the Progressive to indicate the *approach* to a transition, rather than the transition itself:

> David Campbell *was arriving* when the bomb exploded. | Suddenly a helicopter *was landing* on the beach. | Mother *was dying* in hospital.

It might even be argued that a different meaning of the verb comes into play in the switch from Simple Past to Progressive Past: *die* in *she was dying* indicates a process which ends in death; *die* in *She died* pinpoints the actual moment of death, the completion of the process.

a. In the plural these verbs can refer to a multiplicity of events. *The guests were arriving*, for example, can either mean a single arrival, or (more likely) a set of arrivals, in progress. In the latter case the notion of 'approach to a transition' applies differently: it signifies progression towards the final state when all guests will have arrived.

36 Next, here are two classes of verb typically accompanying the Progressive form.

36 C. 'ACTIVITY VERBS' (*drink, eat, play, rain, read, run, talk, watch, work, write*, etc.). Although these verbs can be used with the Simple Tenses in an 'event' sense, they more usually occur with the Progressive, as they refer to a continuing, though time-limited, activity:

> 'What *are* you *doing*?' 'I'm *writing* a letter.' | They're *eating* their dinner. | It's still *raining*.

'Activity' is not altogether a satisfactory term for this class: not all the verbs included refer to human occupations. The important point is that the verb in the Progressive tells us something is 'going on'.

a. Note that activity or 'going on' can include gaps: e.g. *They're working on the car* is fine even if they have paused for a break or a rest.

36 D. 'PROCESS VERBS' (*change, develop, grow, increase, learn, mature, slow down, widen*, etc.). As a process of change ordinarily has duration, but not indefinite duration, these verbs also tend to go with the Progressive Aspect:

The weather is changing for the better; They're widening the road; etc. To these we should add verbs like *become, get* and *go* which frequently have a 'process' meaning when combined with a following word or phrase: *It's getting late.*

37 Most difficulties over the use of the Progressive Aspect arise with classes of verbs which are normally incompatible with the Progressive: these can be called ANTI-PROGRESSIVE verbs, because of their 'unfriendliness' to the Progressive. The most important of these verbs is the main verb *to be*: it is possible to say *He is ill* (state present) but not normally *?*He is being ill,* even though the illness referred to here is presumably a temporary rather than permanent one. Verbs unfriendly to the Progressive can be placed in certain rough semantic categories. Meaning, unfortunately, is not the sole determining factor, since virtually synonymous sentences can be found, one in which the Progressive is allowable, and one in which it is not:

> She's *suffering* from influenza = She *is* ill with influenza.

It seems as if usage in this area is not always logical and systematic, because the language itself is gradually extending the use of the Progressive. There are also dialect differences.

A further point is that many of these anti-progressive verbs can occur with the Progressive Aspect in special contexts. Such special uses can usually be explained by supposing that the verb (perhaps through a special transfer of meaning) can become a member of a different verbal category. First, however, let's consider the straightforward cases of verbs unfavourable to the Progressive Aspect.

37 E. 'VERBS OF INERT PERCEPTION' (*feel, hear, see, smell, taste* – see §§40–1 for exceptions). The term 'inert' can be used for these common verbs, to distinguish perception of the kind denoted by *see*, where the perceiver is merely passively receptive, from that of (say) *look at*, where one is actively directing one's attention towards some object.

I *could feel / felt* something hard under my foot.	(NOT ?*I *was feeling* . . .)
I *could hear / heard* a knocking at the door.	(NOT ?*I *was hearing* . . .)
I *could see / saw* someone through the window.	(NOT ?*I *was seeing* . . .)
I *could smell / smelt* onions cooking.	(NOT ?*I *was smelling* . . .)
I *could taste / tasted* sugar in the tea.	(NOT ?*I *was tasting* . . .)

The difference between the constructions with and without *could* is that the *could* form denotes a state, whereas the Simple Past form denotes an event. Thus *I could hear a door slamming* (*all night*) indicates a continuing and repeated noise; (*At that moment*) *I heard a door slam* indicates a single moment of impact. (*?*I could hear a door slam* seems odd because of the clash between duration in *could hear* and the momentariness in *slam*.) There is a parallel contrast in the Present Tense: *I see a bird of paradise!* is a case of the event use of the Present (where *see* means much the same as *catch sight of*). Here, as elsewhere, the event or 'instantaneous' use is rather unusual and melodramatic. The more natural *can* construction (*I can see a bird of paradise*) stands in place of the state use of the Present.

37 F. 'VERBS OF INERT COGNITION' (*believe, forget, guess, think, imagine, know, suppose, understand*, etc. – see §§42–3 for special uses). These, like the verbs of perception above, are inert, in the sense that they do not involve conscious effort or intention. The Simple Present in this case refers to a mental state, and so belongs to the category 'state', even though a limitation on the duration of the state may be implied:

> I *think* she's getting upset.   (RATHER THAN: I *am thinking* she's getting upset.)
>
> I *believe* in fair play.   (RATHER THAN: *I *am believing* in fair play.)
>
> I *guess* you're right.   (RATHER THAN ?*I *am guessing* you're right.)

As the examples suggest, verbs with this type of meaning are frequently followed by a noun clause. Other examples:

> I *forget* what I paid for the house. | He *imagines* everything to be easy. | We *understand* your difficulty.

37 G. 'VERBS OF ATTITUDE' (including volition and feeling) such as *hate, hope, intend, like, love, prefer, regret, want* and *wish* are similar to 'verbs of inert cognition': *She loves working on a farm*. However, some of these can more easily occur in the Progressive – *enjoy, hope, like, love*, for example – if the emphasis is on temporariness or tentativeness. Compare:

> What *do* you *want* me to wear tonight? | Tim, *are* you *wanting* any fruit?

The second example sounds like a tentative offer – although it would also be perfectly normal to use the Simple Present here: *Tim, do you want any fruit?*

a. Feel, see and *hear*, in addition to being 'verbs of perception' (Class E), can be used as verbs of cognition (Class F): *We FEEL (i.e. it is our feeling or opinion) that you have so much to offer* (not **We are feeling . . .*, etc.). *I SEE your point. I HEAR Kate Jones is engaged to someone called Jack.*

b. Verbs such as *read, tell* and *find*, when they refer to the result of communication (see §16) can also be placed in this class. For example, *John tells me . . .* means 'I understand as a result of John's having told me . . .'.

c. It is significant that *know* is characteristically followed by the Progressive with another verb in sentences like *John KNOWS he IS TALKING nonsense; I like a woman who KNOWS what she's DOING*. The state of knowledge and the activities of 'talking' and 'doing' are here concurrent; the time-spans are comparable, and therefore, but for the inclusion of *know* in Class F, we would expect matching verbal constructions – the Progressive Present in both cases. Similarly, in a sentence like *I think I'm catching a cold*, the temporariness of the situation calls for a Progressive form *I'm catching*, but this does not apply to *think*, which is equally temporary in its reference, but belongs to Class F.

37 H. 'STATE VERBS OF HAVING AND BEING' (*be, belong to, contain, consist of, cost, depend on, deserve, have, matter, own, resemble*, etc. – see §44 for exceptions). In this class, along with the key verbs *be* and *have*, we put verbs which include, as part of their meaning, the notion of 'being' or 'having'. Often a paraphrase with *be* or *have* is possible: *matter = be important; own = have in one's possession; resemble = be like*; etc. (Incidentally, some verbs of Class F can also be paraphrased in a similar way: *I think = My opinion is* . . . ; *I believe = My belief is* . . . ; etc. But in Class H we place only non-psychological verbs.)

> This carpet *belongs* to me. (NOT *This carpet *is belonging* to me.)
>
> I *own* this carpet. (NOT *I *am owning* this carpet.)
>
> Your age *doesn't matter*. (NOT *Your age *isn't mattering*.)

Similarly:

> This bread *contains* too much yeast. | Mangoes *cost* a lot just now. | Whether the play is a success *depends* on you, the audience.

a. The forms of the verb *be* do not always refer to a state. An exception is the past participle *been*, used as past participle of the verb *go*: *Where have you been?* Here *been* is an event verb – see §59*b*.

b. The use of *have* we are considering here is the 'state' *have* of *She has several sisters; I have a bad backache*, etc. (This use of *have* can easily be replaced by *have got* in colloquial BrE, but not by the Progressive *be having*: **She is having several sisters.*) Note there is also an 'activity' *have* which occurs freely with the Progressive Aspect, and which can often answer the question *What are you doing?*: *I'm having lunch / a barbecue / a shower / a singing lesson / some friends to dinner*, etc. In other cases, the Progressive of *have* is used to describe a good or bad experience: *We're having fun / problems / a great time / a hard time.*

38 Finally, there is a small class of verbs which, when referring to a temporary state, can occur either with or without the Progressive:

38 J. 'VERBS OF BODILY SENSATION' (*ache, feel, hurt, itch, tingle*, etc.). There is a choice, without any noticeable change of meaning, between *I feel great* and *I'm feeling great*, between *My knee hurts* and *My knee is hurting*, etc. Notice, here, a difference between this meaning of *feel*, which is a question of INTERNAL sensation, and the meaning of *feel* as a 'verb of perception' (Class E above), denoting EXTERNAL sensation: *I can feel a stone in my shoe*, etc.

a. Notice, however, that a verb like *hurt* can also occur as an event verb. Imagine a doctor examining a patient with a leg injury. Bending the knee, the doctor might say *Does that hurt?* and the patient would probably respond *Ouch! That hurts!* on feeling a sudden jab of pain. In this case, it would be unlikely that either speaker would use the Progressive *is hurting*.

Special cases

39 There are many apparent exceptions to the rule that verbs of Classes E, F, G and H do not go with the Progressive Aspect. Many of these exceptions can be explained by noting that one verb can belong to more than one of the Classes A–J. Such multiple membership has already been noted with the verb *feel*, with its different meanings belonging to Classes E, F and J. Some further examples of multiple membership follow.

40 VERBS IN CLASS E. *Feel, taste* and *smell* can be used to indicate not only 'inert perception', but also 'active perception'. In the second case, they belong to the 'activity' category (Class C) and so may freely take the Progressive form:

INERT	ACTIVE
I (*can*) *smell* the gas.	I'm *smelling* the perfume. It's splendid!
I (*can*) *feel* the heat here.	I'm *feeling* the ground (with my foot).
I (*can*) *taste* the spices in it.	I'm *tasting* the broth (to see if it's spicy enough).

In the first sentence of each pair, the sensation is an experience that simply 'happens' to me; but in the second, I go out of my way, physically, to focus my attention on some object. The second sentence answers the question *What are you doing?* and for clarity, as the examples show, can be supplemented by an adverbial expression of instrument or purpose.

However, the remaining two verbs in Class E, *see* and *hear*, are not used in the active sense, because the separate verbs *look at* and *listen to* are available for that function:

INERT	AGENTIVE
I *can see* a bus in the distance.	I'm *looking* at a bus in the distance.
I *can't hear* what he's saying.	You're *not listening* to what he's saying.

'Inert perception' is a more appropriate term than 'passive perception', since it is merely the absence of agency that is signified by the verb in the left-hand column. Likewise 'agentive verb' or 'doing verb' is a more suitable term for the type represented by *look at* and *listen to*: these verbs are not merely 'activity verbs' in the wide sense of Class C, but in the more precise sense of 'involving animate agency'.

41 A third class of perception verbs can more fittingly be called 'passive', as it consists of those verbs for which the grammatical subject is the object of perception: *That* SOUNDS *like Martha's voice*; *You* LOOK *tired*. Here again, although *see* and *hear* are matched by separate verbs (*look* and *sound*), the three verbs *smell, taste* and *feel* are used for the additional meaning. These three verbs are used in the 'passive' sense in: *This mango feels / smells /*

PROGRESSIVE ASPECT

tastes good. As the type of perception expressed is 'inert' rather than 'active', the Progressive is generally avoided:

That sounds like Martha's voice.   RATHER THAN: ?*That is sounding like Martha's voice.

Strangely, *look* is an exception to this rule: it is possible to say both *You look well* and *You're looking well* without any appreciable difference of meaning, perhaps because of an analogy with *I feel / am feeling well* (see Class J, §38).

Before leaving Class E, we have to reckon with an acceptable use of the Progressive in sentences like *I am hearing you clearly* (spoken, say, by a radio or telephone operator). The meaning here is 'I am receiving your message', and the effect of the Progressive is to place emphasis on the ACTIVATION or AROUSAL of the processes of perception. We can argue, therefore, that in this context *hear* becomes, exceptionally, an activity verb (Class C). A rather different case is *see* in: *I need glasses – I'm not seeing so clearly these days*. Here *see* is more like a 'process verb' describing the speaker's deteriorating eyesight.

a. Also *sound*, *smell* and *taste* could occur with the Progressive in describing a process developing towards completion. A chef, supervising the progress of cooking might say: *That's tasting pretty good*. A technician adjusting the sound quality of a test recording might say: *That's sounding more like it*. These are special usages, comparable to the 'process verb' usage discussed in §45 below.

42   VERBS IN CLASS F are also sometimes found with the Progressive form:

I'm thinking for the moment in plain economic terms. | Surely *you're imagining* things! | *We're supposing* the butler did it.

These examples are comparable to those of §41 in showing the ACTIVATION or AROUSAL of thought processes. In the first example, 'thinking' is felt to be a kind of work or mental exertion, equivalent to 'considering' or 'ruminating'. In the second example, *imagining things* means 'entertaining or indulging yourself with illusions'. In the third, *I'm supposing that...* means 'I am making the temporary assumption that...' Each sentence, that is, suggests some positive mental activity. In other words, in sentences of this kind, verbs normally of Class F seem to function, unusually, as 'activity verbs'.

43   The explanation above in §42 does not meet cases of a special polite use of the Progressive with certain verbs of Classes F and G:

I'm hoping you'll give us some advice. | What *were you wanting*? | You *are forgetting* the moral arguments. | *We're wondering* if you have any suggestions.

In idiomatic colloquial speech, this apparently unaccountable usage is often preferred to the regular Simple Present form *I hope... You forget*, etc.

29

MEANING AND THE ENGLISH VERB

One reason for this preference seems to be that the Progressive is a more tentative, and hence a more polite method of expressing a mental attitude. As we have seen (§30), the Progressive form is associated with 'susceptibility to change' and, in the present context, it is only a small step further to associate the Progressive with 'lack of commitment or confidence in what will happen'. *I hope you'll give us some advice* leaves the addressee little room for polite refusal; but *I'm hoping* ... adds a pessimistic note: it implies that the speaker has not made a final commitment to the hope – there is still scope for a change of mind should the listener's reaction be discouraging.

a. The Progressive fulfils in this case a function similar to that of the Past Tense described in §23: *I just wondered if you could give us some advice*. In fact, the two forms can be combined in a Past Progressive construction with doubly self-deprecatory connotations: *I was just wondering if you could give us some advice; I was hoping you'd look after the children for us*. The form of verb, for politeness, must be matched against the size of favour requested. The Past Progressive (most tentative) is more appropriate to a request which will put the listener to considerable risk or inconvenience. The Simple Present (most direct) is more appropriate when the listener is invited to do something to his/her own advantage: *I hope you'll come and have dinner with us when you're in London next*.

44 VERBS IN CLASS H ('state verbs of having and being') can, like those of Classes E and F, combine with the Progressive Aspect where an 'activity' meaning can be supplied. The verb *to be* itself furnishes many examples. While it is virtually impossible to make sense of **He is being tall* or **The trees are being green*, there is no difficulty with *She is being kind*, because we are able to understand 'kindness' here as a mode of behaviour over which the person has control, rather than as an inherent trait of character. *She is being kind* means 'She is acting kindly towards someone', whereas *She is kind* means 'She is constitutionally good-natured'. Similar differences of meaning are seen in:

He's a fool	(i.e. 'He can't help it – it's his nature').
He's being a fool	(i.e. 'He's acting foolishly').
She's awkward	(i.e. 'She's clumsy, gauche').
She's being awkward	(i.e. 'She's being deliberately obstructive').
The car is difficult to drive	(i.e. 'It's made that way').
The car is being difficult	(i.e. 'It's going out of its way to cause trouble' – the car here is almost personified).

The Progressive also makes sense in *She's being good / useful / helpful / a nuisance / an angel*. But even if no obvious 'activity' meaning is available, we can frequently interpret a sentence *X is being Y*, however improbable the context, by reading into it the idea of someone acting a part. *Today, my uncle is being Napoleon* could be said of an actor or a megalomaniac or – ironically – someone behaving in an imperious manner. *He is being sorry / afraid / happy*, etc. could conceivably mean 'He is pretending to be sorry / afraid / happy'. A parallel though less likely example with the verb *have* is *Deirdre is having a headache*, meaning 'Deirdre is pretending to have a headache'. (On the other hand, no element of showmanship is likely to be present in *Deirdre is having a good time / her hair done / another baby* – these are normal instances of the 'activity' or 'process' use of *have* – see §37Hb.)

a. A more precise analysis should make clear that the contrast between *She is awkward* and *She is being awkward* is more complicated than suggested above. Whereas the Progressive Present here restricts the adjective to the meaning 'obstructionist', the Simple Present is ambiguous, allowing both 'state' and 'activity' interpretations. Two separate conditions of meaning are involved in the Progressive of *be* as main verb: (1) the time-span is temporary rather than permanent; and (2) the verb may be construed as referring to an activity with human agency. The first of these conditions is fulfilled in *She is hungry*, and the second in *She is an angel* (meaning 'She goes out of her way to be kind, helpful, considerate, etc.'). Only when both conditions are present together, as in *She is being an angel*, does one expect the Progressive Aspect with the main verb *to be*.

b. Notice the equivalence of the following sentences with and without the Progressive:

The child *is* asleep = The child *is sleeping*.
The train *is* in motion = The train *is moving*.
The train *is* stationary = The train *is standing* still.

In each case, a sentence containing the Simple Present form *is* is matched in meaning with a sentence (on the right) containing the Present Progressive form of some other verb. In the sentences on the left, the Simple Present *is* counts as an example of the state use of the Simple Present (§§7–8), even though it clearly refers to a temporary state of affairs. As was said in §7, the state present may, for common sense reasons, refer to a limited time-span – in this case the sleeping child will wake up after a few hours. But the interest of these examples is that, with anti-progressive verbs, the Simple Present invades (so to speak) the semantic territory of the Progressive.

45 Certain other verbs of Class H can take the Progressive when accompanied by an expression like *more and more*:

He *is resembling* his father more and more as the years go by. | The income of one's parents *is mattering* less in education these days. | Good food *is costing* more since devaluation.

The meaning of all these sentences (which are felt to be rather unnatural by some speakers) could be vaguely formulated 'This is the way things are going', and the explanation of the Progressive here seems to be that the verbs are no longer 'state verbs', but have transferred to the class of 'process verbs'. *Resemble*, for example here means 'to become like' rather than 'to be like'.

46 Unavoidably, there are some special cases which have not been dealt with here. Some instances that one may hear in colloquial English today seem difficult to fit into any system of rules and classes. It seems likely that some aspects of Progressive usage are unstable at the present time, and are undergoing continuing though gradual change.

For instance, it is difficult to find an explanation for one common application of the Past Progressive in conversation:

> I *was* recently *reading* about an invention which may turn garbage into soil. | Paula *was saying* that Eddie was going to be promoted.

The Progressive Past refers here to fairly recent communicative happenings (*the other day* is a typical adverbial collocation). There is no feeling of a 'temporal frame' round a specific past moment of time; nor does there appear to be any suggestion of the tentativeness of *I was wondering* or *I was hoping* (see §43a). The only parts of the Progressive meaning relevant are 'duration' and 'lack of completeness'. In answer to the question *Did you hear about what happened to Matthew on the tour?* you might reply, *Yes, my daughter Liz WAS TELLING me about it*. This would not imply total knowledge, and so would politely leave the way open for a continuation of the story. But the talebearer might be silenced by a similar reply with the Simple Past Tense (*Yes, Liz TOLD me about it*), as this would assume: 'Yes, I know the whole story, so don't bother to tell me'.

A further peculiarity of this usage is that the Past Tense does not have to be anchored to a specific earlier point of time reference (cf. §§63–4). One could say *Yes, Liz was telling me about it* without mentioning or implying some definite point of time at which the telling happened. The factor of Past Tense meaning that is relevant here, apart from past time, is that there is a time gap between the communication and the present moment. If the Perfect Progressive were used, as in *I have been reading about* . . . the gap would be assumed to disappear – i.e., the reading would be assumed to continue up to the present moment.

Progressive Aspect: other uses

47 Apart from the major use of the Progressive Aspect to refer to single temporary happenings, there are four other less important uses to be considered.

48 First, there are two separate HABITUAL (or iterative) uses of the Progressive, corresponding to the habitual use of Simple Present and Past illustrated in §§13 and 19.

49 Consider the following sentences:

> I'm *taking* dancing lessons this winter. | This season she *is appearing* in the popular musical *Guys and Dolls*. | At the moment Glyn *is cycling* almost twenty miles a day.

In these cases, the Progressive concept of 'temporariness' applies not to the individual events that make up the series, but to the series as a whole. The meaning is 'HABIT IN EXISTENCE OVER A LIMITED PERIOD' – the period often being specified by an adverbial expression, as in the examples above. On the other hand, there may be no adverbial, as in *I'M TAKING dancing lessons*. It is the temporariness of the habit that is important: *I'M TAKING dancing lessons* suggests a shorter period than *I TAKE dancing lessons*. Cf. also: *They are giving him steroids.*

The iterative element of meaning may well be made clear by an adverbial expression of frequency: *I'M GOING to the gym EVERY AFTERNOON this week.*

a. Adverbs of indefinite frequency may not be so used, however: **I am SOMETIMES walking to work until my car is repaired.*

50 The second habitual meaning is REPETITION OF EVENTS OF LIMITED DURATION:

> Whenever I pass that house the dog's *barking*. | Don't call on them at 7.30 – they're normally *having* dinner. | Usually the cramp starts just as I'm *going* to sleep. | You only seem to come alive when you're *discussing* your work.

Here the notion of limited duration applies not to the habit as a whole, but to the individual events of which the habit is composed. The effect of substituting the Progressive for the Simple Present is thus to *stretch* the time-span of the event so that it forms a frame around the recurrent event or time-point: compare the first sentence above with *Whenever I pass that house the dog barks*. Normally, this meaning of the Progressive is accompanied by adverbial modification naming the event or point of time around which the temporary activity is seen as a 'frame'. When no adverbial of time is present, there must nevertheless be a point of time implied by the context. Thus to the second example above we could add the words . . . *at that time* (viz. 7.30), making explicit what is otherwise implicit.

An adverbial phrase of frequency may also be added: OFTEN *when I pass she is sitting there on the doorstep, watching the world go by*. Sometimes, absence of frequency modification leads to ambiguity as to habitual or non-habitual meaning. This is evident in the second example above, which, if *normally* were omitted, could refer either to a single event of having dinner, or to an event regularly repeated on each work day.

a. The point of reference 'framed' by the Progressive in this iterative sense is often indicated by a verb introducing a clause within which the Progressive form occurs: *He rarely LETS us KNOW what he IS DOING; You never LISTEN to what people ARE SAYING; You can always TELL what he's THINKING.*

51 The Progressive Present may, like the Simple Present, refer to anticipated happenings in the future:

> Martin *is coming* over for lunch on Sunday. | She's *staying* over in London next Wednesday night. | I hear you're *moving* to a new job.

Also happenings anticipated in the past may be expressed by the Progressive Past Tense:

As we WERE VISITING them the next day, there was no point in sending the parcel by post.

More will be said of this FUTURATE PROGRESSIVE in §§83, 98–99.

52 Finally, there is a special extended meaning of the Progressive, marked by the absence of the 'temporary' element of the normal Progressive meaning:

The western land mass is always moving towards the water.

The sense here is one of PERSISTENT or CONTINUOUS activity; it is as if, in the 'process' use of the Progressive, the durational element of meaning overrides in this instance the temporary element. The uninterrupted nature of the activity is usually underlined by the presence of adverbs or adverbial phrases such as *always, continually, constantly* and *for ever* (this less common adverb can be written as one word: *forever*):

I'm continually forgetting people's names. | *His mother is always telling him the things he is not allowed to do.* | *They're always cracking jokes.* | *We were continually mending punctures – It was really rough going.* | *He's always giving her expensive presents.*

Notice that *always* in this context is a synonym for *continually*. It does not mean what *always* means in the corresponding Simple Present construction: *He always GIVES her expensive presents*. The sense of this last sentence is 'He gives her an expensive present on every occasion' (i.e. on every occasion when people normally give presents). But with the Progressive, the rough sense is 'There is never a time at which he is not giving her expensive presents'.

Obviously there is an element of colloquial exaggeration in such sentences. Their tone is often one of irritation or amused disparagement. Anyone who talked about *a man who is always giving people lifts* would tend to have a critical attitude towards the man, even though his habit of giving lifts might generally be considered laudable by other people.

CHAPTER 3

The Expression of Past Time

53 introduction. PRESENT PERFECT TENSE: 54 involvement with the present; 55 state-up-to-the-present; 56 indefinite past; 57 'at-least-once-in-the-period-leading-up-to-the-present'; recent indefinite past; 58 'habit-in-a-period-leading-up-to-the-present'; 59 resultative past. PRESENT PERFECT AND SIMPLE PAST: 60 frequency of occurrence; distinguishing characteristics of the Present Perfect; 61 continuation up to the present time; 62 present result; 63 indefinite time. DEFINITE AND INDEFINITE PAST MEANING: 64 what is meant by 'definiteness'. MISCELLANEOUS POINTS: 65 interchangeability of Simple Past and Present Perfect; 66 imaginary Present Perfect; 67 Perfect Aspect with non-finite verbs. ADVERBIALS IN RELATION TO PERFECT AND PAST: 68 primary and secondary points of reference; 69 adverbials associated with Past Tenses; 70 adverbials associated with Present Perfect; 71 adverbials combining with either; 72 adverbials combining with either, but with difference of meaning. PAST PERFECT: 73; 74 Simple Past interchangeable with Past Perfect. PERFECT PROGRESSIVE: 75; 76 duration, limitation of duration and possible incompleteness; 77 Perfect Progressive requires no adverbial, and can be used with a wider range of verbs than the Simple Perfect; 78 potential incompleteness; 79 effects of the activity are still apparent; 80 summary; 81 temporary habit up to the present. PAST PERFECT PROGRESSIVE: 82. FUTURE IN THE PAST: 83 Past Progressive and *was/were going to*; 84 *would* + Infin, *was/were to*. USED TO: 85.

53 It is well known that English has two chief ways of indicating past time by means of verbs: the Past Tense (*I worked, he wrote*, etc.) and the Perfect Aspect (*I have worked, he has written*, etc.); also that these two can be combined to form the Past Perfect (or 'Pluperfect') (*I had worked, he had written*, etc.) signifying 'past in the past'. My main goal, in this chapter, is to show how the Perfect is distinguished in meaning from the Past, first of all concentrating on the Present Perfect Tense. To begin with, it is worth making the point that Present Perfect and Simple Past are not mutually exclusive choices: there are many situations where either of these tenses would be suitable.

MEANING AND THE ENGLISH VERB

At its most general, the Perfect Aspect is used for an earlier happening which is seen in relation to a later event or time as a reference point: in one word, the Perfect represents 'beforeness', or ANTERIORITY. Thus the Present Perfect means 'past-time-related-to-present-time'.

Present perfect tense

54 The Present Perfect, as distinct from the Simple Past Tense, is often described as referring to 'past with present relevance', or 'past involving the present'. There is a great deal of truth in this description, but on its own it is too vague to tell us exactly when and when not to use the Present Perfect. There are actually two distinct ways in which a past event may be related to the present by means of the Perfect: (a) it may involve a TIME PERIOD lasting up to the Present, and (b) it may have RESULTS persisting at the present time. Moreover, we can distinguish not just two, but four different uses of the Present Perfect, one of them occurring with 'state verbs' and three with 'event verbs'. We begin with the 'state' use, which is conceptually the best starting point, although it will turn out that the fourth use (resultative) is the most common (see §§59, 60).

a. The construction *have got* appears to be the Perfect form of the main verb *get*. Although it is possible to use it in this way (as in *Sam's got meaner in the last couple of years*), it is more likely that *have got* is interpreted as a 'state present' equivalent to *have* (*We've got plenty of fruit* = *We have plenty of fruit*). In any case, the usual AmE Perfect of *get* is *have gotten* (*Sam's gotten meaner...*). The semi-modal *have got to* (§148) is also non-perfect in its interpretation. In general, then, *have got* is not Perfect.

Four uses of the present perfect

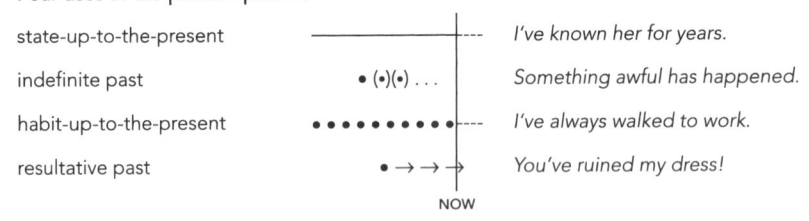

state-up-to-the-present	────────┼---	*I've known her for years.*
indefinite past	• (•)(•) ... │	*Something awful has happened.*
habit-up-to-the-present	• • • • • • • • • •┼---	*I've always walked to work.*
resultative past	• → → →│	*You've ruined my dress!*
	NOW	

--- indicates possible continuation after the present moment.
(•) (•) ... indicates that there may be more than one event.
→ → → indicates that results persist in the present time.

55 STATE-UP-TO-THE-PRESENT. With 'state verbs', present involvement means that the state extends over a period lasting up to the present moment:

I've lived in this neighbourhood since I was a kid ('and this is where I'm living now'). | We've *known* each other for years. | That house *has been* empty for ages.

THE EXPRESSION OF PAST TIME

The *period* mentioned extends up to the present moment, but since 'state verbs' are of undefined time-span, the *state itself* may possibly extend into the future: e.g. *We've kept healthy all our lives, and we mean to stay healthy in the future.*

The Past Tense would be unacceptable in BrE, though not in AmE, in the first of the three examples above (being incompatible with *since* here). In the other two examples the Past Tense would mean that the period is already complete and in the past: *That house was empty for ages* ('... but now it's been sold and occupied').

This 'state' use of the Present Perfect is generally accompanied by an adverbial of duration: the absence of an adverbial (e.g. *We have lived in London*) usually indicates not a state at all, but a completed happening in the indefinite past (see §56 below). There are exceptions, however, where a period leading up to the present, although not actually mentioned, is implied by context or the meaning of the clause. In *He's lived a life of luxury*, duration up to the present is understood, because there is an implicit period 'during his life'; in *You've outstayed your welcome*, the word *outstay* likewise incorporates the durational meaning 'for too long'.

a. A further special case has to be made for verbs used in one of the 'anti-progressive' categories (see §§37–8). With these verbs, the ordinary Present Perfect can also identify a period of 'limited duration' normally expressed with other verbs by the Present Perfect Progressive (see §§76–7), for which the requirement of an accompanying adverbial does not apply. In answer to *Why haven't you been writing to me?* one might reply *I've been too angry to write*, or *I've been ill*. Here the verb *to be* (of Class 37G) describes a temporary situation, for which the Progressive form would elsewhere be appropriate.

56 INDEFINITE PAST. With 'event verbs', the Present Perfect can refer to some indefinite happening (or happenings) in the past:

> *Have you been to Brazil?* | *He's a man who has experienced suffering.* | *I've known love, but not true love.* | *All my family have had injections against measles.*

Often the indefinite meaning is reinforced adverbially, especially by *ever, never* or *before (now)*: e.g. *Have you ever been to Brazil?*

Two things are meant by 'indefiniteness' here: first, the number of events is unspecified – there may have been one or more than one occurrence; second, the time is also left unspecified. To put it more carefully, therefore, the meaning of the Present Perfect here is 'at-least-once-before-now'. The number of events, it is true, can be mentioned adverbially: *I've been to America three times*. But if there is an adverbial of time-when to specify the exact time in the past, the Present Perfect becomes inappropriate, and is normally replaced by the Simple Past: not **I'VE BEEN to America last summer*, but *I WENT to America last summer*.

a. Especially in BrE, there can be cases where the Present Perfect co-occurs with an adverbial specifying a past time. E.g.: '*Have you ever been to Austria?*' '*Yes, I've been to*

37

Vienna in 1980.' Many people would consider such usages as mistakes, even though they sometimes occur in the speech of native speakers.

b. The indefinite past meaning of the Perfect, like the state-up-to-the-present meaning, does not often occur without adverbial reinforcement. On the infrequent occasions when it does so occur, the verb *have* tends to be stressed, and the whole clause tends to imply some kind of reservation:

> I *have* eaten lobster (with a fall of intonation on *have* and a rise on *lobster*) ('... but I can't say I enjoyed it'). | I *have* played tennis ('... but not very often').

57 At first glance, it looks as if there is no element of 'present involvement' in this use of the Present Perfect, any more than there is in the Simple Past. But in fact, a more precise definition of the indefinite past use should indicate that a period of time leading up to the present is involved here, just as in the state use of the Present Perfect. Once again, our 'indefinite past' definition must be revised, and more exactly formulated as: 'at-least-once-in-a-period-leading-up-to-the-present'. This longer wording, when applied to the preceding examples, adds nothing material to the more concise label 'indefinite past'. But consider these other examples:

> Have you visited the Gauguin exhibition? (i.e. 'while it has been on'). | The postman hasn't called at our house (i.e. 'today').

The first of these sentences implies that the Gauguin exhibition is still running, whereas the Simple Past *Did you visit the Gauguin exhibition?* would have suggested that the exhibition is over (or more precisely, that your chance to visit it is over). In the same way, the second sentence is spoken with a special time period (probably a day) in mind: it does not mean that the postman failed to call at least once in the past; it means rather that the postman has not called during a period in which his regular visit is expected. There is a general tendency of self-centredness in human speech, whereby, unless otherwise specified, we understand a word or phrase to refer to something close at hand rather than distant. It is this principle that is at work in these sentences. If we recognise that the indefinite past meaning always involves a period leading up to the present, it is easy to see how this period can become reduced, by subjective assumption, from 'always' to 'within the last few days', or even 'within the last few minutes'. In other sentences, the restricted period is made explicit:

> Have you installed any new software *in the last week*? | Have you taken him to the vet *since the trouble started*?

The assumption of proximity is noticed in a vaguer way in utterances like *Have you seen my car keys (recently)?* or *The electrician has (just) called* (where AmE would be more likely to use the Simple Past). If the adverbs *recently* and *just* are omitted from these sentences, there is scarcely any change of meaning, as they simply make the implicit 'nearness' of the event explicit.

The sense of 'nearness' is quite common, so that it is worth recognising a sub-category of the indefinite past meaning, that of the RECENT INDEFINITE

THE EXPRESSION OF PAST TIME

PAST. This is partly separated from the more general indefinite past meaning by its association with the adverbs *just, already, recently, still* and *yet*. *Always, never, ever* and *before*, on the other hand, single out the more general meaning. Compare, for instance, *Have you* EVER *been to America?* with *Has the electrician called* YET?

a. In AmE, the recent indefinite past is frequently expressed by the Simple Past Tense: *Did your sister phone yet?* (which would be unusual for a British speaker in this context). But the Present Perfect is also used here in AmE – and British speakers show signs of beginning to follow the American use of the Simple Past.

58 HABIT-IN-A-PERIOD-LEADING-UP-TO-THE-PRESENT. The habitual or iterative use of the Present Perfect with 'event verbs' is illustrated by:

> Mr Phipps *has sung* in this choir for fifty years. | I've always *walked* to work. | The news *has been broadcast* at 10 o'clock for as long as I can remember.

Since a habit (as that term has been understood here) is a state consisting of repeated events, this use is similar to the 'state' use of the Present Perfect described in §55 above. As we saw there, the habit or state may continue through the present moment into the future, and an adverbial of duration is usually required: *Mr Phipps has sung in this choir* without the adverbial phrase becomes an example of the indefinite past meaning. Often, the habit element is emphasised by an adverbial of frequency: *The machine has been serviced* EVERY YEAR *since we bought it.*

59 RESULTATIVE PAST. The Present Perfect is also used in reference to a past event to imply that the result of that event is still operative at the present time. This meaning is clearest with 'transitional event verbs' (§35B), describing the switch from one state to another. The resultant (and present) state implied by the Perfect is indicated in brackets in these typical examples:

> The taxi *has arrived* (i.e. 'The taxi is now here').
> She *has been given* a camera ('She now has the camera').
> I've *recovered* from my illness ('I'm now well again').
> Someone *has broken* her doll ('The doll is now broken').

In other examples, the resultative implication is still there, even though it is not quite so obvious from the verb's meaning:

> I've *had / taken* a shower ('So I'm now clean').
> He's *cut* his hand with a knife ('The cut is still there, i.e. has not yet healed').

The resultative meaning needs no support from adverbials. It is sometimes difficult to distinguish from the recent indefinite past use (§57): in fact, it is arguably a special case of the recent indefinite past, in which there is the additional resultative inference. One may argue, for instance, that the question *Have you seen my trainers?* is really a question about the present consequences of seeing the trainers; i.e. 'Do you know where they are?'

a. There is a comparable resultative use of past participles: *a broken doll, a painted ceiling, an injured arm.* For example, *a broken doll* means a doll that has been broken, and is still in the resulting state of being 'broken'. These examples contrast with past participles of 'state verbs', where the meaning is purely stative: *an honoured colleague; a known gambler; a feared opponent.* These cannot be paraphrased by a clause with a Present Perfect verb form; *Hewitt is a feared opponent* means that the opponent *is* feared now, not that he *has been* feared in the past.

b. There are two Perfect forms of the verb *go*: *have* + *gone* and *have* + *been*. The difference in meaning between them is that the first is resultative, indicating transition into a current state of absence, whereas the second is indefinite past (or habitual). *He has gone to America* implies he is still there; *He has been to America* implies that he has since returned (or at least that he has since left America).

c. As the notions of completeness and result are clearly connected, we note at this point the completive emphasis of the Present Perfect in some rather oracular utterances in elevated style: *What I have written, I have written.* Here the effect of the Perfect is 'What I have written must stay there – it cannot be altered or added to'.

Present Perfect and Simple Past

60 Having noted the four principal meanings of the Present Perfect, let's briefly consider factors of frequency. First, it is worth noting that the Present Perfect is much less frequent than the Simple Past tense. Second, the four senses of the Present Perfect are of very different frequency – by far the most common sense is the last of the four: the resultative. The indefinite past sense (without the resultative implication) is next most common. The remaining senses (state-up-to-the-present and habit-up-to-the-present) are considerably less frequent than the other two.

Now let's review the contrasts and points of overlap between these meanings and that of the Simple Past. As a means of referring to the past, the Present Perfect differs from the Simple Past on three counts, viz. continuation up to the present, present result, and indefinite time.

61 CONTINUATION UP TO THE PRESENT TIME. This element of meaning is found in the state-up-to-the-present, in the habit-up-to-the-present and (to a degree – see §57) in the indefinite past meaning. The contrast of the 'state' Perfect with the Past is evident in:

> His sister *has been* an invalid all her life (i.e. 'She is still alive').
>
> His sister *was* an invalid all her life (i.e. 'She is now dead').

The same contrast is made with the habitual use in:

> For generations, Nepal *has produced* the world's greatest soldiers ('The nation of Nepal still exists').

THE EXPRESSION OF PAST TIME

For generations, Sparta *produced* Greece's greatest warriors (This permits, but does not compel, us to infer that 'The state of Sparta no longer exists').

Again, here is the same point illustrated with the indefinite past use:

Has Tom Stoppard *written* any novels? ('Stoppard is still alive – or at least he's still an active writer').

Did Anton Chekhov *write* any novels? ('Chekhov is now dead – or at least he's no longer active').

In all these examples, the period in question is assumed rather than named: it is most likely the lifetime of the person or institution denoted by the subject of the sentence.

a. We do find occasional examples which contradict the rule about continuation up to the present, e.g.:

Over the past six months statistics have been gathered by a new Europe-wide service, but HAVE NOT BEEN PUBLISHED *until yesterday.*

Perhaps the best way to explain such cases as this is to assume that speakers use only an approximate notion of 'up to the present moment', which can stretch to accommodate 'up to the recent past'. (This is more evident with cases of the Present Perfect Progressive such as *It's been raining* – see §79).

62 PRESENT RESULT. The resultative use of the Present Perfect (in BrE) is shown in contrast to the Simple Past in:

Peter *has injured* his ankle ('His ankle is still bad').

Peter *injured* his ankle ('... but now it's better').

The second allows us to conclude that the result of the injury has disappeared.

a. On the other hand, the Simple Past is used for unique historical events, even when their results are still there: *This house was built by Inigo Jones. Tobacco was brought to England by Sir Walter Raleigh.*

b. For present result as for recent indefinite past, the Present Perfect can often be replaced by the Simple Past: *Why are you limping? Did you hurt your foot?* In AmE, in fact, the Simple Past is more natural here.

63 INDEFINITE TIME. Whereas the Present Perfect, in its indefinite past sense, does not name a specific point of time, a definite POINT OF REFERENCE (or anchor point) in the past ('then') is normally required (in BrE) for the appropriate use of the Simple Past Tense. The point of reference may be specified in one of three ways:

(a) By an adverbial expression of time-when:

I *saw* him *Tuesday.*

41

(b) By a preceding use of a Past or Perfect Tense:

> I *saw* / *have seen* him this morning – he *came* to borrow a hammer.

(c) By implicit definition; i.e., by mentally assuming a particular reference point from the context:

> *Did* you *hear* that noise?

(Here the speaker has in mind a particular time when the noise occurred. From the speaker's viewpoint – though not necessarily from the hearer's – the time is definite.)

Definite and indefinite past meaning

64 A little more needs to be said on the concept of definiteness.

The 'definite'/'indefinite' contrast between Simple Past and Present Perfect is exactly parallel to the contrast in meaning between the definite article *the* and the indefinite article *a* or *an*. We say *the cat* rather than *a cat* whenever a particular animal has already been mentioned, or else whenever, even though no cat has been mentioned, we know simply from familiarity with the context, what particular cat is under discussion. If a husband says to his wife *Did you feed the cat?* it is clear to them both (unless they have more than one cat) which cat is meant.

These two conditions of previous mention and uniqueness within the context correspond to conditions (b) and (c) in §63 above.

A further resemblance is this. It is natural to introduce a new topic *indefinitely*, then to progress to *definite* reference (using Past Tense, definite article, personal pronouns, etc.) once a frame of reference has been established:

> Two teenagers and *a 10-year-old girl* were caught in the crossfire. *The girl* was taken to hospital for emergency treatment, but fortunately *her* wounds were not serious.

Similarly, Past follows Perfect:

> There *have been* times when I *wished* you were here.
>
> Where *have* you *been*? I *was looking* for you everywhere.
>
> A: I've only *been* to Switzerland once. B: How *did* you like it? A: It *was* glorious – we *had* beautiful weather all the time.

As the last example shows, after the definite time has been established, the Past Tense can be repeatedly used to denote events happening simultaneously or in succession, just as one may continue to refer to the same person as *the woman* or *she*. A preceding indefinite reference 'licenses' a definite reference.

a. Implicit definiteness can often be clarified by taking the corresponding indefinite statement, and by mentally adding a *when* clause. *Who gave you this tie?* for instance, can be expanded into the following train of thought: 'This tie has been given to you by someone – that much I know already; but *when it was given to you*, who gave it to you?' Other examples are: *Did you have a good journey?* ('... when you came here'); *Did you enjoy your meal?* ('... when you ate it'); *I went to school with Tony Blair* ('... when I was a schoolboy').

b. When the topic of a sentence is unique (e.g. often when its subject or object is a proper name) the definiteness extends to the verb form, so that Past Tense is selected: in *Philadelphia was founded by William Penn*, the Past Tense is only natural, since we know that Philadelphia is a definite place, and was founded at a unique point in history. In this connection, it is interesting to contrast the indefinite *John has painted* A *picture* (*of his sister*) with the definite *John painted* THIS *picture*.

c. The Past Tense, indicating a definite point of reference in the past, is to be expected in temporal clauses introduced by *when, while, since*, etc., because the time specified in such clauses is normally assumed to be already given: *You made a mistake* WHEN YOU BOUGHT THAT DOG; *She hasn't spoken to us* SINCE WE QUARRELLED ABOUT THE WILL. (*When* followed by the Present Perfect is not frequent, and must be understood in a past-in-the-future or habit-up-to-the-present sense.) If the *when* clause contains a Past Tense verb, the main clause must also be in the Past Tense: the *when* clause is classed as an adverbial expression of time-when, just like *last week*, *three years ago*, etc. (see §69).

d. There is an idiomatic exception to the rule that the Simple Past Tense indicates definite meaning: this is the construction with *always* illustrated by *I always said he would end up in jail*; *Timothy always was a man of peace*. It is simply a colloquial variant of the Present Perfect with 'state verbs', and can always be replaced by the equivalent Present Perfect form. There are equivalent question and negative forms with *ever* and *never*: *Did you ever see such a mess?* *I never met such an important person before*.

e. The Present Perfect is used less frequently in AmE than in BrE, and in particular, it is quite common to hear in North America the Simple Past where in Great Britain the Present Perfect in its recent-indefinite-past sense would be standard: *Did you sell your bicycle (yet)?*

f. The Simple Past is sometimes used in comparative sentences where *used to* + Infinitive would be more generally appropriate (see §85): *I'm not so young as I* WAS = *I'm not so young as I* USED TO BE.

Miscellaneous points

65 Although the meanings of the Simple Past and Present Perfect are different in the ways stated, it is worth noting that either of them can be acceptable in the same utterance, with little difference of effect. For example, a person who has mislaid his/her spectacles might exclaim either *Now where did I put my glasses?* or *Now where have I put my glasses?* The difference between these two is merely a slight difference of viewpoint. In the first sentence, the speaker's attention is fixed on the moment when the glasses were lost, in an effort to remember what happened at that time; in the second, the speaker focuses on the present result of this action, and the question uppermost is: 'Where are they now?'

MEANING AND THE ENGLISH VERB

66 Like the ordinary Present Tense, the Present Perfect can be used with reference to an imaginary 'present moment' (see §25*a* where the first part of the following example was quoted):

> Batman responds when Gotham City is threatened by the vengeful Penguin and his gang of crooked circus performers, who HAVE TEAMED up with a corrupt tycoon, Max Schreck.

In this way a writer of a narrative summary gives a retrospective account of previous happenings, using the Present Perfect for events which are 'in the past' from the point of view of the stage of the story now reached.

67 The non-finite verb is strictly outside the subject matter of this book, but one important point has to be made about it. As the Past Tense belongs to finite verb constructions only, the Perfect form does duty, in non-finite constructions, for both Past Tense and Perfect Aspect. Thus it can have both definite and indefinite reference: *Having seen a doctor yesterday* shows the Perfect form of the present participle co-occurring with *yesterday* – something not allowable with a finite verb. Similarly with a *to* + Infinitive construction: *She is believed to* HAVE LEFT *last Monday* means practically the same as *It is believed that she* LEFT *last Monday*. The same point can be made, more relevantly, about the Infinitive in finite verb constructions with modal auxiliary verbs (see §142): *She may* HAVE LEFT *last Monday* is equivalent in meaning to *It is possible that she* LEFT *last Monday*.

Adverbials in relation to Perfect and Past

68 All tenses of the English verb map time by means of points of reference (or 'points of orientation' – also called 'anchor points') which indicate the relation of one time to another.

The primary point of reference is the present moment – the moment 'now' when the speaker is actually speaking, or (sometimes) the moment at which the speaker imagines he/she is speaking. But with the Past Tense, there is a secondary point of reference as well: as we have seen, it is an important difference between the Simple Past and Present Perfect that the Past evokes a past point of reference 'then', whereas the Present Perfect relates past time more directly to the present point of reference 'now'.

It is a consequence of this difference that the range of time adverbials (i.e., adverbs, adverbial phrases and adverbial clauses) combining with the Past Tense is by no means the same as the range of time adverbials combining with the Present Perfect. We have already noticed some of the differences, but it will be useful at this point to summarise usage with regard to adverbials. A rough general rule is that with the Present Perfect, as with Present Tenses in general, adverbials must relate, in one way or

THE EXPRESSION OF PAST TIME

another, to the present point of reference 'now', while with the Past Tenses they must refer to some point or period of time in the past.

69 Adverbials associated with the Past Tenses include *a week ago, earlier this year, last Monday, the other day, yesterday morning* and similar phrases. These, like the single adverb *yesterday*, refer to a specific time in the past, and so cannot normally occur with the Present Perfect.

At four o'clock, in the morning, on Tuesday, then, soon, next, after breakfast, etc. Members of this group, although they refer to a definite time, do not refer explicitly to the past. But when they have past reference they are likely to be found with the Past Tense. With the Present Perfect, they can have only a habitual sense, as in *We've always watched the TV news at 10 o'clock.*

70 In contrast, the following are adverbials associated with the Present Perfect rather than the Past: *So far, up to now, hitherto, since Thursday, since I met you,* etc. Such phrases and clauses normally refer to a time period stretching up to 'now', and so go with the Present Perfect in its state, indefinite past, or habitual sense.

Lately and *latterly* (BrE) go with the recent indefinite past interpretation of the Present Perfect.

For the present, for now, for the time being, etc. indicating present duration can accompany the Present Perfect, but not the Past.

a. Present time-when adverbials such as *nowadays* and *these days* cannot accompany either the Present Perfect or the Past – they require the Simple Present or Present Progressive. (But *now* can be used with the Present Perfect, marking the end point of the period of time during which a particular happening has taken place: *We have now finished the whole project.*)

71 The next group is composed of adverbials combining with either the Present Perfect or the Past.

Today, this month, this year, this century, etc. refer to a period including the present moment: with them, the Present Perfect and Past Tense are virtually interchangeable. If there is a difference of meaning between *I went to the dentist today* and *I have been to the dentist today*, it is that the second focuses on the result aspect of the verb.

This morning, tonight, this March, this Christmas, etc. refer to a period which is part of a larger period including the present moment (as 'this morning', for instance, is part of 'today'). With *this morning / afternoon / evening*, it is sometimes said that the Present Perfect indicates that the period referred to is not yet over – that, for example, it is possible to say *I have been to the dentist this morning* at 11 a.m., but not at 3 p.m. This distinction, if made, accords with the principle that the Present Perfect has to involve a period extending up to the present. But other speakers of English find it is possible to say *I've been to the dentist this morning* in the

45

afternoon or evening: for them, it seems, we can interpret *this morning* as 'today in the morning'.

Phrases of calendar time such as *this March* conform to the general rule that a period that is gone requires the Past Tense. The most natural inference from *I saw him this March* is that March is over, while *I have seen him this March* suggests that March is still with us.

Recently and *just*, as adverbs of the near past, can take either the Present Perfect or the Past: *I've just seen your boyfriend* or *I just saw your boyfriend*. Other adverbials with 'recent' meaning are somewhat varied in their behaviour: *lately* and *latterly* (as we saw in §70 above) normally collocate with the Present Perfect in BrE; *just now*, on the other hand, is like *a moment / second / minute ago*: it goes with the Past Tense.

With *always*, *ever* and *never*, Past and Present Perfect are largely interchangeable when describing a period up to the present (see §64d). Here is an exceptional use of the Past Tense.

72 Finally, we turn to adverbials combining with either Perfect or Past but with a clear difference of meaning.

Now, as we would expect, is principally associated with the Present Tenses: *Now my ambition is / has been fulfilled*. With Past Tense, it is a narrative substitute for *then* (= 'at this point in the story'): *Now my ambition was fulfilled*.

Once with the meaning 'on a certain occasion, at one time', accompanies the Past Tense, despite its indefinite meaning. It can refer to a long period of time in the past: *I was once an honest man*. With the Present Perfect, it is a numerical adverb contrasting with *twice*, *three times*, etc.: *I have visited the Highlands only once*.

Already, *still*, *yet* and *before* occur with the Present Perfect in the sense '[surprisingly,] as early as now', '[surprisingly,] as late as now', etc.: *I've seen him already*; *I still haven't seen him*. With the Past, they must have a meaning involving a past point of reference: *I was already* (= 'as early as then') *very hungry*.

Past Perfect

73 The Past Perfect Tense (*I had written*, etc.) has the meaning of past-in-the-past, or more accurately, 'a time further in the past, seen from the viewpoint of a definite point of time already in the past'. That is, like the Simple Past Tense, the Past Perfect demands an already established past point of reference. This is why it is difficult to begin a conversation with the Past Perfect Tense.

We would hardly need to give separate attention of the Past Perfect if it were merely a question of adding the Perfect Aspect meaning to Past Tense meaning. But in fact the Past Perfect covers an area of meaning (further in the past) equivalent to both the Past and Perfect. It is like the

Perfect Aspect of non-finite verbs (see §67) in being capable of referring to both indefinite and definite time: contrast *The parcel had already arrived* (indefinite) with *The parcel had arrived on April 15th* (definite).

In discussing the Past Perfect, it is useful to distinguish between the ordinary past point of reference 'then' (T) and the previous point of time 'before then' (B):

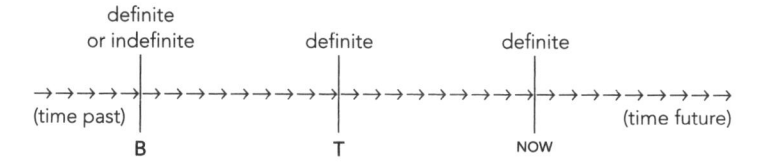

```
        definite
      or indefinite       definite          definite
→→→→→|→→→→→→→→→→→|→→→→→→→→→→→|→→→→→→→→→→→
(time past)                                              (time future)
        B                T              NOW
```

Whereas T (by its very nature as a point of reference) is definite, B is either definite or indefinite. The following examples show the Past Perfect paralleling the four uses of the Present Perfect as discussed in §§55–9:

The house had been empty for ages. (state-up-to-then, cf. §55)

Had they visited Brazil before? (indefinite past-in-past, cf. §56)

Mr Phipps had sung in that choir for fifty years. (habit-up-to-then, cf. §58)

The goalkeeper had injured his leg, and couldn't play. (resultative past-in-past, cf. §59)

For *The parcel had arrived on April 15th*, however, there is no corresponding Present Perfect sentence, because a definite time B ('before then') is mentioned.

It is worth noting that an adverbial of time-when with the Past Perfect can refer to either T ('then') or B ('before then'):

When the police arrived, the thieves *had run away*. ('By the time the police arrived, the thieves had run away.')

The thieves *had run away* when the police arrived. ('The thieves had run away at the time when the police had arrived.')

In the first of these sentences, the *when* clause is likely to identify T, whereas in the second sentence it is likely to identify B.

74 In some contexts, particularly following the conjunction *after*, the Simple Past and Past Perfect are interchangeable. These two sentences could well be describing the same sequence of events:

(1) I ate my lunch after my wife *had come* back from town.

(2) I ate my lunch after my wife *came* back from town.

After itself places the wife's arrival before the eating, so the Past Perfect in (1) is, in a way, redundant. What difference there is between these two statements can be represented as follows:

MEANING AND THE ENGLISH VERB

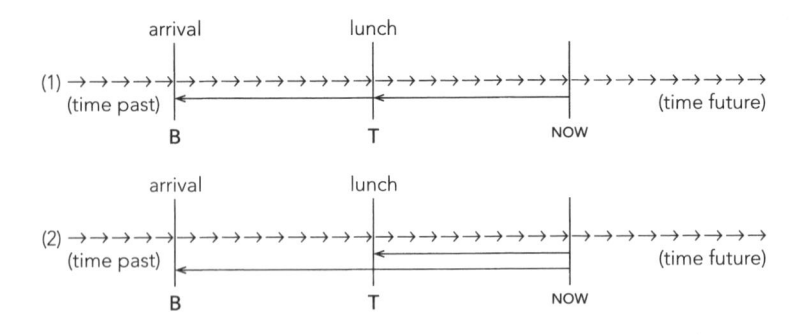

```
              arrival              lunch
                 |                   |                 |
(1) →→→→→→|→→→→→→→→→→→|→→→→→→→→→|→→→→→→→→→→
 (time past)   |←                 →|←             →|              (time future)
              B                   T                NOW

              arrival              lunch
                 |                   |                 |
(2) →→→→→→|→→→→→→→→→→→|→→→→→→→→→|→→→→→→→→→→
 (time past)   |←                                   →|              (time future)
              B                   T                NOW
```

Statement (1) measures the 'beforeness' of the arrival from the event of eating lunch; statement (2) measures it directly from the present moment, treating it as another 'then', not as a 'before then'. Statement (1) is the more explicit choice.

From this illustration, we see that the fact that one happening is further in the past than another happening already mentioned makes the use of the Past Perfect appropriate, but not necessary. (BrE favours this use of the Past Perfect more than AmE.)

Perfect Progressive

75 Like the Past Perfect, the Perfect Progressive (*I have been working*, etc.) has a range of meaning that is not entirely predictable from the meanings of its components. However, all features of meaning associated with the Perfect Aspect and the Progressive Aspect considered separately come into play in one way or another.

76 The main features associated with the Progressive in §§28–31 were DURATION, LIMITATION OF DURATION and POSSIBLE INCOMPLETENESS. The second of these gives the Perfect Progressive its meaning of 'temporariness', seen in these examples:

> I've *been writing* a letter to my nephew. | How *have* you *been getting* on? | It's *been snowing* again.

The verbs here are 'activity verbs' which typically go with the Progressive Aspect. The meaning of the Present Perfect Progressive is roughly that of A TEMPORARY SITUATION LEADING UP TO THE PRESENT MOMENT, and is comparable to the state-up-to-the-present meaning of the non-progressive Present Perfect. There is, however, a difference between a temporary and a permanent time-scale:

> Lynn and Josh *have lived* in that house since their marriage.
>
> Lynn and Josh *have been living* in that house since their marriage.

The second statement describes a situation which the speaker regards as temporary; it is therefore more appropriate when Lynn and Josh have not been married very long. It also hints that the situation is liable to change.

Because of the semantic element of duration, the Perfect Progressive is difficult to use with verbs which normally refer to momentary events:

> He has been starting his car.
> ?*He has been starting his book.

The first of these makes sense, but reflects badly on the car's reliability. The second sentence, on the other hand, seems nonsensical because it gives duration to something which cannot have duration: the only way to make sense of it is to construe it as an ironical remark with the interpretation 'He has been meaning / trying / pretending to start his book'.

77 Two further differences between the Present Perfect Progressive and the Present Perfect meaning state-up-to-the-present are:

A As examples above show, the Progressive does not have to be accompanied by an adverbial of duration. The sentence *?*It has snowed* without any adverbial qualification sounds very odd, while *It has been snowing* is perfectly acceptable.

B The Progressive can be used with many verbs which cannot be used with the non-progressive Present Perfect in this sense, because they cannot act as 'state verbs': *You've been reading that book for ages* is allowable, but not **You've read that book for ages*.

Once again, however, there is virtually a free choice between the two forms in many contexts: *Jack has been looking after the business for several years* and *Jack has looked after the business for several years* are both acceptable.

a. There seems to be a tendency to avoid the ordinary Present Perfect with verbs such as *sit, lie, wait* and *stay*, which generally refer to temporary states. Thus *I've been sitting here all afternoon* is more idiomatic than *I've sat here all afternoon*. The same preference is exercised even with very long periods of time: *The inscription has presumably been lying here for thousands of years* is more likely to be used than *The inscription has presumably lain here for thousands of years*.

b. The Perfect Progressive, however, is almost never found with the Passive Voice: *Volunteers have been running the organisation* could scarcely be turned into the Passive form of *The organisation has been being run by volunteers*. (The Perfect Progressive Passive, although not impossible in present-day English, is extremely rare.)

c. Naturally enough the anti-progressive verb classes listed in §37 do not normally appear with the Perfect Progressive: **I've been knowing Dr Mason for some time* is unacceptable (see §55a).

d. Although as a general rule a *since* clause requires the Present Perfect instead of the Simple Present (see §7a), we not infrequently find *since* with the non-perfect Present Progressive in sentences such as *I'm cycling to work since my car broke down*. The usual construction is, however, the Present Perfect Progressive: *I have been cycling to work since my car broke down*.

MEANING AND THE ENGLISH VERB

78 The element of POTENTIAL INCOMPLETENESS in the meaning of the Perfect Progressive becomes important when one thinks about the possibility of adding a statement predicting the continuation of the activity into the future:

> The business *has been losing* money for years ('. . . and will probably continue to lose money').

With 'bounded' verbs ('event verbs', including some 'activity verb' or 'process verbs', whose meaning entails eventual fulfilment or completion – see boundedness, §31*a*), the 'incompleteness' option in the Present Perfect Progressive contrasts crucially with the ordinary Present Perfect, which specifies that the conclusion has already been reached:

> Who's *been eating* my dinner? (This usually implies 'Some of it is left').
>
> Who's *eaten* my dinner? (This usually implies 'It's all gone').
>
> They've *been widening* the road (?'They're still at it').
>
> They've *widened* the road ('The job's finished').

Where finality is not likely to be an issue, the two can be equally acceptable in similar situations. There is little to choose between *I've taken the dog for a walk* and *I've been taking the dog for a walk*, except that the former places emphasis on the present result, the latter on the recent activity, as suggested by these two snatches of dialogue:

> 'I've taken the dog for a walk.' 'Oh thanks, that means I can take a rest.'
>
> 'Where have you been?' 'I've been taking the dog for a walk.'

79 Although 'present result' is not a noticeable part of the meaning of the Perfect Progressive in the examples above, in other circumstances there is a trace of it in the implication that THE EFFECTS OF THE ACTIVITY ARE STILL APPARENT:

> You've been fighting again ('I can tell that from your black eye').
>
> It's been snowing ('Look, the ground is white').
>
> She's been crying again ('Look, her eyes are red').

In these cases, as in general with the Perfect Progressive, it is not necessary for the activity to continue right up to the present moment. In fact, we frequently understand that THE ACTIVITY HAS RECENTLY STOPPED. The meaning-components 'effects still apparent' and 'recently finished' are closely connected, and it is very difficult to tell whether one of them is dependent on the other. Recentness is sometimes stressed by the adverb *just*: *I've just been listening to a programme on Vietnam.*

a. The 'recently stopped' component of meaning need not be in conflict with the element of 'non-completion'. *I've just been painting the house* implies 'I have recently stopped painting the house', but it may also mean that the job as a whole is incomplete and will be resumed later.

THE EXPRESSION OF PAST TIME

80 In summary, we may say that the main use of the Present Perfect Progressive combines elements 'continuation up to the present', 'recent indefinite past', and 'resultative past' found in the use of the non-progressive Present Perfect; and that, in addition, it combines these with the concepts of temporariness and possible non-completion associated with the Progressive Aspect. Let us list these elements as follows:

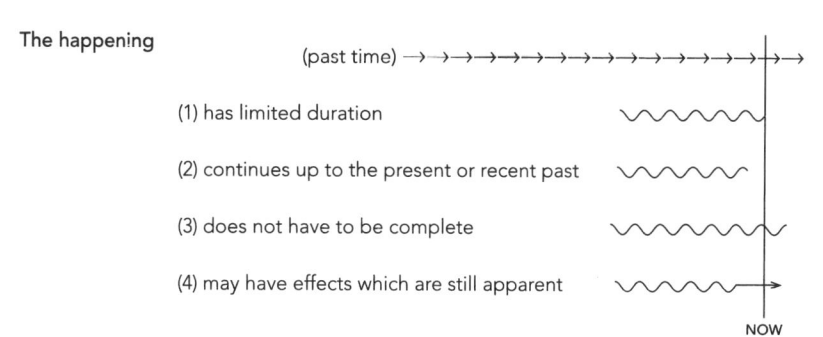

The happening

(past time) →→→→→→→→→→→→→→→→→

(1) has limited duration

(2) continues up to the present or recent past

(3) does not have to be complete

(4) may have effects which are still apparent

NOW

81 The above description applies to the Present Perfect Progressive referring to a single unbroken activity or situation. Less commonly, this tense is also used in the habitual sense of TEMPORARY HABIT UP TO THE PRESENT:

He's been scoring plenty of goals so far this season. | I've been going to hospital every week for tests.

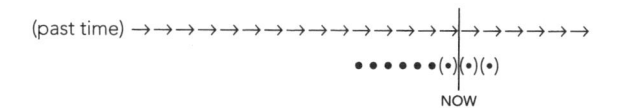

(past time) →→→→→→→→→→→→→→→→→→→→
• • • • • •(•)(•)(•)
NOW

Examples can also be found of the second habitual meaning of the Progressive, that which involves stretching the time-span of each event rather than compressing the time-span of the habit as a whole (see §50): *Whenever I've seen her, she's been wearing that preposterous old hat.*

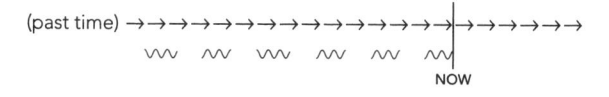

(past time) →→→→→→→→→→→→→→→→→→→→
NOW

Past Perfect Progressive

82 The rare Past Perfect Progressive (*Sam had been drinking*, etc.) can be used in all the ways illustrated above with the Present Perfect Progressive and, what is more, may have the definite past-in-the-past meaning discussed in §73; that is, it may be a shift further into the past than the meaning of the ordinary Past Progressive *was dancing*, etc. Hence it is possible to join the Past Perfect Progressive, like the non-progressive Past Perfect, with an adverbial of time-when: *I had been speaking to her at 4 o'clock*. (The corresponding example with the Present Perfect Progressive would be unacceptable: **I have been speaking to her at 4 o'clock*.) Hence, also, there is an ambiguity in the sentence:

> The inscription had been lying there for a thousand years.

This can mean (a) that the thousand years led up to 'then', the point of reference (a use corresponding to the Present Perfect Progressive, as in *The inscription has been lying there for a thousand years*); or (b) that there was a gap between the thousand years and 'then' (a use corresponding to the ordinary Past Progressive, as in *The inscription was lying there for a thousand years*).

a. Although I described the example as 'ambiguous' above, it is probably better to think of the Past Perfect Progressive as simply more general in its meaning than either the Present Perfect Progressive or the ordinary Past Perfect. It combines the temporariness of the Progressive with the past-in-the-past meaning of the Past Perfect. This is all that needs to be said about this tense of infrequent occurrence.

Future in the past

83 To balance the Past Perfect, we might expect the English language to possess a 'future in the past' tense for describing happenings which are in the future from some vantage point in the past. But there is no regular verbal construction with this meaning in everyday use.

Past Progressive forms or *was / were going to* + Infinitive with future-in-the-past reference are coloured by the notion of 'intention' or 'imminence' (see §§92–100), and so do not guarantee that the event foreseen in the past actually did take place:

> The beauty contest *was taking place* on the next day.
>
> The beauty contest *was going to take place* on the next day.

To both of these one could add: 'This was the plan – but in fact it had to be cancelled because of bad weather'. These are therefore not true future-in-the-past tenses.

84 The language comes nearest to possessing a future-in-the-past tense in the constructions *would* + Infinitive and *was / were to* + Infinitive, when these are interpreted 'was / were destined to':

> Twenty years later, Dick Whittington *would be* the richest man in London.
>
> This strange, nervous individual *was* later *to be* defendant in one of the most notorious murder trials of all time.

Both these usages are uncommon, and are largely restricted to a rather literary style of historical narrative. In neither case can the events foretold be in the future from the *present* point of view of the narrator: they must take place between the 'then' of the narrative and the 'now' of the narration.

The use of these constructions in the sense 'was / were destined to' is so limited that in practice English speakers manage without a future-in-the-past construction, and use the ordinary Past Tense when they wish to anticipate some later event in past narrative:

> Pitt, who later *became* Britain's youngest Prime Minister, was at this time Chancellor of the Exchequer.

a. Both *would* + Infinitive and *was / were to* + Infinitive are more commonly used in senses other than 'was destined to'. *Would* + Infinitive can be used as the equivalent of *will* + Infinitive in indirect speech (see §157), and indeed, the sentence about Dick Whittington above is ambiguous. It can be interpreted not only in the 'was destined to' sense, but as free indirect speech, as if a parenthetic 'he said to himself' were added (see §160). Likewise, *was to* can be the Past of *is to* in the sense of 'is due / intended to'. Hence *Pitt was to be the next Prime Minister*, read in one way, is a prophecy with the benefit of historical hindsight, but read in another way, reports a plan which perhaps was never fulfilled (see §149).

Used to

85 Before we leave the subject of past time, there is the auxiliary *used to* (pronounced /juːstuː/ or /juːstə/) + Infinitive construction to consider. This construction is not to be confused with the adjectival idiom *(be) used to* meaning '*(be) accustomed to*'. It indicates:

1 A PAST STATE (with 'state verbs'):

> Cigarettes *used to cost* fifty pence a packet – now they cost nearly ten times as much. | Before they built the hotel, this place *used to be* a Chinese garden.

2 A PAST HABIT (with 'event verbs'):

> I *used to go* for a swim every day. | When I was young, my grandfather *used to tell* me frightful stories of the war.

Three points are to be noted about this construction.

(a) *Used to* has no equivalent present construction **uses to*, and can only have durative past meaning. Because of its state or habit meaning, it typically implies a contrast with a present state or habit, which can be expressed by a verb in the Simple Present: *I used to be rich* ('... but now I am poor').

(b) *Used to* is not normally accompanied by an adverbial of time-when. Instead, it seems to have its own 'built-in' adverbial *once* (= 'at one time'), in that the *used to* construction can be paraphrased by *once* with the Simple Past Tense:

> the man who *used to be* organist of St Paul's = the man who *was once* organist of St Paul's.

Thus an element of 'indefinite past' is normally present in the meaning of *used to*. Nevertheless, the combination of *used to* with an adverbial of time-when, though unusual, is not unacceptable: *He used to live here during the war years.*

(c) The 'indefinite past' meaning of *used to* discourages combination with an adverbial naming the actual duration of the state or habit:

> ?*She used to live in the green house for ten years, and then moved to the one on Mill Street.

a. On the other hand, an adverbial of duration can be employed if it specifies the period of each event making up a habit: *He used to go home for several weeks during the summer* is permissible, because *for several weeks* here refers to each of the series of occasions.

b. Used to does not occur with the Perfect Aspect: **I used to have worked all afternoon*. With the Progressive Aspect, too, it is rare, but can be used in a habitual sense corresponding to that of §50 'repetition of events of limited duration': *Often when I passed she used to be sitting there on the doorstep.*

c. On the use of *would* (= 'predictability') with habitual past meaning similar to that of *used to*, see §140.

CHAPTER 4

The Expression of Future Time

86 five ways of expressing future. WILL (ALSO *'LL* AND *SHALL*): *87* prediction; *88* will, 'll and shall; *89* forecasting use; *90* past in future; *91* future use of *shall*. BE GOING TO: *92* future outcome of the present; *93* future of present intention; *94* future of present cause; *95* be going to less appropriate in future conditional sentences; *96* 'soonness' not a necessary element of meaning; *97* does not guarantee fulfilment of the event. FUTURATE PRESENT PROGRESSIVE: *98–9* future of present plan, programme or arrangement; *100* 'soonness' frequently implied; *101* mainly restricted to 'doing' verbs. SIMPLE PRESENT WITH FUTURE MEANING: *102* Simple Present with conditional, temporal and manner conjunctions; *103* futurate Simple Present: future as 'fact'; *104* plan or arrangement regarded as unalterable; *105* sequential use. WILL (ALSO 'LL AND SHALL) + PROGRESSIVE INFINITIVE: *106* normal use; *107* 'future-as-a-matter-of-course'; *108* tactful use; *109* interchangeability with *will* + Simple Infinitive. CONCLUDING REMARKS: *110* list in order of importance; *111* list in order of certainty; *112* other methods of referring to the future: *am / is / are to*; *be about to*; *113* meaning differences can be overemphasised.

86 There are a number of ways of expressing future time in English. The most important of them are:

- *Will* (or *shall*) + Infinitive: The parcel will arrive tomorrow.
- *Be going to* + Infinitive: The parcel is going to arrive tomorrow.
- Present Progressive: The parcel is arriving tomorrow.
- Simple Present: The parcel arrives tomorrow.
- *Will* (or *shall*) + Progressive Infinitive: The parcel will be arriving tomorrow.

These verb forms all have their subtle nuances of meaning, and cannot be regarded as simply interchangeable. The task of this chapter is to explain the differences, beginning with the most common construction, that of *will* (or *shall*) followed by the infinitive.

Shall as an alternative to *will* is becoming uncommon, especially in AmE. Since *will* is at least 10 times more frequent than *shall*, I treat *will* as the normal auxiliary for the future, and deal with future *shall* more briefly in a separate section. The contracted form *'ll* (see §88 below), like the negative contraction *won't*, will also be treated as a variant form of *will*.

Will (also 'll and shall)

87 *Will* (with *'ll* and *shall*) has the function of a modal auxiliary as well as an auxiliary of the future. In fact, these two functions are so closely intermingled that it is difficult to separate them. This chapter, however, will deal with only the main future use of *will*, leaving its volitional and other modal uses to the next chapter (§§125, 126).

A good reason for putting together the future and modal uses of *will* lies in the very nature of futurity. We cannot be as certain of future happenings as we are of events in the past and present, and even the most confident prediction about the future must reflect something of the speaker's uncertainty and so be tinged with modality. *Will* is no exception. The word which most usefully characterises the future meaning of *will* is PREDICTION – something involving the speaker's judgement. Thus, although the *will* construction provides English with its nearest approximation to a neutral or colourless future, we should not describe it as a 'future tense' on a par with the Past and Present Tenses.

88 The full auxiliary form *will* is frequently contracted in speech (especially after pronoun subjects) to the form written *'ll*, which can combine with subjects of all three persons to express future meaning:

> *I'll* see you soon. | *You'll* have to work quickly. | *She'll* be at home when you get there.

Shall, however, can express this predictive meaning only with a first-person pronoun as subject:

> *I shall* have to tell the truth at last. | *We shall* explore this topic in the next chapter.

With a second-person or third-person subject, *shall* has a modal meaning, which we discuss later (§127). *You shall receive what you deserve* is a threat or promise rather than a prediction in present-day English, but in fact this usage is rare and old-fashioned.

Will, like its contracted form *'ll*, is used with all three persons to express futurity:

> *I will* be here until five. | *You will* be here until five. | *He/she will* be here until five.

THE EXPRESSION OF FUTURE TIME

With the first-person pronouns, however, according to tradition English-speaking people feel that *shall* is the correct form, and so *I will* and *we will* are sometimes avoided by more 'grammatically conscious' writers, particularly in situations (such as in writing business letters) where people are on their best linguistic behaviour.

89 The *will* future is used in a wide range of contexts in which it is appropriate to make predictions:

> Tomorrow's weather *will be* cold and cloudy. | You*'ll feel* better after this medicine. | The next budget *will need to be* a severe one. | Perhaps I*'ll change* my mind after I've spoken to my wife.

Will is particularly common in the main clause of conditional sentences:

> If you press this button, the roof *will slide* back.

(In the *if-clause*, however, the future condition is usually expressed by the ordinary Present Tense – see §102 – as the verb *press* illustrates above.)

Will is suitable for both long-range and short-range forecasts about the future:

> In twenty years' time, no one will work more than a thirty-hour week. | There *will be* a fire-alarm drill at 3 o'clock this afternoon.

a. Will can refer to either an indefinite or a definite time in the future. In *Sarah will keep her promise*, *will keep* is the future counterpart of the Present Perfect Tense (*Sarah has kept her promise*); in *Next year we'll have a good harvest*, *'ll have* is the counterpart of the Simple Past (*Last year we had a good harvest*).

b. Frequently, however, a sentence with *will* describing a future event feels incomplete without an adverbial of definite time: ?*It will rain; ?**The room will be cleaned*. These sentences are relatively unacceptable on their own, because of their factual emptiness. We all feel certain that 'it will rain' at some time in the future, so there is no point in saying *It will rain* unless an actual time can be forecast. ?*It has rained is slightly odd for a similar reason. (On the other hand *It is going to rain* is fine without the adverbial – see §94*a*.)

c. It can be taken for granted in the rest of this chapter that *will*, as well as other methods of referring to future time, can be employed in reference to a narrative future: *Will John Jennings escape from the clutches of Red Reagan's gang? Find out in next week's* Conquest. (Compare similar uses of Present and Present Perfect Tenses, §§25*b* and 66.) Here time is seen in terms of the 'virtual reality' of imaginary narrative sequence. *Will* also often denotes a 'virtual' future in referring forward to a later part of a book or article: *The sensory apparatus of bats will be examined later, in Chapter 25*. (However, the Simple Present can also be used here: . . . *is examined* . . . .)

d. A special adapted use of *will* (= 'prediction') occurs in military or quasi-military orders: *Officers will report for duty at 0300 hours. You will not move a muscle until I say so* (see §126D*a*).

90 *Will* followed by the Perfect Infinitive, though not common, is the usual means of expressing PAST IN FUTURE in English; i.e., of referring to a state or event seen in the past from a viewpoint in the future: *By the age of 20, as*

57

a typical American child you will have watched 700,000 TV commercials. The time looked at retrospectively can either precede or follow the present moment, as is shown by the adverbials in this imaginary speech of a disgruntled student:

> By next weekend I'll be sick of exams; I*'ll have had* eight exams in two weeks.

There is a similar construction with *will* + Perfect Progressive Infinitive:

> When she moves out in August, she*'ll have been staying* here in my house for six months.

The 'future progressive' form is another possible construction with *will*: *Who will be driving? I'll be waiting for you*. This is discussed in §§106–9 below.

91 SHALL is an alternative to *will* with first person subjects in more formal styles of speaking and (especially) writing:

> We *shall* see. | I hope we *shall* meet again quite soon. | I *shall* ask my lawyer to be present at the hearing.

a. Shall is very occasionally used for future reference with second- and third-person subjects: *The earth shall be filled with God's glory. The time shall come when the poor and the oppressed shall rise against the oppressor*. This is the old-fashioned language of prophecy. (See also §127.)

b. In AmE, *I shall* and *we shall* are largely confined to very formal situations, as in the orator's *We shall never surrender*.

Be going to

92 After *will*, the next most important way of expressing future time is the construction *be going to* + Infinitive, which is especially common in informal spoken English. (In fact informally *going to* is reduced to /'gənə/, a pronunciation reflected in the non-standard spelling *gonna*.) If there is one general meaning that can be attached to this construction, it is FUTURE AS OUTCOME OF PRESENT CIRCUMSTANCES. In fact, though, it is useful to distinguish between two meanings, the FUTURE OUTCOME OF PRESENT INTENTION and the FUTURE OUTCOME OF PRESENT CAUSE.

a. Be going to + Infinitive here is a single construction, not to be confused with a combination of the verb of motion *go* with the infinitive of purpose. *I am going to see my grandmother* can mean either 'I intend to see . . .' or 'I am going [there] in order to see . . .' The first alternative is our present concern: it can be reduced to the pronunciation represented *gonna*, where the second cannot.

93 The FUTURE OF PRESENT INTENTION is illustrated in these sentences:

> 'What *are* you *going to do* today?' 'I*'m going to stay* at home and write letters.' | My ex *is going to vote* for Pat Buchanan. | They*'re going to get* married in a registry office.

This is found chiefly with human subjects, and with 'doing' (or agentive) verbs which imply conscious exercise of the will.

a. There is a slight difference of meaning, however, between *I am going to leave tomorrow* and *I intend to leave tomorrow*. The latter does not tell us whether the departure will take place or not; but *be going to* brings with it a strong expectation (if not quite a prediction) that the intention will be carried out. *I'm going to cut down on junk food* is stronger than *I intend to cut down on junk food* – it implies confidence in my power to put the resolution into effect – and sooner rather than later.

b. The intention communicated by *be going to* is usually ascribed to the subject of the sentence – but not invariably. In passive sentences, it is often the intention of the IMPLIED agent that is in question: *This wall is going to be repainted* (= 'We or somebody else intend to repaint it').

94 THE FUTURE OF PRESENT CAUSE is found with animals and inanimate subjects, as well as with human subjects; it is also common to both 'agentive' and 'non-agentive' verbs. It thus covers a wider range of contexts than the intentional meaning of *be going to*:

> She's going to have twins.   (i.e. 'She's already pregnant')
> I think I'm going to faint.   (i.e. 'I'm already starting to feel ill')
> There's going to be a storm   (i.e. 'I can see the black clouds gathering')
> in a minute.

In each of these there is the feeling that factors giving rise to the future event are already present; or (to be more exact) it is as if THE TRAIN OF EVENTS LEADING TO THE FUTURE HAPPENING IS ALREADY UNDER WAY. The first sentence may be contrasted with *She will have twins*, which is the pronouncement of a fortune-teller, rather than a piece of news.

From this, it is easy to see why *be going to* is often used in reference to the immediate future:

> Watch it! That pile of boxes is going to fall! ('I can see it already tottering')
>
> Just look! She's definitely going to win the race! ('She's starting to overtake the other runners')

Is going to win here is almost equivalent to *is about to win* or *is on the point of winning*.

a. When the clause with *be going to* contains no time adverbial, immediate future is almost certainly implied. *We're going to buy a house in the country* implies 'soon', unless some adverbial indicates otherwise: *We're going to buy a house in the country when we retire.*

b. It is generally clear which of the two variant meanings of *be going to* applies to a given context, but ambiguities can arise: *He's going to arrive late at the concert* can mean either 'That is his intention' or 'That is what will happen, if he goes on like this'.

95 *Be going to* is less appropriate than *will* in most future conditional sentences:

> If you pay by cash you *will* normally *obtain* a receipt as proof of payment.
>
> ?*If you pay by cash you *are* normally *going to* obtain a receipt as proof of payment.

The second of these sentences is less likely because the eventuality described in the main clause in such sentences depends on future rather than present circumstances. *Be going to* is suitable, however, if present circumstances are mentioned in the *if-clause*; i.e., if the condition is a present one rather than a future one:

> We*'re going to find* ourselves in difficulty if we go on like this.
>
> If you're expecting Wales to win, you*'re going to be* disappointed.

Be going to implies that the conditions for the future event already exist. However, *will* could replace *be going to* in these two examples with little difference of meaning.

96 Imminence ('soonness') is not a NECESSARY semantic accompaniment of *be going to*, as we see from the remote periods mentioned in these statements:

> Present intention: I'*m going to do* what I like when I retire.
>
> Present cause or train of events: If Winterbottom's calculations are correct, this planet *is going to burn itself out* 200,000,000 years from now.

If we take a fatalistic view of the future, of course, any coming event, however remote, can be thought to have its seeds in the present. In any case, there is often in people's speech a sense of destiny vague enough to bring *be going to* almost as close to a neutral 'future tense' as *will*. The two constructions can often be substituted for one another with little change of effect:

> The whole idea of the digital computer *will be* obsolete in fifty years.
>
> The whole idea of the digital computer *is going to be* obsolete in fifty years.

Will can be replaced by *be going to* even more generally if the nearness of the event is signalled by an adverb, or is made clear by the situation:

> What *will happen* now? = What *is going to happen* now?
>
> *Will* you *be away* long? = Are you *going to be away* long?

Following these trends, it seems that in more informal styles of English (particularly in speech) *be going to* is beginning to rival *will* as a fairly neutral future auxiliary. The following two examples show *be going to* being used in contexts where there is no particular reason to feel that the 'future is an outcome of the present':

I wonder if she *is going to* recognise us? (Anticipating a meeting with a long-lost cousin)

But closing seven excellent schools *is* not *going to save* anything. (Arguing against a proposal to save money)

97 *Be going to* does not guarantee that the anticipated happening will actually come to pass. This is illustrated most clearly in Past Tense examples:

He *was going to sue* me, but I persuaded him it would be pointless. | The car *was going to crash*, but with the last wrench of the wheel I brought it to safety.

With the Past Tense, indeed, a frequent interpretation is that fulfilment did not take place, or at least was not evident. Non-fulfilment is also characteristic of the Present Perfect form of *be going to*: *He's been going to fix that window-catch for months* ('... but he hasn't got around to it').

a. This Perfect form *He's been going to . . .* is unusual, and is likely to be accompanied by a strong stress on '*go*-. More usual would be: *He has been meaning to fix . . .*

b. Be going to has no non-progressive variant **go(es) to*, and so it cannot really be considered a Progressive form, nor can it follow a Progressive: **I'm being going to*. But it can follow a Perfect: *I've been going to finish that job for ages*. In principle it can also precede a full range of grammatically permissible tenses and aspects: *Are you sure you're going to have finished the job by the time they arrive? I guess they're going to be watching the World Cup all week*. With a preceding *will*, *going to* can even express 'future in the future': *Call on me at lunchtime on Monday – I'll be going to speak to the boss about it that afternoon*. These complex constructions are rare.

Futurate Present Progressive

98 Like *be going to* + Infinitive, the Present Progressive can refer to a future happening anticipated in the present. (This use is termed FUTURATE – see also §103). But there is a subtle difference from *be going to*: it is not a present intention or cause, but rather a PRESENT ARRANGEMENT that is signalled by the Progressive.

99 A reasonably precise definition of the Present Progressive futurate is: FUTURE EVENT ANTICIPATED BY VIRTUE OF A PRESENT PLAN, PROGRAMME OR ARRANGEMENT. Here are examples:

She's *getting married* this spring. | The Chelsea–Arsenal match *is being played* next Saturday. | We're *having* fish for dinner. | I'm *inviting* several people to a party. | When *are* we *going* back to France?

In each there is the implication of an arrangement already made: the marriage has been arranged, the football match has been fixed, the menu has been chosen, the party has already been decided on.

The difference between 'arrangement' and 'intention' is a very slight one; so *be going to* + Infinitive could be substituted for the Present Progressive in all these examples. There is, however, a small change of emphasis, as is illustrated in this pair of sentences:

I'm *going to take Mary out* for dinner this evening.
I'm *taking Mary out* for dinner this evening.

An intention is part of one's present state of mind, while an arrangement is something socially predetermined in the past, regardless of how the speaker feels now. So the second sentence, but not the first, could conceivably be uttered with some reluctance by someone who now regrets the arrangement. It could very readily be used as an excuse: *I'm sorry, I'd love to have a game of billiards with you, but I'm taking Mary out for dinner.* The social nature of an arrangement also means that it is somewhat strange to use the Progressive to refer to an activity which the speaker will perform alone: *I'm watching TV this evening* (unlike *I'm going to watch TV this evening*) is a little odd, and seems to suggest that watching TV is an arrangement that has been made by the speaker with others. For example, several football fans may have arranged to meet and watch their favourite team on the television.

100 It is understandable that the notion of 'fixed arrangement' comes to be associated with the near rather than distant future. The element of IMMINENCE ('soonness') often accompanying the future use of the Present Progressive is illustrated in the examples just given. As with *be going to*, however, the possibility remains of referring to the more remote future if it is seen as determined in advance: *When I grow up, I'm joining the police force.*

Another resemblance between the Present Progressive future and the *be going to* future is that time adverbials can be omitted. The following sentences without adverbial modification are in fact ambiguous out of context, as they can be given either a present (in progress) or future (imminent) interpretation:

I'm *taking* Mary out for a meal. | We're *starting* a bridge club. | Buffy and Rex *are leaving*. | My aunt's *coming* to stay with us. | They're *being made* redundant.

(To get the present in-progress meaning, it helps to imagine the speaker talking into a mobile phone in the middle of the mentioned activity!) Without an adverbial, a time in the near future rather than remoter future is generally intended: one could insert the adverb *just* or *soon* in these sentences to make the imminence explicit.

The future use of the Present Progressive without a time adverbial seems to be chiefly limited to verbs of motion and some other verbs signifying single events. It is difficult, for example, to see any ambiguity in *I'm attending evening classes in Spanish.* Because of its habitual meaning, this sentence must almost certainly refer to the present rather than the future, unless we add a future adverbial such as *next year.*

a. 'Transitional event verbs' such as *arrive, die, land* and *stop* in any case have an anticipatory element in their meaning when used with the Progressive Aspect (see §35B). *The aeroplane is landing, Our team is winning,* etc. referring to an event already under way, are probably best regarded as exemplifying the in-progress present rather than the future use of the Present Progressive. But *The aeroplane is landing at Amsterdam* could easily be interpreted as 'future by arrangement'.

101 The factor of 'plan' or 'arrangement' in the future meaning of the Present Progressive restricts its use in the main to 'doing' verbs involving conscious human agency:

John's *getting up* at 5 o'clock tomorrow. | *The sun *is rising* at 5 o'clock tomorrow.

The second sentence is absurd because it suggests that the rising of the sun could be deliberately planned, instead of being determined by natural law. In this respect, the *be going to* future has wider application than the Present Progressive future: we can say *It is going to rain tomorrow* (a forecast on the basis of present circumstances), but not **It is raining tomorrow.*

a. This does not mean, however, that the Present Progressive is entirely limited to 'doing verbs'. In *I'm getting a present tomorrow,* the verb *get* is ambiguous – it can have either the active, agentive meaning 'acquire', or the passive, inert meaning 'receive'. The inert meaning is possible because in this case the plan is understood to have been made and carried out by someone other than the subject of the sentence: the meaning is approximately 'Someone has arranged to give me a present tomorrow'.

b. A further, unsurprising restriction on the future use of the Present Progressive is that it does not occur with verbs (such as *to be,* see §37H) that are normally incompatible with the Progressive Aspect: we can very well ask *Who is captaining the team next Saturday?* but not *?*Who is being captain of the team next Saturday?*

Simple Present with future meaning

102 A SUBORDINATE FUTURE use of the Simple Present occurs in DEPENDENT CLAUSES introduced by conditional, temporal and manner conjunctions *if, unless, when, as soon as, as,* etc.:

I'll tell you if it *hurts.* | When you *wake up,* you'll remember nothing. | Jeeves will announce the guests as they *arrive.* | Phone me as soon as you *get* there. | Next time do as she *tells* you.

Here the future is indicated by the ordinary Present Tense, instead of the construction with *will* that might be expected. Apparently this is because the situation indicated in the dependent clause is not a prediction in its own right, but something given or assumed to be the case, a contingency of the future reference in the main clause. It can be said that in *I'll tell you if it hurts*, there are not two future references, but one – signalled by the *'ll* in the main clause. In this sense, the Simple Present in the dependent clause is a 'subordinate future', depending on the future reference in the main clause.

The Simple Present as subordinate future also occurs in some *that*-clauses, *wh*-clauses and relative clauses of future reference:

> Just suppose we *miss* the plane. | Make sure you *get* up early. | The press is bound to report what she *says* tomorrow. | I mustn't forget to ask her how much she *wants*! | The man she *marries* will have to be rich.

The Simple Present is used especially where the main clause clearly suggests futurity, and so we can say again that the sentence makes only one reference to the future through verbs like these, and a (further) use of *will* would be redundant. But some verbs like *hope* and *bet* offer a choice between the Simple Present and *will*: *I hope we (will) win. I bet you (will) lose.*

The future subordinate use of the Simple Present applies to other classes of verbs and adjectival expressions, followed by *that*-clauses and typically used in the imperative: *make sure, be sure, be careful, mind, ensure, see*. With these, it is impossible to use *will* in the *that*-clause: *Be careful you don't spill it* is fine, but not **Be careful you won't spill it*. Perhaps this is again because the independent clause clearly places the time-zone of the dependent clause in the future, and no separate reference to the future in the dependent clause is needed.

a. Notice the following ambiguity where both the present and future interpretations of a state verb are possible: *If you already know the answers, you will pass the exam*. Here the *if*-clause can mean 'know the answers now' or 'know the answers when you take the exam'.

b. Compared with the Simple Present, *will* is rather rare in *if*-clauses. When it does occur, it can have a volitional interpretation: *If you'll* (i.e. 'are willing to') *come this way, I'll show you some of our latest products*. On the other hand, the neutral 'prediction' meaning of *will* is not impossible in *if*-clauses, as this example shows:

> If you'll be alone at the New Year, just let us know about it.

The effect of using *will* here is to make the relation between the *if-clause* and the independent clause a matter of present rather than future contingency. The above sentence means 'If you can predict *now* that you will be alone at the New Year, let us know about it *now* (or at least before the New Year)'. The effect of the Simple Present is quite different: *If you are alone this New Year, just let us know about it*. This means: 'If, at the New Year, you find yourself alone, let us know about it *at that time*'. Here the condition exists in the future. (In the above sentence, *If you are going to* . . . could replace *If you'll* . . . .)

c. The future subordinate use of tenses is not confined to the Simple Present alone. It can also be found occasionally with (1) a Present Progressive form, (2) a Present Perfect form, and (3) even a Simple Past form. These are illustrated below:

THE EXPRESSION OF FUTURE TIME

(1) A mother, saying goodbye to her daughter about to spend a month abroad, might say: *Don't forget to phone me tomorrow and let me know how* YOU'RE GETTING ON. The Present Progressive here refers to a future scenario.

(2) In the following, *have been welcomed* denotes the past-in-future: *As soon as the guests* HAVE BEEN WELCOMED, *show them into the garden.*

(3) In the following, the Simple Past *missed* refers to something that is to happen in the past-in-future: *If you don't take this job, you'll always regret that you* MISSED *your chance.*

103 The name FUTURATE is given to a (rather infrequent) use of the future Simple Present in INDEPENDENT CLAUSES. This represents FUTURE ASSUMED TO BE FACT; that is, it attributes to the future the same degree of certainty we normally accord to present or past events. Statements about the calendar are the most obvious illustrations:

Tomorrow's Saturday. | Next Christmas *falls* on a Thursday. | This Friday *is* Abigail's birthday. |

But any aspect of the future which is regarded as immutable can be similarly expressed:

The semester *starts* on 1st February. | Next year the United Nations *celebrates* the sixtieth anniversary of its charter. | The train *leaves* at 7.30 this evening.

Since most future happenings are in principle subject to doubt, the present futurate, which describes a future event by a categorical statement of fact, is a special or 'marked' form of reference. It overrides the normal feeling that the future is less certain than the present or past. A statement like *Next week John fails his driving test* is unthinkable except as an ironical comment, suggesting that John's failure is as sure as the rising of the sun, or the fact that Wednesday will succeed Tuesday.

104 From this it is an easy step to the Simple Present signifying a PLAN OR ARRANGEMENT REGARDED AS UNALTERABLE:

We *start* for Istanbul tonight. | I *get* a lump sum when I retire at sixty-five. | Her case *comes* before the magistrate next week. | The President *gives* his inaugural address tomorrow afternoon.

The Simple Present is a 'marked' future here also: it carries a special, rather decisive overtone similar to that of the event present (see §10). It would weaken the force of the above sentences to substitute the Present Progressive: *We are starting for Istanbul tonight* announces a present plan which could, conceivably, be altered later. Here the Present Progressive's connotation 'susceptible to change' comes to the fore. But in *We start for Istanbul tonight*, changing the plan is out of the question.

A further difference between the two constructions is that the arrangement conveyed by the Present Progressive is generally (though not necessarily) assumed to have been made by someone named in the subject of the sentence. *I'm starting tonight* almost always means '*I* have arranged to start tonight'. But with the Simple Present, the plan is often felt to be an impersonal or collective one – made, for example, by a committee, a court of law, or some unnamed authority.

a. However, this difference is not always felt: *The match starts at 2 o'clock* and *The match is starting at 2 o'clock* are more or less equivalent statements. In both we suppose that it is the organisers of the match that have made the arrangement.

105 In its FUTURATE use, the Simple Present refers to a definite future occasion in the same way as the Simple Past Tense (see §64) refers to a definite occasion in the past. This means it has to be accompanied by an adverbial referring to future time, unless it occurs in a narrative sequence, or in a context where some definite point of time in the future is assumed. An example of such a narrative sequence is:

> Right! We *meet* at Victoria at 9 o'clock, *catch* the fast train to Dover, *have* lunch at the Castle Restaurant, then *walk* across the cliffs to Deal.

The tone of this statement, as well as suggesting an irrevocable decision to follow the planned programme, also has something in common with the 'dramatic present' of stage directions (see §25*a*): the speaker seems to enact in advance the events as they will take place.

a. A related use of the Simple Present is the expression of inexorable determination in some conditional sentences: *If they reject the appeal, we'RE FINISHED. One more step, and I SHOOT you!* The latter example shows a style of threat familiar from popular crime and adventure stories. Similar also is the quasi-imperative use of the Simple Present with the inversion of Verb and Adverbial Complement in *Into bed you go! Up you get!* Such commands have a rather patronising air, and are directed mainly at pets and young children. These are examples of the Present futurate with a strong 'immediate future' connotation: the child or pet is expected to respond straight away.

b. Note the ambiguity of sentences like *His train leaves at 5 o'clock*, which can indicate either future (= '... at 5 o'clock today') or habitual present (= 'at 5 o'clock every day'). Compare a similar ambiguity in travel instructions, §26(b).

Will (also *'ll* and *shall*) + Progressive Infinitive

106 The construction *will* (*'ll* or *shall*) + Progressive, following the normal in-progress use of Progressive Aspect, can refer to temporary situations in the future (see §§28–31):

> This time next week they *will be sailing* across the North Sea. | Don't phone me at 7 o'clock – I'*ll be watching* my favourite TV programme.

As these examples show, the activity is often associated with a future point of time round which it forms a 'temporal frame' (see §32). In this, the 'future progressive' with *will* is entirely comparable to the Past Progressive: *This time last week they were sailing across the North Sea.*

On the other hand, in other examples there is no framing effect, and instead *will* + Progressive conveys the idea of an ongoing happening or state of affairs in the future: *The whole factory will be working overtime next month.*

107 There is also, however, a special use of *will* + Progressive: a use which applies to a single happening viewed in its entirety (and therefore without the characteristic 'framing effect' or non-completeness normally associated with the Progressive). This use requires separate attention, as it cannot be regarded just as a combination of the future meaning of *will* with the 'in progress' meaning of the Progressive. Examples are:

> I'*ll be writing* to you soon. | When *will* you *be moving* to your new house? | Next week we'*ll be studying* Byron's narrative poems. | The parties *will be meeting* for final negotiations on July 25th.

The meaning of the verbal construction here can be roughly summed up in the phrase FUTURE-AS-A-MATTER-OF-COURSE: it suggests that the predicted happening will come to pass without the interference of the volition or intention of anyone concerned.

It is tempting to speculate that this usage has grown up through the need to have a way of referring to the future uncontaminated by factors of volition, plan or intention which enter into the future meanings of *will* + Infinitive, the Present Progressive, and *be going to*. It appears to combine the future meaning of *will* ('prediction') with the 'arrangement' meaning of the Progressive futurate, so that, for example, *I'll be seeing you* can be glossed: 'The arrangement is such that I predict I will see you'.

Although the volitional uses of *will* and *shall* have not so far been discussed (see §§126–7 below), we need to notice here that with human subjects and 'agentive' or 'doing' verbs, *will* frequently combines prediction with overtones of volition (see §§126B–D). Hence there is a clear distinction of meaning in these pairs:

(a) *I'll drive* into London next week ('I've made up my mind. That's what I've decided').

(b) *I'll be driving* into London next week ('This will happen as a matter of course').

(c) *Will* you *put on* another play soon? ('Please!' – this sounds like a request).

(d) *Will* you *be putting on* another play soon? ('Is this going to happen?').

In principle, it is possible to use (a) in the neutral predictive sense of *I'll die one day*; but in practice, it is difficult to avoid suggesting at the same time that HERE AND NOW I AM DECIDING to drive to London. The possibility of volitional colouring is avoided in sentence (b), which is understood simply as a statement that 'such-and-such is predicted to happen'. There is a similar contrast between examples (c) and (d). As a question, (c) implicates the intentions of the listener, and therefore sounds almost like a cajoling request; but (d) simply enquires whether a further production will take place.

a. To illustrate the difference between the in-progress and special meanings of the *will* + Progressive construction, notice that the following sentence may be interpreted either with or without the 'framing effect': *I'll be visiting my aunt at lunchtime.* Let's define *lunchtime* as the period 12–2 p.m. The 'framing' interpretation is that lunchtime is included in a longer period (say, 11 a.m. to 7 p.m.) during which I am at my aunt's house. The matter-of-course interpretation is that I will turn up at my aunt's house sometime during lunchtime (say, 12.15 p.m.) and stay for a while.

b. The matter-of-course meaning does not seem to occur with 'state verbs', as is argued by the lack of ambiguity of a sentence like *We'll be living in London next year.*

108 One reason why the *will* + Progressive usage has become quite common in everyday speech is that it is often a more polite and tactful alternative to the non-progressive form. Sentence (b) §107 could easily precede the offer *Can I give you a lift?* as it would forestall any awkward feeling of indebtedness on the listener's part: 'I'll be making the journey anyway, so don't feel you will be causing me trouble'. Similarly, sentence (d) expresses polite interest in the future theatrical programme, while avoiding any suggestion of putting pressure on the person questioned.

109 In confirmation of the above comments, *will* + Progressive is found to be largely restricted to clauses with human subjects and with implications of agency. A sentence like *The lights will be coming on in a minute* (referring to an automatic lighting system), although acceptable enough, is unlikely. In this case there is no personal involvement, and so a disclaimer of volition is irrelevant. *The lights will come on in a minute* is a simpler way of expressing virtually the same meaning.

a. The 'matter-of-course' connotation helps to account for a temporal restriction which has been noted in the *will* + Progressive construction: viz., that it generally refers to the near, but not too immediate future. If we think of the underlying notion 'this will happen in the natural course of events', we shall not expect it to refer to events too far in the future nor to events too close to the present moment. This is only a rough guideline, however.

b. A second restriction consists in the avoidance of this Progressive form in describing abnormal or sudden or violent events which could not be said to happen 'in the natural course of things'. Remarks like *?*Margot will be poisoning her husband when he gets home* or *?*We shall be blowing up the Houses of Parliament tonight* have a crazy, semi-comic air which arises from the incongruity of treating such outrages as 'a matter of course'.

c. On the other hand, there is an idiomatic exploitation of such incongruities in colloquial English: *You'll be losing your head one of these days* (said to a very forgetful person) or *He'll be buying himself an island in the Bahamas next* (said to someone

THE EXPRESSION OF FUTURE TIME

aspiring to a life of luxury). The message, with allowance for a certain amount of comic hyperbole, runs: 'This is what things will come to in the natural course of events if things carry on in this absurd way'. In the same spirit of comic exasperation is the routinely heard question *Whatever will they be doing next?*

Concluding remarks

110 Leaving aside the subordinate future use and focusing on the futurate use of the Simple Present (§§102–3), I will subdivide the five major types of future construction listed at the beginning of this chapter into six, which can be placed roughly in the following order of frequency:

(1) *will* + Infinitive

(2) subordinate future Simple Present

(3) *be going to* + Infinitive

(4) {futurate Present Progressive
     futurate Simple Present

(5) *will* + Progressive Infinitive.

Probably the most significant point to notice is the relative infrequency (except in dependent clauses) of the futurate Simple Present Tense as an expression of future time in independent clauses, in comparison with the corresponding construction in other prominent European languages. However, in dependent clauses (as discussed in §102), where the occurrence of the Simple Present is syntactically conditioned, the subordinate future use is much more frequent: in fact, frequent enough to make the Simple Present the second most common future construction after *will* + Infinitive. The *will* + Progressive 'future as a matter of course' construction is the least frequent of the five constructions, although becoming more common. The three constructions *be going to*, Present Progressive, and *will* + Progressive are more likely to occur in speech than in writing.

111 Another list, this time ordering the five main-clause constructions according to the degree of certainty ascribed to the future happening, may also help to give guidance on the choice between these six options:

(1)	futurate Simple Present	'future as fact' – the most certain option
(2)	*will* + Infinitive *will* + Progressive Infinitive subordinate future Present	'future as predicted to happen' – the most neutral way of referring to the future
(3)	*be going to* + Infinitive futurate Present Progressive	'future as outcome of present intention, cause, arrangement, etc.' – the least certain option

69

Even those marked 'least certain', however, convey at the least a strong expectation of the future event. There are other infinitive constructions with cognitive verbs such as *intend, hope* and *expect* which are less certain than those listed under (3) above: *I intend / hope / expect to arrive tomorrow*, etc.

112 Yet further ways of expressing future time include *am / is / are to, be about to* + Infinitive, *be on the point of* + Ving, and *be destined to* + Infinitive. Of these *am / is / are to* and *be about to* are the only two common enough to be worth comment.

- AM / IS / ARE TO consists of a Present Tense form of the verb *be* followed by the infinitive marker *to*. This verb construction is like a modal auxiliary in that it has no non-finite forms (*be to, being to, been to*). It is used in rather formal written style, and is used to refer to something that is going to happen in the future as a result of a plan or decree, normally by some authority other than the subject of the sentence:

    (a) The new play *is to* be staged at the Century Theatre next week.
    (b) All school-leavers *are to* have the chance to attend a university.

  Am / is / are to is thus similar in meaning to the present futurate. But unlike the futurate, it can occur without an adverbial (or some other indicator) referring to future time. It can also occur with 'state verbs' and lacks the sense of certainty that accompanies the futurate. As a result, example (a) above could not happily occur with the Simple Present (*?*The new play is staged ... next week*), and example (b) could not occur at all with future meaning with the Simple Present. *Am / is / are to* also has additional uses, more appropriate to consider later under the heading of modality (§149).

- BE ABOUT TO refers to the immediate future, and is close to the meaning of *be going to*, except that it suggests greater immediacy:

    I *am about to hypnotise* you. Don't be afraid! ('I am going to hypnotise you right now') | Keep your seat belts fastened, everyone – we're *about to land*.

  a. *Was / were* (the Past Tense of *am / is / are*) commonly expresses a 'plan' in the past: *The meeting* WAS TO *take place at Oxford the next day*. (There is no claim here that the meeting actually did take place.) In addition, *was / were to* has a factual future-in-the-past meaning 'was / were destined to': *Little did Jenny know that the peace of her life* WAS TO *be shattered* (see §84). Again, these forms are formal, and would rarely be heard in spoken English.

  b. *Am / is / are to* with the interpretation 'plan for the future' is characteristic of newspaper reports, and in headlines, the construction is abbreviated to *to* + Infinitive through the ellipsis of the form of the verb *to be*: UNESCO CHIEF TO VISIT AFRICA; MISS UNITED KINGDOM TO MARRY FILM BOSS.

c. There is a special use of *am / is / are to* with the verb *come* (or, in elevated literary style, with the verb *to be*): *The best is still to come. The best is yet to be.* Both of these could be paraphrased 'The best is still ahead of us, in the future'. They can be compared with a similar construction with *have*: *I have yet to see him smile.* However, in all three cases, the infinitive is a complement rather than part of the finite verb construction.

113 Two final comments. First, the ways of referring to the future dealt with in this chapter illustrate the point made in §5: that the Present Tense, from the semantic point of view as well as syntactically, would be best described as 'non-past'. We have seen that all these future-referring constructions are variations on the Present Tense, with the very minor exception of the future subordinate use of the Past (see §102c) – even including the 'non-past' modal auxiliaries *will / 'll / shall*, to which we turn again in the next chapter. In other words, the Present Tense, in a broad sense, encompasses both present and future domains of time. The future uses of the Simple Present and the Present Progressive are special cases of this.

The very final comment is this. While this chapter has naturally focused on differences of use between these constructions, it appropriately finishes by observing that these differences can be overemphasised. The following sentences, varying only in the choice of future construction and in their consequent connotations, are all entirely acceptable:

The parties will meet for final negotiations on July 25.

The parties are going to meet for final negotiations on July 25.

The parties are meeting for final negotiations on July 25.

The parties meet for final negotiations on July 25.

The parties will be meeting for final negotiations on July 25.

CHAPTER 5

The Primary Modal Auxiliaries

114 six auxiliaries, Primary and (Secondary) Past. CAN: *115* A 'possibility', B 'ability', C 'permission'. MAY: *116* A 'possibility', B 'permission', C quasi-subjunctive uses. MUST: *117* A 'obligation', B 'requirement', C 'logical necessity'. HAVE TO: *118* A 'obligation', B 'requirement', C 'logical necessity'. RELATIONS BETWEEN CAN, MAY, MUST AND HAVE TO: *119* permission, possibility, obligation, requirement and necessity; *120* inverseness; *121* may and can (= 'possibility'); *122* may and can (= 'permission'); *123* must and have to (= 'obligation' or 'requirement'); *124* must and have to (= 'logical necessity'). ROOT AND EPISTEMIC MODALITY: *125*. WILL: *126* A 'prediction/predictability', B 'intention', C 'willingness', D 'insistence'. SHALL: *127* A 'prediction', B 'intention', C 'other volitional meanings', D 'rules and regulations'.

114 Many pages, chapters, books have been written about the modal auxiliary verbs in English. One thing that can make it difficult to account for the use of these words (called 'modal auxiliaries' or 'modals' for short) is that their meaning has both a logical (semantic) and a practical (pragmatic) element. We can talk about them in terms of such logical notions as 'permission' and 'necessity' but, this done, we still have to consider ways in which these notions become remoulded by the social and psychological influences of everyday communication between human beings: factors such as motivation, condescension, politeness, tact and irony. Condescension, for example, in the right context makes the *can* of *You can go now* (which in logical terms means no more than 'permission') into something approaching a command (see §115c*b*).

These factors influence not only the modal auxiliaries, but also main verbs: we can compare the ways in which *Would you* MIND . . . ? and *Would you* LIKE . . . ? (as face-value questions about the listener's wishes) are typically used as polite commands.

This chapter looks at the meanings of the six verbs *can, may, must, have to, will* and *shall*, together with the similarities and contrasts between them. These I will call the Present Tense or PRIMARY modal auxiliaries. It is

THE PRIMARY MODAL AUXILIARIES

important to remember two points about these meanings. First, some meanings are very much more common than others. In fact, for all modals except *must*, one meaning is decidedly the most common and most important meaning. These facts about frequency are indicated in the following sections. Second, the distinctions between the meanings are not so clear-cut as their separation in the lists suggests. It is often better to think of contrasts of meaning as scales of similarity and difference. For example, we can see the three meanings of *can* as forming a diagram as follows:

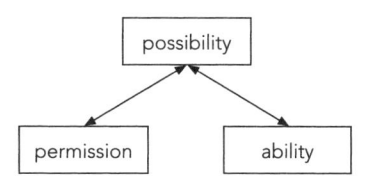

```
              ┌─────────────┐
              │ possibility │
              └─────────────┘
               ↗↙        ↖↘
      ┌────────────┐  ┌─────────┐
      │ permission │  │ ability │
      └────────────┘  └─────────┘
```

The reason for representing the difference between *can* = 'possibility' and *can* = 'ability' (for example) as a scale is that we often find it difficult to decide whether a given instance of *can* belongs to one category or the other. For example, *No one can see us here* could be paraphrased 'It isn't *possible* for anyone to see us here' or 'No one is *able to* see us here'.

In the next chapter, we will turn to the relation between Present (or primary) forms *may, can*, etc. and the Past (or secondary) forms *could, might, would, should*. It is as well to remember, however, that 'Present' and 'Past' are misleading titles for these forms. The 'Present' auxiliaries might more properly be called 'Non-past', as they can refer to future as well as to present time (see §139). The Past auxiliaries, on the other hand, have more important functions than that of simply indicating past time: some of these functions will be postponed until Chapters 7 and 8. Hence I prefer to call modals like *can* PRIMARY and modals like *could* SECONDARY rather than Present and Past.

The meanings of the modals as stated below apply primarily to positive statements; questions and negative forms are dealt with in §§129–38.

a. In grammatical terms, *have to* is not a modal auxiliary verb on the same footing as the others. It has, for example, an infinitive form, which means that it can combine with other modals (as in *We may* HAVE TO *go*) and can combine with *will* to express future time: *We'll* HAVE TO *go*. In terms of meaning, however, it is closely linked to *can, may* and *must*.

b. The modal auxiliaries themselves vary a great deal in terms of frequency. They divide conveniently into three classes:

VERY FREQUENT:	*will* (including *'ll*), *would, can, could*
QUITE FREQUENT:	*must, should, may, might, have to*
INFREQUENT:	*shall, ought (to), need*

This list includes the 'marginal modal' verbs *need* and *ought (to)*, which are less important than the other modals, but will also need some discussion in this and

73

MEANING AND THE ENGLISH VERB

the following chapters. (*Need* is infrequent as an auxiliary, but not as a main verb – see §§133, 147.)

Can

115 The meanings of *can* are:

115 A. POSSIBILITY (very common)

> Even expert drivers *can* make mistakes (= 'It is possible for even expert drivers to make mistakes'). | I don't understand how he *can* be so stupid. | If it rains, we *can* hold the meeting indoors (= '... it will be possible for us to ...').

This sense of *can* is often found in the negative with *cannot* or *can't* (see §§136–8): *She can't be working at this hour!* ('It is not possible, i.e. impossible, ...'). Sometimes *can* (= 'possibility') has a habitual meaning which can be paraphrased by the use of the adverb *sometimes*:

> Lightning *can* be very dangerous = Lightning is sometimes very dangerous.

a. Colloquially, *can* (= 'possibility') is very often a proposal for future action: *We can see about that tomorrow.* In fact with second- and third-person subjects, *can* expresses a familiar though tactful imperative – the type of imperative that might be used by the captain of a sports team to the team members, or by the producer of a play to its cast: *Mike and Willy, you can be standing over there; and Janet can enter from behind that curtain.* It is as though the speaker does not like to exert authority openly, so, counting on co-operation from Mike and Willy, he/she merely suggests that a certain plan of action is POSSIBLE. This is a democratic imperative, to be used in addressing a person regarded as one's equal. This *can* occasionally occurs with the Progressive Aspect (*you can be standing ...*), which is a sign that it belongs to the 'possibility' rather than to the 'permission' sense (see §143). An equivalent usage with a first-person subject can function as an offer: *I can give you a hand for a few minutes, if you need help.*

b. In questions such as *Can you come inside?* or more indirect equivalents such as *I wonder if you can help me? can* (= 'possibility') takes on the force of a (rather polite) request. Note that the adverb *possibly* can intensify such a request: *Can you possibly lend me an umbrella?*

115 B. ABILITY (common)

> Paula *can't* sing, but she *can* play the guitar (= 'knows how to ...'). | You *can* work harder than this (= 'are capable of ...'). | 'Can you read and write?' 'Of course I *can.*'

Can in this sense is more or less synonymous with *be capable of*. When it refers to an acquired ability (as in *Can you speak Greek?*), *can* is also more or less equivalent to *know how to*.

a. With verbs of 'inert perception' and 'inert cognition' (§§37E, 37F) there is little difference between BEING ABLE TO DO something and ACTUALLY DOING it, so *can* tends to lose its distinctive modal meaning. *I can remember* scarcely differs from *I remember* as a means of referring to a state of recall. Similarly, there is little difference between *I can't understand it* and *I don't understand it*. With 'verbs of inert perception', furthermore, *can* not only loses its distinctive modal value, but has the additional special function of denoting a state rather than an event. As the Simple Present with these verbs has only an 'instantaneous' event meaning (see §37E), the main difference between *I can hear* and *I hear*, *I can see* and *I see*, etc. (referring to visual or auditory perception) is one of 'perception as a state' versus 'perception as a (momentary) event'.

b. There is no clear-cut distinction between *can* (= 'ability') and *can* (= 'possibility') as discussed in §115A above. The two meanings are especially close because 'ability' implies 'possibility' – that is, if someone has the ability to do X, then X is possible. However, as *can* (= 'ability') and *can* (= 'permission') require a human or at least animate subject, the 'possibility' sense is the only one available when the subject is inanimate, as in *Appearances can be deceptive*. Another distinguishing mark of the 'possibility' meaning is its likelihood in passive clauses: *This game can be played by young children* means 'It is possible for this game . . .', but the active sentence *(Even) young children can play this game* is more likely to be interpreted in the 'ability' sense.

c. The common verbal construction *be able to* is not always associated with the 'ability' meaning. Like *can*, it can be used to express possibility and even permission: *When the children are grown up, you will be able to live more cheaply*. The most appropriate paraphrase for this remark is '. . . it will be possible for you to live . . .'. As this example shows, *be able to* has an advantage over *can*, in that we can use it as an infinitive after a modal auxiliary, or as a participle, e.g. *The British have never been able to understand the Americans' devotion to baseball*.

115 C. PERMISSION (less common)

> You *can* stay here as long as you like (= 'You're allowed to . . .'). | Residents *can* use the car park without a permit. | '*Can* I see the letter you wrote?' 'Sure, you *can* keep it.'

Linguistic law-makers of the past have considered *may* to be the 'correct' auxiliary of permission, and have condemned the use of *can*. Generations of English-speaking schoolchildren have been reprimanded for saying *Can I . . . ?* instead of *May I . . . ?* Yet in fact, *can* is much more widely used as an auxiliary of permission than *may*. In asking and giving permission, *can* and *may* are almost interchangeable, except that *may* is more formal, and is sometimes felt to be more polite.

a. One place where *can* cannot replace *may* (= 'permission') is in the fixed phrase *if I may*, used as a polite formula: *I'll leave my car in the garage, if I may*.

b. The meaning of 'permission' is strengthened to something like 'strong recommendation' in more or less joking or offensive remarks such as:

> You *can* forget about your holiday. | If he doesn't like it he *can* lump it. | This chicken is half-cooked. Take it back to the cook and tell him where he *can* put it.

A possible explanation for the impolite tone of *can* here lies in a touch of irony: the speaker sarcastically offers someone the choice of doing something that cannot be avoided, or something no one would choose to do anyway.

May

116 Although *may* is one of the middle-frequency modals, its use is declining in present-day English. The only meaning of *may* which is still flourishing is the first sense of 'possibility'. The uses of *may* are:

116 A. POSSIBILITY (common)

> Careful, that gun *may* be loaded. (= 'It is possible that it is loaded.') | You *may* lose your way if you don't take a map. | Don't wait for me – I *may* be a few minutes late.

This use of *may* is common in statements, but does not occur in questions. *May* in this sense, as well as in the 'permission' sense below, usually indicates a future event when it combines with an 'event verb': *may lose, may go, may become*, etc. (see §139).

May in the sense of 'possibility' can be replaced by *might* with little or no difference of meaning – see §183. In fact, spoken AmE shows a preference for *might* in the sense of possibility over *may*. For example, *might* could easily be substituted for *may* in the three examples above: *That gun* MIGHT *be loaded. You* MIGHT *lose your way. I* MIGHT *be a few minutes late.*

a. There is a concessive use of *may* (= 'possibility') in remarks like: *The buildings may be old, but academically it's an excellent school* (i.e. 'I admit that the buildings are old, but . . .').

b. There is generally a difference between *can* and *may* in the sense of 'possibility'. Notice, for example, that in *We may see you tomorrow, can* could not replace *may* without a considerable change in meaning. There is, however, a rather formal use of *may* where the meaning of 'possibility' is the same as for *can*. Thus in *Transitive verbs in English may be either active or passive, can* could be substituted for *may* with no change of meaning. This use of *may* is typically found in formal contexts such as in academic writing. This difference between the 'possibility' senses of *can* and *may* is discussed in §121.

116 B. PERMISSION (less frequent)

> *May* I offer you a drink? | If you wish to consult another doctor, you *may* do so. | Visitors *may* park their vehicles in the main square.

May characteristically signals permission given by the speaker or writer, or (in questions) by the hearer. *May* (= 'permission') is traditionally considered more polite and 'correct' than *can*, but is now increasingly restricted to formal contexts where writers (or speakers) are on their best linguistic behaviour. A guidebook might say *Visitors may ascend the tower for £2*, but *can* would be more natural in speech: *You can go up the tower for £2*. Especially in AmE and in spoken English, *may* (= 'permission') is losing ground to the more popular form *can*. In part this may be because *may* suggests a difference of power between the giver and the receiver of permission – for example, the power of a schoolteacher over children in class.

a. In *if*-clauses, as in questions (see §129), *may* typically indicates not permission given by the speaker, but permission to be given by the hearer. Thus approximately, *May I join you?* means 'Will you allow me to join you?' and *I'll pay you tomorrow, if I may* means '... if you will allow me'.

b. The 'permission' and 'possibility' meanings of *may* are close enough for the distinction to be blurred in some cases. We should not conclude from this, however, that the 'permission' / 'possibility' distinction is unreal. There are important grammatical differences between the two senses of *may*. Only the 'permission' sense, for example, is found in questions (see §129), and the negation of the 'possibility' sense (= 'It is possible that ... not ...') is different in kind from the negation of the 'permission' sense ('You are not permitted to ...') (see §§137–8).

c. Writers of academic literature are fond of impersonal phrases such as *It may be noted ... We may now consider ....* It is particularly difficult to say whether 'be permissible' or 'be possible' is intended here. These are rather empty formulae soliciting and focusing the reader's attention.

116 C. QUASI-SUBJUNCTIVE USES (becoming even rarer than B)

Under the heading QUASI-SUBJUNCTIVE I am grouping three rare uses of *may* which appear as alternatives to old-fashioned subjunctive forms (see §162). The first is the EXCLAMATORY WISH construction, where *may* is placed in front of the subject, and is separated from the Infinitive verb:

May he never set foot in this house again! | *May God grant you happiness!*

This use of *may* is very formal and is more or less limited to the expression of blessings and curses. It is marked by the inversion of the subject and the auxiliary verb. There are no interrogative, negative or Past Tense forms. The *may* construction here is an alternative to the equally rare FORMULAIC SUBJUNCTIVE, expressing an exclamatory wish in utterances like *God be praised, Heaven forbid, God grant you happiness*.

A second rare use of *may*, again resembling an old-fashioned use of the subjunctive, is found in concessive subordinate clauses, especially those beginning with *whatever, whenever, however*, etc.: *Our task is to deal with the customer's complaints, however unreasonable they* MAY *be*. (Another variant of this kind of clause has a pre-posed complement: *... unreasonable though they* MAY *be*.) Like the present subjunctive in general, this is truth-neutral (see §163); i.e. the speaker expresses a relatively open mind as to whether any customer's complaints are unreasonable. It is synonymous with the archaic subjunctive *however unreasonable they be*, and is slightly more open-minded than the indicative form of *however unreasonable they are*, which would suggest that at least some customers' complaints *are* unreasonable. This 'quasi-subjunctive' use of *may* is similar to *may* (= 'possibility'), and could in fact be regarded as a variant of it.

Yet another, very rare, formal and old-fashioned use of *may* is found in dependent clauses of purpose beginning with *in order that* or *so that* (or occasionally *that* alone): *The object is to preserve these monuments, in order that the achievements of the past* MAY *not be forgotten*. Again, this has an affinity to the archaic subjunctive (. . . *that the achievements of the past* BE *not forgotten*), and also to the *may* of 'possibility'.

Must

117 *Must*, like *may*, is a middle-frequency modal which is suffering a decline in use in present-day English. Its 'obligation' meaning, in particular, is used less frequently than it used to be. The meanings are:

117 A. OBLIGATION [SPEAKER'S AUTHORITY] (quite common)

> You *must* be back by 10 o'clock ('You are obliged [by me] to . . .'). | Tell Betty she *must* be more careful with her money. | I *must* go now, or I'll be late.

The usual implication of *must* (= 'obligation') is that the speaker is the person who exerts authority over the person(s) mentioned in the clause. Consistent with this principle, *I must* and *we must* convey the idea of SELF-OBLIGATION: the speaker exerts power over himself/herself (and possibly others), e.g. through a sense of duty, through self-discipline, or merely through expediency. Especially in spoken AmE, the 'obligation' use of *must* is giving way to the more common 'obligation' use of *have to* (see §118).

a. Like *may* (§116B), *must* in questions and *if*-clauses involves the hearer's authority, instead of that of the speaker: *Must I answer those questions?* means 'Is that what you require?' Here we note a special sarcastic use of *must* with *you*: *Must you make that ghastly noise?* ('For heaven's sake stop it!') *If you must behave like a hoodlum, at least make sure the neighbours aren't watching.* Remembering that *must* here indicates obligation (i.e. self-obligation) by the hearer, we can see in this an element of irony, as if the speaker pays lip-service to the idea that the hearer acts under internal compulsion rather than by free will. *If you must smoke, use an ash-tray* could be expanded 'If you are under compulsion to smoke (but of course you aren't – smoking is just a nasty habit you could break if you wanted to) . . .'. *Must* in such sentences could be replaced by *will* in the sense of 'insistence' (see §126D), and like *will* in that sense, is invariably stressed. But nowadays in AmE it is more likely to be replaced by *have to* (e.g. *Do you have to make that ghastly noise?*), which here appears to avoid a flavour of pomposity associated with *must* (see §118A*b*).

117 B. REQUIREMENT (quite common)

Often the meaning of *must* is more impersonal than in the examples above, and is better captured by the label of 'requirement':

> Old people *must* be treated with sympathy and understanding. | All students *must* register for the examinations by Monday 10th March. | As a crime has been committed, there *must* now be a trial. | The wine *must* be well chilled before it is served.

In paraphrasing these sentences, we might say 'It is essential that . . .' or 'It is necessary to . . .'. But it is difficult to draw a dividing line between this use and that of 'obligation': they are arguably two variants of the same meaning, which extends along a scale from personal authority at one end to general regulations, instructions, moral imperatives at the other.

a. A variant of the 'requirement' meaning of *must* is found in examples like these:

(1) *If we want to change society,* we must be prepared for struggle and sacrifice.
(2) *To compete with the world* our workforce must adapt to the twenty-first century.

The italicised *if*-clause in (1) or *to*-infinitive clause in (2) describes a desirable goal – and the main clause with *must* then specifies a pre-condition that has to be achieved. In brief, the pattern is: if goal X is to be reached, condition Y must be fulfilled. Again, a paraphrase 'It is necessary to . . .' can be used instead of *must* here, and this 'requirement' meaning can be alternatively labelled 'practical necessity', to distinguish it from the 'logical necessity' meaning in §117c below.

117 C. LOGICAL NECESSITY (common)

> He's not home yet – he *must* be working late at the office (. . . 'That is necessarily the case – no other explanation is possible'). | Her head is hot and clammy: she *must* have a temperature. | There *must* be some mistake. | You *must* have left your handbag in the theatre.

Must is used here of knowledge arrived at by inference or reasoning rather than by direct experience. For each example we could add the comment 'Given the evidence, there can be no other conclusion'. In each case, too, a chain of logical thinking can be imagined. For *I must be dreaming*, the stream of thought could run something like this: 'Here I am watching a fight between a lion and a unicorn; but unicorns do not exist; therefore, the unicorn I see cannot be real; therefore, I cannot really be watching it; therefore I MUST be dreaming'.

This use of *must* normally has no negative or question form; but see §137*b*.

a. There is an understandable feeling that knowledge acquired indirectly, by inference, is less certain than knowledge derived from direct experience. Hence 'logical necessity' can easily be weakened to 'reasonable assumption'. This weakening is evident in remarks like *You must be Mr Jones* (i.e. 'I assume / take it that you are Mr Jones'). There is a further weakening in estimations like *You must be taller than Sue; His mother must be well over eighty*: these express no more than an informed guess.

Have to

118 The meanings of *have to* correspond closely to those of *must*.

118 A. OBLIGATION (common)

> You *have to* be back by 10 o'clock ('It is obligatory...'). | She'll *have to* sleep in the kitchen. | I *have to* take five of these pills every day.

The meaning of *have to* differs from sense A of *must* above in that the authority or influence of the speaker is not involved. *Have to* expresses obligation or requirement without specifying the person exercising power or influence. The constraining power may be some authority figure such as a doctor or an employer, the government, or simply the power of 'circumstances'.

a. By an evasive strategy of politeness, however, *have to* can indirectly imply the speaker's involvement: *Someone will have to do the shopping* (e.g. spoken by one spouse to the other) can be taken to imply 'I want *you* to do it'.

b. Furthermore, there is an ironic use of *have to* in conversation, whereby someone's wilful behaviour is disguised as something they can't avoid: *I don't know why that guy has to try out his new car on a Sunday afternoon. My ex-husband just had to buy the most expensive one.* (Compare the similar use of *must* in §117Aa.)

118 B. REQUIREMENT (common)

As with *must*, there is the closely related meaning of *have to* in which the required course of action is general or public, and for which a paraphrase with 'it is essential to...' or 'it is necessary to...' is more appropriate:

> The Department of Education will *have to* rethink its policy (= 'The Department of Education will be compelled to rethink its policy'). | The garden *has to* be watered every day. | Pensioners *have to* be careful with their money.

Also, as with *must*, *have to* in this sense can express a 'practical necessity', where to reach some goal (expressed by an *if*-clause, *to*-Infinitive, or some other adverbial), some kind of action is a necessary or required condition: TO KEEP WARM, *elk have to eat and move around. She had to wait five minutes* BEFORE BEING SERVED. Sometimes, the goal is obvious, and does not need to be stated: *Mrs Harris has to please her customers*. The missing implied goal here is: 'if her business is to succeed'. The examples above can also be interpreted in terms of such an implicit goal: e.g. *The garden has to be watered every day* IF THE PLANTS ARE TO FLOURISH. There is no absolute boundary between sense B and sense A.

118 C. LOGICAL NECESSITY (chiefly colloquial AmE)

> There *has to* be some reason for his absurd behaviour ('That is necessarily the case – no other explanation is possible'). | You *have to*

be joking. | Everybody *has to* die sometime, pal [a jokingly obvious statement].

Although gaining in popularity, *have to* in the 'logical necessity' sense is less usual than *must*, especially in BrE – where it is still felt to be an Americanism. (The alternative construction *(have) got to*, especially in its reduced form *gotta*, is a likely substitute for *have to* ('logical necessity') in AmE: e.g. *You('ve) gotta be joking* – see §148.)

a. Have to has question and negative forms both with and without the auxiliary *do*: *Do you have to go now? Have you to go now?* The second of these, however, is now rare, and is confined to BrE.

b. The meanings of *have to* tend to merge, especially in scientific and mathematical writing, for the same reason as applies to the different meanings of *may* (§116BC). To take a linguistic example: *Every clause has to contain a finite verb* could be interpreted either 'Every clause is obliged/required (by the rules of the language) to contain a finite verb', or 'It is necessarily the case that every clause contains a finite verb'. In examples like this, the boundary between 'obligation', 'requirement' and 'logical necessity' is an indistinct one.

c. Have got to (often reduced in speech to *gotta*) is a verbal construction similar to *have to*, favoured in informal usage. (See §148 for examples and discussion.)

Relations between *can*, *may*, *must* and *have to*

119 What should be clear by now is that there are close relations of meaning between the four verbs *can*, *may*, *must* and *have to*. In fact, the relationships between all four can be summarised in the diagram:

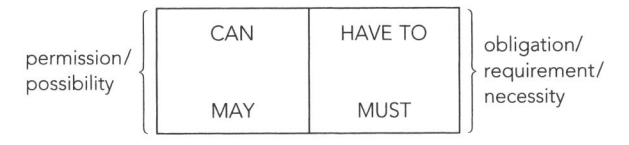

	CAN	HAVE TO	
permission/ possibility			obligation/ requirement/ necessity
	MAY	MUST	

May and *can* share the same box because both express 'permission' and 'possibility'; *must* and *have (got) to* likewise both express 'obligation', 'requirement' and '(logical) necessity'. But we cannot consider any two verbs actually interchangeable: there are always some slight differences of meaning or effect, and these we now consider.

120 First, however, there is another question to be answered: 'What is the horizontal relation of meaning between the left-hand box and the right-hand box?' There is a special kind of meaning contrast between 'permission' and 'obligation', and between 'possibility' and 'necessity': this contrast may be termed INVERSENESS (the two senses may be imagined as opposite sides of the same coin). So:

'permission' is the inverse of 'obligation'

'possibility' is the inverse of 'necessity'

What is meant by 'inverse' is made clear by these equations:

1 Some of you *can* stay out late = Not all of you *have to* be in early.
2 Someone *has to* be telling lies = Not everyone *can* be telling the truth.

Pair 1 shows the connection between 'permission' and 'obligation', and pair 2 shows a similar connection between 'possibility' and '(logical) necessity'. Further, this interesting relationship of meaning is reversible: exchanging the positions of subject and modal in pair 1, we arrive at another pair of sentences with the same logical meaning:

Some of you *have to* be in early = Not all of you *can* stay out late.

A great deal more could be said about such relations of meaning. One puzzle in the diagram in §119, to which I will return in §125, is: Why are there just two terms ('permission' and 'possibility') on the left side of the diagram, but three terms ('obligation', 'requirement' and '(logical) necessity') on the right side? But let's now turn to differences of meaning between *may* and *can*, *must* and *have to*. The following is an overview of the differences (some of which have been mentioned in §§115–18 above).

121 MAY and CAN (= 'possibility') (see §§115A, 116A)

In general (but see Note *a* below), *may* represents 'factual possibility', and *can* represents 'theoretical possibility'. The difference is clarified by these sets of equivalent statements:

(A) FACTUAL: The road *may* be blocked = 'It is possible that the road is blocked' = 'Perhaps the road is blocked' = 'The road might be blocked'.

(B) THEORETICAL: The road *can* be blocked = 'It is possible for the road to be blocked' = 'It is possible to block the road'.

As we see, *may* is paraphrased by *It is possible* followed by a *that*-clause, but *can* is paraphrased by *It is possible* followed by a (*for* + Noun Phrase +) *to* + Infinitive construction.

The second sentence describes a theoretically conceivable happening, whereas the first feels more immediate, because the actual likelihood of an event's taking place is being considered. The situations they conjure up are quite different:

(A) The road can be blocked by police ('and if we do this, we might intercept the criminals' – said by one detective to another).

(B) The road may be blocked by flood water ('that possibly explains why our guests haven't arrived' – dialogue between husband and wife expecting visitors).

'Factual possibility' is stronger than 'theoretical possibility':

This illness *can* be fatal. | This illness *may* be fatal.

The second of these statements is likely to be far more worrying than the first. It is not hard to see why this is: CAN *be fatal* merely postulates a theoretical possibility; MAY *be fatal* envisages the event actually happening. If a doctor used the second statement in addressing a patient, the patient would have reason to be pessimistic.

a. Can (= 'possibility') is associated with general statements. Contrast *A friend can betray you*, an observation about friends in general, with *A friend may betray you*, which is more likely to be a warning about one person (uttered, for example, by a fortune teller).

b. It would be pleasant if the auxiliaries *can* and *may* corresponded exactly with the 'factual' and 'theoretical' types of possibility. But in formal English, *may* is sometimes used for theoretical, as well as for factual possibility. E.g.: *During the autumn, many rare birds may be observed on the rocky northern coast of the island.* A suitable paraphrase for this is: . . . *it is possible to observe* . . . ; or the original sentence with *can* replacing *may*: . . . *many rare birds can be observed* . . . . This type of 'theoretical *may*', unlike the usual *may* of factual possibility, is rather uncommon and is normally unstressed.

122 MAY and CAN (= 'permission') (see §§115C, 116B)

The normal auxiliary for 'permission' is *can*. *May* tends to be used in formal and polite contexts, especially in polite formulae such as *if I may; May I speak to . . . ? How may I help you?* with a first-person subject.

123 MUST and HAVE TO (= 'obligation' or 'requirement') (see §§117A/B, 118A/B)

Must (= 'obligation') is generally subjective, in that it refers to what the *speaker* thinks it important or essential to do. *Have to*, on the other hand, is more 'objective', i.e. the obligation or compulsion tends to come from a source outside the speaker. Contrast:

> You *must* save that money to buy a house (= 'I'm telling you').
>
> You *have to* save that money to buy a house (= 'This is a financial requirement').

In addition, since *have to* has past and non-finite forms, it can be used in variable tenses and aspects, and also after modal auxiliaries, including *will* in reference to the future:

> I've *had to* go to hospital every week for tests. | Families *are having to* hold down two – sometimes three – jobs to make ends meet. | You'll *have to* fill out this form to borrow the money.

124 MUST and HAVE TO (= 'logical necessity') (see §§117C, 118C)

Must is the normal verb to use for this meaning. *Have to* is much less common, and is particularly associated with AmE. But it is growing more common in BrE. There is a further difference, in that *have to* can give a slightly stronger meaning of necessity than *must*:

> Someone *must* be telling lies.
>
> Someone *has to* be telling lies.

The second of these has the uncompromising effect of:

> It's impossible for everyone to be telling the truth.

Since 'logical necessity' and 'possibility' are inverse concepts (see §119), *have to* and *must* can be paraphrased by a doubly negated use of *can*:

> These lines *have to* be by Shakespeare = These lines *can't* be by anyone *but* Shakespeare. [*but* = 'who is not', 'other than']

Root and epistemic modality

125 This section is an exception. The general policy of this book is to avoid technical terminology, and to use only terms that have a relatively transparent meaning in everyday English. The discussion of modality, however, can be full of technicalities, and terms such as 'deontic', 'dynamic' and 'epistemic' are commonplace in classifying the meanings of modal auxiliaries. Here I will make use of just two technical terms for modal meaning, ROOT MODALITY and EPISTEMIC MODALITY.

ROOT MODALITY is the ordinary, more basic type of modality denoting constraint and lack of constraint in situations (typically situations involving human behaviour) in our universe of experience: it includes 'permission', 'obligation', 'theoretical possibility' and 'requirement' as discussed in the preceding sections. EPISTEMIC MODALITY is more oriented towards logic, dealing with statements about the universe, and constraints of likelihood on their truth and falsehood. It includes 'practical possibility' (*may*) and 'logical necessity' (*must*, *have to*) in the preceding sections. The diagram in §119 can be refashioned as follows:

	WEAK MODALITY		STRONG MODALITY	
ROOT { permission ↕ possibility	CAN, MAY	MUST, HAVE TO	obligation ↕ necessity } ROOT
EPISTEMIC − possibility	MAY	MUST, HAVE TO	necessity − EPISTEMIC

There was a lack of symmetry in the labelling of the diagram in §119: two labels appear on the left of the diagram ('permission' and 'possibility'), whereas three labels appear on the right ('obligation', 'requirement' and 'necessity'). This can be explained by the fact that the term 'possibility' on the left of the diagram should be subdivided into two categories, designated 'theoretical possibility' and 'factual possibility' in §120. These now enter into the following set of terminological equivalences:

'permission' = (ROOT) PERMISSION	'obligation' = (ROOT) OBLIGATION
'theoretical possibility' = (ROOT) POSSIBILITY	'requirement' = (ROOT) NECESSITY
'factual possibility' = EPISTEMIC POSSIBILITY	'logical necessity' = EPISTEMIC NECESSITY

There is an INVERSE relation, as already described in §119, between a modal term on the left side of the diagram, and its corresponding modal term on the right. The terms in single quotes on the left of '=' are the terms I have chosen to be as reader-friendly as I can in this book. But the terms on the right are more technically correct, as they show equivalences and contrasts which would otherwise be obscured.

A good test of epistemic modality is a paraphrase in which a modal sentence about a statement is expanded as follows:

> She may be hungry = It may be *that she is hungry* = It is possible *that she is hungry.*
>
> She must be hungry = It must be *that she is hungry* = It is necessarily the case *that she is hungry.*

The statement that the modal sentence is about is the italicised part of the expanded paraphrases above. Notice that it shows up as an Indicative clause introduced by *that* – the hallmark of a proposition. In contrast, root modality is paraphrased by a non-indicative construction – either an Infinitive construction or a *that*-clause containing a Subjunctive (see §162):

> Anyone can make mistakes = It is possible (for anyone) *to make mistakes.*
>
> The treaty must be signed = It is necessary for the treaty *to be signed.*
>
>   = It is necessary *to sign the treaty.*
>
>   = It is necessary *that the treated be signed.*

In the table above, the distinction between root and epistemic modality enables us to see that there are two kinds of possibility and two kinds of necessity – and that possibility and necessity are inverse concepts which balance one another. Similarly, 'permission' and 'obligation' are inverse concepts (although there are no epistemic variants of these two meanings). What the table does not show is that the root distinction between permission and possibility or between obligation and necessity is not an absolute one – but a gradient or scale.

Will

126 In the last chapter (§§87–91), we looked at *will* and *shall* as auxiliaries of future time. Our task now is to look at the full range of the meanings of these modal auxiliaries. *Will* has meanings of PREDICTION/PREDICTABILITY, INTENTION, WILLINGNESS and INSISTENCE.

126 A. PREDICTION/PREDICTABILITY (very common)

Usually *will* with this meaning makes reference to the future (see §§87–90), but there is also a kind of 'prediction' that refers to the present or past:

> By now they*'ll* be eating dinner [looking at one's watch]. | That*'ll* be the electrician – I'm expecting him to call about some rewiring [on hearing the doorbell ring]. | They*'ll* have arrived home by now. (Note the use of the Perfect here.)

It is only a small step from the 'future prediction' of sentences like *You will feel better after a good night's sleep* to the more general idea of prediction illustrated in the three sentences above. In *By now they'll be eating dinner*, the speaker makes a 'forecast about the present', based on previous experience, concerning an event not directly observable. In the same way, someone who says *That'll be the electrician* 'predicts' the identity of someone at that moment invisible.

To this extent, *will* (= 'prediction') belongs to contexts similar to those of *must* (= 'logical necessity'). In fact, *must* could replace *will* in all three examples above with little change of effect.

This 'prediction' meaning may be broadened still further to include general or habitual predictions: a use for which the label 'predictability' is more appropriate. Examples are common in scientific or quasi-scientific statements such as *If litmus paper is dipped in acid, it will turn red*. The meaning of such conditional sentences is roughly: 'Whenever *x* happens, it is predictable that *y* happens'.

In many general statements, including scientific and proverbial statements, habitual 'predictability' comes to have the force of 'typical or characteristic behaviour'. Thus:

> A lion *will* attack a human being only when hungry (= 'It is predictable or characteristic of lions that they attack . . .'). | Truth *will* out (a proverb meaning 'Truth has a habit of making itself known').

'Predictable or characteristic behaviour' is also the meaning of such descriptions of human habit as:

> She*'ll* go all day without eating. | At weekends, he*'ll* be in the club by 7 o'clock, and there he*'ll* stay till they close. | That parrot *will* chatter away for hours if you give him a chance.

Will (= 'predictability') is normally without stress, and can be contracted to *'ll*.

a. The *will* of predictability is found in a number of traditional proverbs: *Accidents will happen. Boys will be boys. When the cat's away the mice will play. A drowning man will clutch at straws. Faith will move mountains. Love will find a way.* These have a rather dated feel – but one proverb with *will*, dignified by the name of 'Murphy's Law', remains popular: *If anything can go wrong, it will.*

b. The choice of adverbial is often crucial for distinguishing 'present prediction' from the more common 'future prediction'. Compare: *The plane will be ready for its test flight by now* with: *The plane will be ready for its test flight tomorrow.*

c. The use of *will* in general scientific statements is comparable with the Simple Present in its 'event' and 'habitual' senses (see §§9, 13): *Oil floats on water* and *Oil will float on water* are more or less equivalent statements. There are, however, no 'predictability' statements equivalent to habitual statements like *Deciduous trees lose their leaves in autumn*; *The Kyoto train leaves at 4.20 daily.* This must be because the recurrent events described in such sentences are thought to be so certain or predetermined that to talk in terms of their predictability is to introduce an inappropriate element of doubt. It would be a poor train service in which departure times were 'typical' only. The notion of 'prediction' (see §87) admits a possibility of non-occurrence, and the same seems to apply even more strongly to the related notion of 'predictability'.

d. There is a type of sentence where *will* indicates 'disposition': *The auditorium will seat 500* (= 'One can seat 500 people in the auditorium'); *This watch won't work* (= 'I can't make this watch work'); *Will that window open?* (= 'Can one open that window?'). As the parentheses show, this use of *will* is closely connected with the 'possibility' sense of *can*. It can, however, be treated as a type of 'predictability' meaning, in which a conditional clause is understood: *The auditorium will seat 500* (if required), etc.

126 B. INTENTION ('INTERMEDIATE VOLITION') (common)

This meaning and the following two meanings are all concerned with 'volition', which often combines with *will*'s future implication of 'prediction'.

> I'*ll* write tomorrow. | You *won't* get any help from us. | She says she'*ll* be back next week. | The board members have assured us that they *will* give the matter their full consideration.

Occurring mainly with first-person subjects (except in indirect speech), *will* in this sense can convey a promise, a threat, an offer or a shared decision. The volitional element is reinforced by a feeling that in the act of speaking, a decision is made, and that the fulfilment of the intention is guaranteed. There is thus a superimposition of predictive and volitional meanings, which could justify the inclusion of this use in Chapter 4 as a 'volitionally coloured future'. This *will* is frequently contracted to *'ll*.

a. Note that there is a slight difference between *will* and *be going to* (see §93) in their expression of a future intention: *I'll give you a hand* expresses the speaker's present resolve to do something in the (near) future; *I'm going to give you a hand* reports what the speaker may have already decided to do. In this sense, *will* is more 'performative' whereas *be going to* is more 'premeditative'.

126 C. WILLINGNESS ('WEAK VOLITION') (quite common)

> What *will* you pay me if I mend this radio? | Jim'*ll* help you – he's always ready to oblige a friend. | Give it to the dog – she'*ll* eat anything. | I'*ll* lend you some money, if you like.

Although 'intention' is the most common type of volition, we can also distinguish a weaker and a stronger version of volitional *will*. Weak-volitional *will* is normally unstressed, and is frequently reduced to *'ll*. This meaning is particularly common in second-person requests: *Will you guys play a game with me?*

a. *Will you . . . ?* in requests, although in logical terms a question about the listener's willingness, is in effect a politer substitute for an imperative. But there are even politer ways of making requests, and so *Will you?* can sound peremptory unless toned down by further markers of politeness, including the use of the hypothetical Past Tense (see §176): *Will you please . . . ? Won't you . . . ? Would you . . . ?* When spoken with falling intonation, *will you . . .* can sound positively impolite: *Will you be quiet!*

126 D. INSISTENCE ('STRONG VOLITION') (rare)

He 'will go swimming in dangerous waters ('He insists on going swimming . . .'). | Janet, why 'will you keep making that awful noise? | 'I'm soaked to the skin.' 'Well, if you 'will go out without an umbrella, what can you expect?'

This variant meaning is uncommon, and is virtually unused in AmE; it carries strong emotional overtones. With second- and third-person subjects, the feeling of annoyance at someone else's obstinacy is uppermost. With a first-person subject, the speaker makes his/her own uncompromising determination felt, with a force the verbal equivalent of banging one's fist on the table: *I 'will go to the dance!* ('you can't stop me!') *I 'won't have you telling lies!* ('it's intolerable').

Strong-volitional *will* is always stressed, and cannot be contracted to *'ll*.

a. There is a difference between the *will* of insistence above and a QUASI-IMPERATIVE *will* found with second- and third-person subjects: *You will do as I say. The Duty Officer will report for duty at 0700 hours.* This *will* is a stronger equivalent of *must*, and expresses the will of the originator of the message, rather than of the subject. It also differs from the *will* of insistence in that it is not strongly stressed. The quasi-imperative *will* seems to be a special use of the future *will* of 'prediction', the implication being that the speaker or writer has so much authority over the addressee that failure to perform the predicted action is out of the question. Hence it has military and despotic associations. (Compare *shall*, §127D below.)

Shall

127 The use of *shall* is declining, especially in AmE. In fact, *shall* occurs nowadays only in a few rather restricted linguistic contexts. In virtually all these contexts, *shall* could be replaced by a different modal or other verbal construction.

127 A. PREDICTION (with first-person subjects)

In statements with *I* or *we* as subject, *shall* is a more formal equivalent of *will* (see §§87–90):

Unless business improves, we *shall* have no alternative but to close the factory.

127 B. INTENTION ('INTERMEDIATE VOLITION') (with first-person subjects)

I *shall* inform you if the situation changes. | We *shall* succeed where others have failed. | We *shall* overcome [the words of a campaigning song].

Again, this is more formal than the equivalent use of *will* (§126B). *Shall*, rather than *will*, is traditionally considered the 'correct' form here, as in §127A above.

127 C. OTHER VOLITIONAL MEANINGS (with second- or third-person subjects in statements, or with first-person subjects in questions)

There is a (now) rare volitional use of *you shall*, *he shall*, etc. in granting favours:

You *shall* stay with us as long as you like. | Good dog, you *shall* have a bone when we get home. | Very well, Minister, it *shall* be done [spoken by a senior civil servant in mock-obedience to a government minister in the BBC satire *Yes, Minister*].

The meaning is 'I am willing...' and the implication is that the speaker is YIELDING TO THE WISHES of another. For this reason, this use often has a connotation of condescension, and is used in reference to pets or young children. Often (as in the first two examples above) this use of *shall* can be replaced by *can*. Another, very rare and old-fashioned, use of *shall* is to express strong volition, especially in making threats: e.g. *No one shall escape!*

Although rare in statements, the volitional use of *shall* (*Shall I? Shall we?*) is quite common in questions in BrE (see §130).

127 D. RULES AND REGULATIONS (with second-person or third-person subjects)

A player who bids incorrectly *shall* forfeit fifty points [rules of a card game]. | The hood *shall* be of scarlet cloth, with a silk lining of the colour of the faculty [rules for academic dress].

This usage is found only in legal or quasi-legal documents. Here *shall* could be replaced by *must* (= 'obligation'), or by the 'quasi-imperative' *will* (§126Da).

CHAPTER 6

Modality Continued

128 introduction. MODAL AUXILIARIES IN QUESTIONS AND *IF*-CLAUSES: *129 may* and *must*; *130 shall*; *131 if*-clauses; *132 may* ('possibility'); *133 need* as an auxiliary; *134 must, need,* and *do . . . have to*; *135* complaining questions. THE MODAL AUXILIARIES AND NEGATION: *136–7* auxiliary and main verb negation; *138* meaning similarities and differences associated with negation. MODAL AUXILIARIES IN RELATION TO TENSE AND ASPECT: *139* future time; *140* past time; *141* meanings not available with the Past Tense; *142* Perfect Aspect; *143* Perfect and Progressive Aspects. SHOULD AND OUGHT TO AS WEAKER EQUIVALENTS OF *MUST*: *144*; *145 should*; *146 ought to.* SOME SEMI-MODALS OF 'CONSTRAINT': *147 need to*; *148 (have) got to*; *149 am / is / are to*; *150 (had) better.* OTHER SEMI-MODALS: *151 be bound to, be supposed to, may as well,* etc.

128 This chapter continues the discussion of modal auxiliaries begun in Chapter 5. The major topics we explore in this chapter are:

- How modals are used in questions and *if*-clauses
- How modals are combined with negation by *not* or *n't*
- How modals behave in relation to tense and aspect
- The so-called 'semi-modals': a range of verbal constructions (e.g. *need to, had better*) related in meaning and behaviour to the primary modals, but also sharing to varying extents the characteristics of main verbs.

In this chapter the discussion begins again with the primary modals (*can, may,* etc.), but the second half of the chapter gives attention to the secondary or Past Tense modals (*could, might,* etc.).

Modal auxiliaries in questions and *if*-clauses

129 The use of modal auxiliary verbs in questions is somewhat different from their use in statements.

MODALITY CONTINUED

In §§122 and 123, we noted a 'subjective' tendency in the use of *may* (= 'permission') and *must* (= 'obligation'). This means that in statements, these modals are often used for *giving permission* and *imposing obligation*, with the speaker acting as the 'authority figure':

You may Verb = 'You are permitted (by me) to Verb'.

You must Verb = 'You are obliged (by me) to Verb'.

But in questions, the role is reversed, and typically the 'authority figure' is the hearer:

May I Verb? = 'Do you permit me to Verb?'

Must I Verb? = 'Do you oblige me to Verb?'

In other words, when we ask questions, we anticipate the attitude of the person being asked, and use the form appropriate for the reply:

May I ask you a few questions? [Yes, you may.]

Must I answer these questions? [Yes, (I'm afraid) you must.]

However, remember *must* is rare in questions (see §§134, 135): in practice it is more common to use *Do I have to* .... Similarly, *May I* ... is less common than *Can I* ....

130 Such a change of roles is also found in questions with *shall*:

Shall I carry your suitcase? ('Do you want me to carry your suitcase?') |
Shall we have dinner? ('Do you agree with my intention to have dinner?')

Questions beginning *Shall I* or *Shall we*, which are a way of offering help, an invitation or a suggestion to another person, obviously consult THE WISH OF THE HEARER, not that of the speaker. In this they again reverse the role of volitional *shall* in statements (§§127B, 127C). However, volitional *shall* is more common in questions than in statements, because it is in keeping with good manners. It is more polite to consult the wishes of the listener than to assert one's own wishes as speaker. With first-person subjects, then, *shall* has survived in questions more robustly than it has in statements.

a. Even this use of *shall*, however, can be avoided by other constructions, e.g. *Do you want (me) to* ... ? or *Would you like (me) to* ... ?

b. In questions with *shall we? shall* generally includes reference to the listener (= 'you and I / we'). *Shall we?* is therefore used in suggestions about shared behaviour. This accounts for the use of *shall we?* as a tag question (in BrE) after imperatives beginning *Let's* ... : *Let's have an ice-cream, shall we?* (In AmE *shall we?* is sometimes heard as a complete utterance equivalent to *Shall we go?*)

131 *If*-clauses are in many ways like questions (e.g. in co-occurring with *any, anyone, ever*, etc. rather than with *some, someone, sometimes*), so it is not strange to find modal auxiliary usage in *if*-clauses imitating the rules for questions rather than for statements. An example from BrE is the frequently heard tag of politeness *if I may* (e.g. *I'll have another biscuit, if I may*), which obviously means 'if you will permit me' rather than 'if I will permit myself'. Similarly, *if you must go* implies self-compulsion by the listener; *Go skating if you must, but make sure you wrap up nice and warm.*

132 *May* in its 'possibility' sense does not occur at all in questions, where its function is usurped by *can* or *could*. Thus the statement *They may be asleep* ('It is possible that they are asleep') has no corresponding question **May they be asleep?* Instead, *can* or (more likely) *could* is used: *Can / Could they be asleep?* = 'Is it (just) possible that they are asleep?' Factual possibility and theoretical possibility therefore become indistinguishable in questions, as they do also in negative sentences.

133 *Need* as an auxiliary verb (i.e. *need* followed by the main verb without *to*) is now rare, especially in AmE. Where it occurs, it can be considered the negative and interrogative counterpart of *must*. In questions, however, the semantic distinctions between *must* and *have to* (§§123–4) seem to fade away, so that *do . . . have to* is a more common equivalent of *need*.

    Need you be so strict?   [Yes, I'm afraid I must.]   (rare)
    Do you have to be so strict?   [Yes, I'm afraid I do.]

Notice that *need* does not normally occur in positive statements, so a reply *?*Yes, I need* is impossible, except as a joke.

a. But the auxiliary *need* does occur in some non-question constructions which resemble questions in other ways: e.g. in *if*-clauses: *I doubt if we need buy any extra food*.

b. This auxiliary *need* should be carefully distinguished from the full verb *need* occurring in the semi-modal construction *need* + *to* + Infinitive (see §147).

c. A distinction is sometimes felt between *do . . . have to*, which can convey a habitual meaning, and *have . . . got to* (see §148), which refers more typically to a single present or future occasion. For example: *Do you have to be at work by 8 o'clock?* can mean 'Is that what you have to do every day?' but *Have you got to be at work by 8 o'clock?* means 'Is that what you have to do this morning?'

134 *Must* occurs alongside *need* and *do . . . have to* in questions, but only rarely and in rather special circumstances, i.e.:

1 to express an obligation or requirement imposed by the listener (see §129): *Why must you leave so early?*

2 in questions with what we may call 'positive orientation': i.e. when the question form presupposes some positive assertion mentioned or suggested by the preceding conversation:

    Rob: Well, the purse isn't here, so we'd better look for it at the train station.
    Sue: (Why) *must* it be at the station? I could have dropped it anywhere, you know.

MODALITY CONTINUED

The purpose of Sue's question is to get Rob to reconsider his assumption 'the purse must be at the station'. This use of *must* is often preceded by *why*: *But why must doctors be so much better treated than nurses?*

135 *Must, need* and *do...have to* are all used in a complaining type of question (usually with a second-person subject) already mentioned in §117A*a*:

> Need you be so rude? | Do we have to have rice pudding every day? | Must you drop ash all over my carpet?

Although the logical meaning of these verbs is 'Is it obligatory / necessary...?' the force of the question is probably ironic, communicating at two levels: 'Is it a fact that you can't help this annoying behaviour? (But, of course, I know very well that you *could* help it if you wanted to!)'

a. Again, we can compare a similar ironic usage in *if*-clauses: *If you must smoke...* (see §131).

b. Complaining questions beginning *Must you...* are avoided in AmE, probably because of the superior, mocking tone they convey.

The modal auxiliaries and negation

136 If we look at the following pairs of sentences, we see that *not* can have two very different effects, according to which auxiliary verb it is combined with:

(a) He can't be serious   ('It is *not* possible [that he is serious]').
(b) He may not be serious   ('It is possible [that he is *not* serious]').
(c) You don't have to go yet   ('You are *not* required [to go] yet').
(d) You must not go yet   ('You are required [*not* to go yet]').

The meaning of each sentence containing a modal can, as we see here, be broken down into the modal statement itself (the statement of possibility, necessity, etc.) and the statement on which the modal statement comments (that within square brackets above). Sometimes the insertion of *not* (or *n't*) after the modal auxiliary negates the modal statement – in examples (a) and (c) above, *not* falls outside the square brackets. In other cases (examples (b) and (d)), the main verb statement is negated. The first type of negation may be called AUXILIARY NEGATION, the second type MAIN VERB NEGATION.

a. An occasional case of 'double negation' is observed with modal auxiliaries, especially with *can*: *I can't not tell her about it*. In such cases, auxiliary negation and main verb negation are combined in the same clause. The meaning is 'It is *not* possible for me *not* to tell her about it'. (Because of inverseness – see §120 – this 'double negative' is an emphatic equivalent to *I have to tell her about it*.)

93

137 The following are examples of AUXILIARY NEGATION (where allowable, I will cite the colloquial contracted forms *can't, needn't*, etc. rather than the full forms):

May not (= 'permission'): You may not go until you've finished your work
('I do not permit you [to go]').

Cannot, can't (all senses): You can't smoke in here
('You are not permitted [to smoke in here]').
You can't be serious
('It is not possible [that you are serious]').
He can't drive a car
('He is not able [to drive a car]').

Don't / doesn't have to (all senses):
You don't have to pay that fine
('You're not obliged [to pay that fine]').
It doesn't always have to be my fault
('It is not necessarily the case [that it is always my fault]')
(= 'It isn't necessarily [always my fault]').

Need not, needn't: You needn't pay that fine.
It needn't always be my fault.

(*Need not / needn't* is equivalent in meaning to *Don't / doesn't have to*, but is now rare, especially in AmE.)

Examples of MAIN VERB NEGATION are:

May not (= 'possibility'): They may not come if it's wet
('It is possible [that they won't come if it's wet]').

Must not, mustn't (in all senses):
You mustn't keep us all waiting
('It is essential [that you do not keep us all waiting]').
She must not be on campus today
('It's necessarily the case [that she's not on campus today]).

Will not, won't (in all senses):
Don't worry – I won't interfere
('I'm willing [not to interfere]').
He won't do what he's told
('He insists on [not doing what he's told]'
i.e. 'He refuses').
They won't have received your letter yet
('It is predictable [that they haven't received your letter yet]').

Won't in the strong-volitional sense of 'refusal' is more common than the rare corresponding sense of *will* (= 'insistence').

There is no logical difference between auxiliary and main verb negation with *will* (= 'intention'): *I won't go if it rains* means indifferently 'I do not intend to go' or 'I intend not to go' (cf. §138*a* below).

a. When the meaning of *may not* is 'permission', the stress normally falls on *not*; when the meaning is 'possibility', the stress normally falls on *may*. Thus: *You may 'not disturb us* (= 'You are not permitted to disturb us') contrasts with *You 'may not disturb us* (= 'It is possible that you will not disturb us').

b. Must not (= 'logical necessity') has a dubious status in BrE, but seems to be gaining ground, particularly in AmE. Notice the logical equivalence of *must not* in this sense and *can't* (= 'impossibility'): *She must not be on campus today* is virtually equivalent to *She can't be on campus today*. Less problematic in BrE is the use of the contracted form *mustn't* in tag questions following *must* in the 'logical necessity' sense: *They must have hundreds of people looking for jobs,* MUSTN'T THEY?

c. Shall not (shan't), like *will not (won't)*, follows the pattern of main verb negation. But the negative of *shall* is too rare to be illustrated, except in a footnote: *We shall not be moved by these entreaties. Don't worry – you shan't lose your reward. You shan't escape my revenge!* The contraction *shan't* is rare in BrE, and even rarer in AmE.

138 A number of differences between positive and negative interpretations of the modals need to be noted.

Because *can* and *may*, *have got to* and *must* are not generally comparable in their negative and question forms, the 'factual'/'theoretical' contrast we have noted in positive statements is not discernible in negative statements or questions. On the other hand, for permission and obligation, *may not* and *mustn't* often keep the implication of the speaker's authority in contrast to *cannot* and *don't have to*. *You may not* typically means 'I do not allow you...' and *You mustn't* 'I forbid you...'.

The type of meaning-contrast called 'inverseness' (see §120) leads to a curious equivalence, in the negative, of auxiliaries which in a positive context have opposite meanings:

You may not smoke in here (= 'You are not permitted to smoke [by me]...').

You mustn't smoke in here (= 'You are obliged [by me] not to smoke...').

Both these statements are prohibitions, but differ in that the second sounds rather more forceful, positively forbidding instead of negatively withholding permission. The secret of this equivalence is that the 'inverse' opposition of the two meanings is cancelled out by the contrast between auxiliary and main verb negation. There is a logical equivalence, for the same reason, between *There doesn't have to be an answer to every question* and *There may not be an answer to every question*. ('It's not necessary that X' = 'It's possible that not-X'.)

a. Shan't (= volition) is residually used with first-person subjects, so that *I shan't!* (the cry of a disobedient child in a dated novel) is synonymous with *I won't*. Both express strong refusal.

b. The fact that a different type of negation neutralises inverseness of meaning makes it difficult to decide whether *won't* and *shan't* in their 'strong' and 'weak' volitional senses are instances of auxiliary or main verb negation. We can paraphrase the 'refusal' meaning in *He won't do what he's told* either by 'He insists on not doing what he's told' or by 'He is not willing to do what he's told', the difference between the two being only a matter of emphasis.

Modal auxiliaries in relation to tense and aspect

139 FUTURE TIME. None of the modal verbs we have been considering has a special construction for combining future with modality, except *have to*, which combines with *will / shall* and *be going to* (and shows, by that fact, that it is not, syntactically speaking, a modal auxiliary verb):

We'll *have to* meet again next week.

This is to be contrasted with:

We *must / can / may* meet again next week.

These true modal auxiliary verbs are unchanged for the expression of future time.

When an 'event verb' (see §12) is combined with an auxiliary, we generally assume that the event referred to is in the future, even when there is no time adverbial to point in that direction:

The weather may improve. | *You must give me all the information you have.* | *They can catch the bus right over there.*

a. There is also, however, the possibility of interpreting an 'event verb' as 'habitual present': *She can cook very well.* This may well be the more common interpretation with *can* (= 'ability') and *will* (= 'predictability').

b. Must ('logical necessity') is exceptional: it does not normally permit future reference. Note the contrast between the 'obligation' interpretation of *The building must be demolished*, which refers to an event in the future, and the 'logical necessity' interpretation of the same sentence, which refers to a state in the present (*demolished* being here adjectival). When the event is located in the future, the meaning of 'logical necessity' can be expressed by *be bound to*: *The building is bound to be demolished* (= 'It is necessarily the case that the building will be demolished') (see §151).

c. Along with *We* WILL HAVE TO *meet next week* above, it is also possible to say *We* HAVE TO *meet next week*. There is a slight difference of meaning between the two sentences, which can be explained as follows. We have already noted, in discussing negation, that a sentence containing a modal can be thought of as expressing two statements: a modal statement, and the main verb statement on which the modal statement comments. Thus any modal statement can be represented as one statement within another, like this: [*We must* [*meet next week*]]. Modal auxiliaries in themselves are 'state verbs', and so a sentence with a primary modal like *must* is regarded as in the 'state present'. Thus the obligation exists in the present (or more precisely non-past) time zone. But the event to which the obligation applies can exist in a different time zone, especially the future: *We must meet next week* expresses a present obligation regarding a future action. With *have to*, this possibility exists too: *We have to meet next week* describes a present obligation about a future action. But there is also the further possibility, expressed by *We will have to meet next week*, where the modality (obligation), as well as the obligated event, are temporally located in the future. Notice that *will have to* is the only option if the obligation is conditional on another event that happens in the future: *If we miss the bus tonight we* WILL HAVE TO *walk home*, but not *?*If we miss the bus tonight we* HAVE TO *walk home*.

140 PAST TIME. To express past time, most primary modals have special Past Tense (or secondary) forms:

PRESENT		PAST	PRESENT		PAST
may	~	might	need	~	—
can	~	could	will	~	would
must	~	—	shall	~	should

The two exceptions, as we see from the above list, are *must* and *need*, both of which have no Past Tense counterpart (there is a Past Tense form *needed to*, but this belongs to *need to* as a semi-modal – see §147).

The following are examples of Past Tense forms used in reference to past time in direct speech (indirect speech will be separately considered in Chapter 7, §§156–60):

May (= 'permission') (*might* in this use is now rare and old-fashioned, chiefly BrE)
  The prisoners *might* leave camp when they wished.
Can (= 'permission')
  The prisoners *could* leave camp when they wished.
Can (= 'possibility')
  In those days, a transatlantic voyage *could* be dangerous.
Can (= 'ability')
  Not many of the tourists *could* speak French.
Have to (= 'obligation')
  Children *had to* behave themselves when I was a boy.
Have to (= 'requirement')
  Someone *had to* be the loser.
Will (= 'willingness')
  In those early days my parents *would* lend me the money.
Will (= 'insistence')
  'What did she think of the new boss?' 'I don't know – she *wouldn't* tell me.'
Will (= 'predictability')
  At the end of the day, I *would* return to my mother's house, where she was preparing the dinner.

In this last sense of 'predictability', *would* is probably more commonly used than *will*, as it is popular in historical or fictional descriptions of characteristic, habitual behaviour:

> In his last years, the King *would* spend whole days in morose solitude, speaking only to his immediate family and refusing all official audiences. At such times he *would* behave with the utmost churlishness to his ministers, and *would* fly into a violent rage whenever his will was crossed.

In its role of describing habitual events in the past, this *would* overlaps in function with *used to* (see §85).

a. The most common meaning of *will*, prediction, has a comparatively uncommon past time counterpart in *would* used as a future-in-the-past auxiliary (see §84): *Sama was my benefactor, and would become my guardian for the next decade.*

b. The rules of stress for *will* apply also to *would*: with the strong-volitional meaning, *would* has to be stressed; otherwise it is generally unstressed, and can be contracted to *'d*.

c. Could being a modal auxiliary has 'state' meaning, while the roundabout expressions *was permitted / allowed to, was able to,* etc. can denote events, and can add a sense of 'fulfilment' to the ordinary meaning of the modal auxiliary. *We were able to reach camp that night* implies 'We were able to, and moreover we did'; in a similar way, *We were permitted to leave camp early* suggests the extra information that we actually *did* leave camp early.

d. As noted in *c* above, *was able to* replaces *could* to express the 'fulfilment' of a past ability. But *couldn't* can negate *was able to* in this sense. There is thus an asymmetry between *could* and *couldn't*. We can say: *I ran hard, but couldn't catch the bus.* We cannot say: **I ran hard, and could catch the bus.* Here *couldn't* is equivalent to *wasn't able to*, but *could* is not equivalent to *was able to*.

141 MEANINGS NOT AVAILABLE WITH THE PAST TENSE. Gaps are left in the expression of past modality not only by the absence of Past Tense forms for *must* and *need*, but by the non-occurrence of certain meanings of *might* and *should*. *Might* is virtually unused in senses A and C of *may* in §116 ('possibility', 'quasi-subjunctive'), and *should* is not used at all as the ordinary Past Tense of *shall* (although it functions occasionally as the Past form of *shall* in indirect speech, and in hypothetical clauses – see Chapters 7 and 8).

Even in the 'permission' sense, *might* in direct speech is so rare as to be discounted. We can therefore present a simplified picture of past modal meanings as follows: for semantic purposes, neither *may, must* nor *shall* have Past Tense equivalents, and their special nuances of meaning cannot therefore be expressed in the Past Tense. Instead, *could* and *had to* are the best available Past Tense translations of *may* and *must*:

> Visitors *may* ascend the tower for £2 this summer →
> Visitors *could* ascend the tower for £2 last summer.
>
> I *must* confess that his latest novels bore me →
> I *had* to confess that his latest novels bored me.

The most suitable Past Tense equivalent of *shall* (with first-person subjects, meaning prediction or intention) is *would*, which, as noted in §140a, has a future-in-the-past meaning corresponding to the prediction or intention meaning of *will*:

We shall always be grateful → We *would* always be grateful.

Would here is understood in the sense of 'be destined to'. (Another interpretation of the same sentence, as FREE INDIRECT SPEECH, will be dealt with in §160.)

142 PERFECT ASPECT. The Perfect Infinitive following a modal auxiliary assigns past time to the meaning of the main verb and what follows it (the included main verb statement), as distinct from the meaning of the auxiliary itself (the modal statement). There is thus a difference between *In those days voyages could be dangerous*, which informs us of a PAST POSSIBILITY (see §140), and *The voyage may have been dangerous*, which informs us of the (PRESENT) POSSIBILITY of a PAST DANGER. It may be a little misleading, though, to talk of 'present possibility', as a possibility (as an example of the 'state present') tends to be a timeless thing, akin to the 'eternal truth' of scientific and proverbial statements (see §8). It is for this reason that expression of past possibility by means of *could* is rather unusual.

In its Infinitive form, the Perfect Aspect (see §67) is a general marker of past time, without respect to the 'definiteness' and 'indefiniteness' which distinguish Past Tense and Present Perfect with finite verbs. Thus it covers the whole area of meaning which, in finite verbs, is subdivided between Perfect and Past (see §64). Note the use of different tenses in these two paraphrases of *may have come*:

They may have come already.   (= 'It's possible that they *have come* already.')

They may have come last year.   (= 'It's possible that they *came* last year.')

143 PERFECT AND PROGRESSIVE ASPECTS. After a modal, the Perfect and Progressive Aspects are ordinarily incompatible with the meanings of 'ability', 'permission' and 'obligation', and also with the volitional meanings of *will* and *shall*. It makes no sense, for instance, to give someone present permission to do something in the past: *You may have seen me yesterday* (as opposed to *You may see me tomorrow*) necessarily has the meaning of 'possibility', not 'permission'.

The remaining meanings, those available to occur with the Perfect and Progressive Aspects, are exemplified below. Some of these are called EPISTEMIC uses of the modals (see §125): they concern the likelihood of truth and falsehood, expressed through such notions as possibility, necessity and predictability. In these modal usages, the modal itself expresses a current state of the mind, while the main verb and what follows it describe an event or state which has variable time and aspect. The Perfect or Progressive construction applies not to the modal meaning itself, but to the meaning of what follows.

May (= 'possibility')
The heat *may* have affected the cables.   She *may* be bluffing.

Can (= 'possibility')
What *can* have happened? (rare, BrE)   They *can't* be telling the truth!

Must (= 'necessity')
He *must* have misunderstood you.   I *must* be dreaming.

Have to (= 'necessity')
You *have to have been* in a coma. (rare)
To speak excellent English, you *don't have to be living* in an English-speaking country.

Will (= 'prediction', 'predictability')
They *will have* read your letter by now.
Don't phone him yet – he *will* still *be eating* his breakfast.

a. Can is rarely used with the Perfect outside negative statements. *Could* may be used instead: *What could have caused her death?*

b. Although the examples of modal + Progressive above show the normal Progressive meaning of temporariness, this construction can, as we have seen in §§105–08, also convey the 'future-as-a-matter-of-course' meaning with *will* (and *shall*). The same meaning can arise with other modals such as *may*, or even semi-modals such as *had better*. E.g. *I may not be coming this afternoon*, as an expression of future possibility, differs from *I may not come this afternoon* in suggesting that the coming is not a matter of personal choice or decision. In a similar way, *I'd better be going soon*, spoken by a guest to a host or hostess, seems to place the choice of whether to go or stay outside the speaker's control, and is to that extent more polite than *I'd better go soon* (cf. §108).

Should and *ought to* as weaker equivalents of *must*

144 Something must now be said about a number of verbs and verb constructions that express constraint, and therefore have meanings in some ways similar to *must* and *have to*. Of these, *should* and *ought to* are the first to be considered, as they are members of the modal auxiliary category (although, in the case of *ought to*, only marginally so).

145 SHOULD is a secondary modal which, as hinted earlier (§141), nowadays has very little common ground with *shall*, the modal of which it is historically the Past Tense. In its most important uses, *should* has the same kind of meaning as *must*, except that it expresses not confidence, but rather lack of full confidence, in the fulfilment of the happening described by the main verb. For example, if someone says *You must buy some new shoes*, it is assumed that the purchase will be carried out: the tone of *must* tolerates little argument. But *You should buy some new shoes* is a different matter – the speaker here could well add in an undertone 'but I don't know whether you will or not'. This meaning can be called WEAKENED OBLIGATION: and the weakening often reduces 'obligation' to something like 'desirability'. *Should* is less categorical than *must* both in this sense of 'obligation' and its sense of 'logical necessity' (see §117):

'OBLIGATION OR REQUIREMENT (BY SPEAKER)'
  Milo *must* pay for that broken window
    ('... and moreover he *will* do so, because I say so').
  Milo *should* pay for that broken window
    ('... but he probably won't').

'LOGICAL NECESSITY'
  Our guests *must* be home by now
    ('I conclude that they are, in that they left half-an-hour ago, have a fast car, and live only a few miles away').
  Our guests *should* be home by now
    ('I conclude that they are, in that ..., but whether my conclusion is right or not I don't know – it's possible they had a breakdown, for instance').

Should weakens the force of *must* (= 'logical necessity') by indicating that the speaker has doubts about the soundness of his/her conclusion. An optimistic treasure-seeker would say, after working out the position by the aid of maps, *This is where the treasure* MUST *be*. A more cautious one would say *This is where the treasure* SHOULD *be*, so acknowledging that there could be something wrong with his/her assumptions or his/her calculations. This sense of *should* can often be equated with 'probability': here it will be called WEAKENED LOGICAL NECESSITY.

a. The negative form *shouldn't*, parallel to *mustn't* (see §§136–7), is a further instance of main verb negation. *We shouldn't complain* is a weakening of *We mustn't complain*, carrying the supposition '... but maybe we do'. *Shouldn't* can also have the second interpretation 'logical necessity'. (On the rare use of *must not* in this sense, see §137*b*.) Hence *You shouldn't have any difficulty getting the tickets* means approximately 'If my suppositions are correct, it is unlikely that you will have any difficulty'.

146 *Should* is one of the middle-frequency modals, and weakened obligation is its most common meaning. In contrast, OUGHT TO is nowadays rather rare. It is a less common alternative to *should* for both (a) weakened obligation and (b) weakened logical necessity:

(a) Milo *ought to* pay for the broken window = Milo *should* pay for the broken window.

(b) Our guests *ought to* be home by now = Our guests *should* be home by now.

Should is normally unstressed, whereas *ought to*, being disyllabic, tends to receive more accentuation. Both these modals are historically Past Tense forms, but nowadays have little connection with past time. To express 'weakened obligation' or 'weakened logical necessity' in the past, we have to combine these modals with the Perfect: e.g. *I should* HAVE BROUGHT *an umbrella*. This describes a desirable (but unfulfilled) action in the past.

The 'logical necessity' meaning of *should* and *ought to* differs from the corresponding meanings of *must* and *have to* in that the former modals express a favourable attitude towards the event or state referred to. Thus these are quite normal:

> Our candidate *ought to* win the election. | Roses *should* grow pretty well in this soil.

But there is something decidedly strange about sentences with the opposite meaning: *?*Our candidate ought to lose the election. ?*Roses should grow badly in this soil.* It appears that the 'logical necessity' meaning here is tinged with the connotation of 'desirability' that naturally accompanies the meaning of 'weakened obligation'.

a. *Should* + Perfect and *ought to* + Perfect referring to past time often have a stronger negative connotation of 'contrary to fact'; *She should / ought to have seen the car coming* has the implication '... but in fact she didn't'.

Some semi-modals of constraint

147 NEED TO. In the construction *need* + *to* + Infinitive, *need* behaves like a full lexical verb, forming question and negative forms with *do*: *Does she need to...? We didn't need to...* etc. It also takes Present and Past Tense endings (*She needs to rest. She needed to rest.* etc.). In these respects it shares the characteristics of *have to*. While the modal auxiliary *need* (see §133) has been becoming a rarity in present-day English, the *need to* construction has been becoming much more common. Since *need* as an auxiliary is practically confined to questions and negative statements, it is only the *need to* construction that can be used in ordinary positive statements: **We need wait. We need to wait.*

In terms of meaning, *need to* is somewhere between *must* and *should / ought to*: it asserts obligation or necessity, but without either the certainty that attaches to *must* or the doubt that attaches to *should / ought to*:

SCALE OF INTENSITY

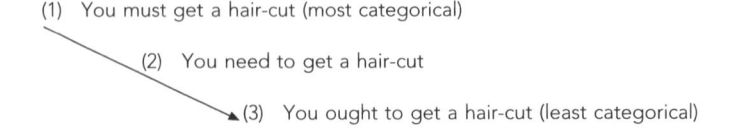

(1) You must get a hair-cut (most categorical)

(2) You need to get a hair-cut

(3) You ought to get a hair-cut (least categorical)

Yet there is a difference in the quality, as well as in the degree of constraint. For *must* and *should / ought to*, the constraint comes from outside the obligated person rather than inside (except for *I / we must* – see §117A). If I say to you *You must get a hair-cut*, I am exerting my own authority over you. But if I say *You need to get a hair-cut*, I am primarily pointing out to you the constraint that your own situation imposes upon you – that your hair is too long, that you look untidy, so that it is for your own sake that a hair-cut is to be recommended. We can make a similar comparison of *She ought to feel wanted* and *She needs to feel wanted*, the one expressing an external and the other an internal constraint.

It is useful to note that in this construction, the main verb *need* has the same meaning as when it is followed by a direct object. The following sentences are virtually synonymous:

My boots need to be cleaned   =   My boots need a clean.
He needs to practise more   =   He needs more practice.

The auxiliary verb *need* and the main verb *need to* scarcely differ in effect on many occasions: *You needn't wake her up* and *You don't need to wake her up* are semantically alike.

a. But in other contexts we can detect a clear distinction between them. Let us suppose that Mrs P. addresses her gardener with the words: *The hedges needn't be trimmed this week, John.* This means 'You are excused the task – I don't want you to trim the hedges this week' (perhaps because Mrs P. is feeling kind, or has more important jobs for John). But the meaning is different if she says: *The hedges don't need to be trimmed this week, John.* The point she makes here is that the hedges do not require attention – because, we presume, they have not grown enough to make them look untidy. (Bearing in mind the infrequency of *needn't*, particularly in AmE, this point and the following one in Note *b* are of minor importance.)

b. There is also a difference between the modal and semi-modal constructions referring to past time, *needn't* + Perfect and *didn't need to*. The *needn't* + Perfect construction is 'contrary to fact': e.g. *We needn't have sold the car* implies 'We did sell it'. But *We didn't need to sell the car* allows us to continue: *. . . and so we didn't sell it*. (Compare *should* + Perfect, §146a.)

148 (HAVE) GOT TO is a fairly common construction in colloquial English. I have placed the (*have*) in brackets here because it can very easily be omitted: in statements, either the *have got to* is contracted to *'ve got to* (or in the third-person singular *'s got to*) or the verb is entirely elided. What we hear is *I got to* or *you got to*, etc., often represented in writing as *I gotta, you gotta*, etc. But the *have* appears in questions: *Have you got to go now?*

In meaning, (*have*) *got to* is similar to *have to*, expressing 'obligation' or 'logical necessity' (see §118):

They*'ve got to* decide what to do = They *have to* decide what to do. (obligation)

You*'ve got to* be joking = You *have to* be joking. (logical necessity)

However, it has no non-finite forms: *(to) have got to, *having got to do not occur. Thus got cannot be inserted in the following: *We may have to leave earlier. I regret having to refuse your offer.*

Although it is tempting to treat *have got to* as a variant of *have to*, it is sometimes important to distinguish the two forms. *Have got to*, lacking non-finite forms, is closer to being a modal auxiliary than *have to*; and this goes with its tendency to share the 'subjective' connotation of *must* (= 'obligation'). E.g. *International crime is a problem all governments have got to face.* Here *have got to* could be replaced without noticeable change of meaning by *must*, but not by *have to*, which would suggest a general state of affairs, rather than a strong expression of personal opinion.

a. Although *(have) got to* on the whole is more common in BrE, the variant *gotta* seems to be more common in AmE.

b. Have to can be used in a habitual sense (see §13), whereas *have got to* normally cannot. Compare:

> Hotel guests have to check out by 12 noon.
>
> Hotel guests have got to check out by 12 noon.

The first statement is likely to be habitual, describing a general rule of the hotel (= 'every day'); the second is more likely to be non-habitual, probably meaning 'by 12 noon today').

c. There is no usual Past Tense of *have got to*: *had to* can be used instead. *Had got to* (BrE) is rare and limited to indirect speech: *She realised that she'd got to find some way out* (see Chapter 7).

149 AM / IS / ARE TO, consisting of a finite form of the verb *be* followed by *to* + Infinitive, has already been discussed as referring to a future plan (§112), as in *The Queen is to undergo surgery on her ankle this evening.* This semi-modal is unusual, compared with other semi-modals, in being rather formal in its style and in showing signs of declining frequency in present-day English.

Am / is / are to covers a shifting range of modalities. In the following examples, it could be approximately replaced by *can* in (a), by *should* or *has to* in (b), and by *is appropriate* (*to hope*) in (c):

(a) Nowadays no such concentrations of geese are to be found on Rockliffe Marsh.

(b) What is to be done then? We must find some solution.

(c) It is to be hoped that the UN will re-establish its authority.

As (a)–(c) show, these modalities are associated with the Passive.

a. A special use of *am / is / are to* in *if*-clauses adds to the notion of 'condition' that of 'purpose or goal': *If we are to win the competition, we must start training now* (cf. §117вa). The meaning of the *if*-clause here is close to 'In order to win the competition . . .' or 'If we are going to (i.e. intend to) win the competition . . .' *Was / were to* can also be employed in *if*-clauses as a marker of future hypothetical meaning (see §173).

150 (HAD) BETTER. This construction is often abbreviated in colloquial English to *'d better* or (in casual speech) just *better*. Although it is Past Tense historically and in outward form, in current English it has no Present Tense equivalent, and its meaning is 'non-past' (present or future) rather than 'past'. In these respects it is like *ought to*.

(Had) better expresses 'ADVISABILITY'. It is like *must* in being 'subjective': it represents the speaker's assessment of what has to be done. But it is not so strong in its coercive force as *must*; it signifies exhortation or strong recommendation rather than compulsion:

You'*d better* be quick (roughly = 'I urge you to be quick').

The negative of *(had) better* is *(had) better not*:

He'*d better not* make a mistake (roughly = 'I advise him not to make a mistake').

With *I* or *we* as subject, it is as if the speaker is giving advice for the benefit of himself/herself (and possibly others):

I think I'*d better* tell you the truth.

We'*d better* clear up this mess before the others come home.

a. A construction with the Progressive is possible: *You'd better be working harder than this when the boss comes back.*

b. In rare negative questions with *(had) better*, the negative word is placed in front of *better*, rather than after it. It is attached, as a contraction, to *had*: *Hadn't we better phone the police?*

Other semi-modals

151 There are a number of other verbal constructions used to express modality. Some of them, such as *be bound to, be supposed to* and *would rather* (see §171) are idiomatic, in that their form does not clearly reflect their meaning. Others are more transparent: e.g. *be allowed to, be permitted to, be willing to, be able to, want to*. However, all the forms listed here have some characteristics which make them similar to modal auxiliaries. For example, *want to*, especially in AmE, is increasingly pronounced as if it were a single word: *wanna*. In its meaning, too, *want to* is expanding to include meanings that would otherwise be expressed by modals:

The last thing you *want to* do is replace the dishwasher (= '. . . you *should* do . . .').

Another matter of interest is that some 'semi-modals' can be used both in an epistemic and a non-epistemic (root) sense, just like the modal auxiliaries (see §125). For example, *be supposed to* and *be bound to* both have meanings approximating to 'obligation' and 'logical necessity', and in this respect are similar to *should* and *must*:

> Civil servants, as the name suggests, *are supposed to* be servants of the public.
> (compare *should* = 'obligation')
>
> They say *it's supposed to* snow here by the end of the week.
> (compare *should* = 'probability', weakened 'logical necessity')
>
> Everyone has these rights, and I*'m bound to* respect them.
> (compare *must* = 'obligation')
>
> Working in the same building, they*'re bound to* meet fairly often.
> (compare *must* = 'logical necessity')

The parallel between *be bound to* and *must* is not exact. This is, first, because *be bound to* can change from Present to Past tense, and can also have non-finite forms. For example, there is no comparable way of expressing the following with *must*: *I was bound to find out sometime* (a logical necessity in the past). A second difference is that *be bound to* can refer to something which will inevitably happen in the future:

> 'I've lost my car keys.' 'Don't worry – someone*'s bound to* find them.'

Must cannot be easily substituted for *be bound to* here, but if the necessary event is placed in the past, *must* + Perfect can be used: *Someone must have found them.*

From a general perspective, it may be said that semi-modals are typically more versatile than core modals in allowing combinations with Tense, Aspect and non-finite forms. This is because the modals are particularly irregular and restricted in such combinations. On the other hand, the core modals are still, in general, far more frequent in their use than semi-modals. However, it appears that semi-modals are increasing in frequency at the same time as core modals are declining in frequency. This trend is especially noticeable with the important semi-modals such as *have to* and *be going to*.

a. We can extend the loosely defined class of semi-modals to include idiomatic combinations beginning with one of the true modals such as *can* or *may*. Two interesting examples are *can't help* + Ving and *might as well* (also *may as well*) + Infinitive. Although not common, these idioms fill what would otherwise be gaps in the semantics of modality in English. *Can't help* is used as a 'strong' or inverse equivalent of *can* (= 'ability'): Consider: *It's so funny – I can't help laughing*. Here *can't help* means 'I can't avoid it' or, in ability terms, 'I'm not able not to laugh'. *Might as well*, on the other hand, is a 'weak' or inverse equivalent of *had better*: whereas *had better* recommends some action as advisable, *might as well* recommends it only in the weak sense of 'there's no good reason not to do it'. The difference between them can be compared in these examples:

> I've started the job, so I*'d better* finish it.
> I've started the job, so I *might as well* finish it.

CHAPTER 7

Indirect Speech

152 direct and indirect speech. BACKSHIFT: *153* backshift in reported clauses; *154* ignoring the rule of backshift; *155* reported feelings and thoughts. AUXILIARY VERBS AND INDIRECT SPEECH: *156* auxiliaries in reporting clauses; *157* auxiliaries in reported clauses; *158 must, should,* etc. in reported clauses; *159* involvement of the speaker of the reported speech with *must,* etc. FREE INDIRECT SPEECH: *160.*

152 The distinction between DIRECT SPEECH and INDIRECT SPEECH (or reported speech) is shown in these two sentences:

(A) DIRECT SPEECH   (B) INDIRECT SPEECH

I enjoy playing football → Jim said that he enjoyed playing football.

Sentence (A) specifies the words actually uttered by Jim, while sentence (B) reports the fact that he uttered something to the effect that he enjoyed playing football. Sentence (B) is similar in meaning to: (C) *Jim said, 'I enjoy playing football'*. But actually, there is a difference between sentences (B) and (C): whereas (C) indicates the actual words spoken by Jim, (B) only reports the MEANING or FORCE of what he said. Thus (B) could be a report of an utterance *I like playing football* or *I love a game of football* or *Playing football – it's great!* which is not identical to (A), but like it in meaning.

Backshift

153 If the verb in the main or REPORTING CLAUSE is in the Past Tense, it is usual for a verb in the reported clause to be BACKSHIFTED:

[A] 'I understand' → Zoe said that *she understood.*

[A] 'I don't want to frighten you' → The officer told the passengers *he didn't want to frighten them.*

[A&] 'I've forgotten his name.' → She said *she had forgotten his name.*

[B] 'Did you see the accused on the night of the 25th?' → She was asked *whether she had seen the accused on the night of the 25th.*

107

There are two possible types of backshift: [A] PRESENT → PAST (including [A*] PRESENT PERFECT → PAST PERFECT) and [B] PAST → PAST PERFECT. The first three examples above show Present → Past backshift. The last example shows Past → Past Perfect backshift.

In semantic terms, backshift can be explained quite simply as follows. The time of the original speech, which is 'now' for direct speech, becomes 'then' for indirect speech, and all times referred to in the speech accordingly become shifted back into the past.

The rule of backshift

	'now'	PAST REPORT OF	'then'
SPEECH ABOUT	(Present Tense)	→ SPEECH ABOUT... (Past Tense)	(Past Tense)
SPEECH ABOUT	'then' (Present Perfect or Past)	PAST REPORT OF → SPEECH ABOUT... (Past Tense)	'before then' (Past Perfect)

a. If the utterance in direct speech contains a verb in the Past Perfect, no backshift is possible, as English has no means of expressing 'past before past before past': *'Before his death, my father had made a new will'* → *She explained that before his death, her father had made a new will*. There is no double Perfect *had had made, so the Past Perfect remains unchanged in the indirect speech report.

b. The term 'indirect speech' is traditionally used for reported discourse in general, whether the original discourse is in spoken or in written form. For our purposes, then, *She wrote in her diary that she had fallen in love with Leo* is an example of indirect speech.

154 Although backshift is the rule when the reporting verb is in the Past Tense, the speaker can sometimes BREAK THE CONCORD between reporting verb and reported verb, keeping the tense form of the original utterance:

(A) 'I hate spiders' → (B) John admitted that he *hates* spiders.

(A) 'The police are still looking for him' → (B) We were told that the police *are* still looking for him.

(A) 'No one has ever spoken to me' → (B) She complained that no one *has* ever spoken to her.

The implication of this avoidance of backshift is that the time of the original utterance ('then') and the time of the report ('now') are both included within the time-span during which the statement in the reported clause remains valid. Thus, in the first example above, the person who utters (B) supposes, at the time of uttering (B), that John still claims to hate spiders.

So it is still appropriate to use the Present. The circumstances in which backshift can be broken are best illustrated by historical statements:

'Virtue is knowledge' → Socrates said that virtue *was* knowledge
OR Socrates said that virtue *is* knowledge.
'I am blameless' → Socrates said that he *was* blameless
BUT NOT ?*Socrates said that he *is* blameless.

The obvious difference between these cases is that the statement *Virtue is knowledge*, if true, is true for all time: it is an 'eternal truth' (see §8), and can therefore have reference to the present day (the time of report) as well as to the time of Socrates. But the declaration *I am blameless*, as spoken by Socrates, has no reference to the present time, since Socrates is now dead. So backshift cannot be avoided in this case. Here is an everyday example:

'Where do you get your hair done?' → I asked her where she *got* / *gets* her hair done.

Both *got* and *gets* are possible here. But *gets* implies that (when 'I' am speaking) 'she' still has her hair done at the same place. *Got* does not have this implication – although it does not exclude the possibility that she still has her hair done at the same place.

a. When the Past Tense has a global indefinite meaning in combination with *ever*, *always*, etc. (see §64d), backshift is virtually compulsory: *I always said he was a liar* (NOT ?*I always said he's a liar*). With the Present Perfect, however, backshift can be avoided: *I've always said he's a liar*.

b. There is an interesting parallel between backshift of tense and the shift from first- and second-person to third-person pronouns in cases like

I don't believe you → She told Tom she didn't believe him.

Just as the backshift of tenses can be broken in special circumstances, so the third-person rule may be broken in cases where people mentioned in the reported clause are identical with speaker or hearer in the reporting situation. For example, *'You're a fraud, Sam'* → *He told me I was a fraud* (spoken by Sam).

c. The backshift from Simple Past or Present Perfect to Past Perfect can also be avoided: *I once met President Kennedy* can be rendered in indirect speech as either *She said she HAD once MET President Kennedy* or *She said she once MET President Kennedy*. This can be explained as follows: the same past happening can either be viewed as 'past in past' (related to another, more recent point of reference in the past) or it can simply be viewed as 'past' (related directly to the present time as its point of reference) – see the diagram in §74.

155 The backshift rule applies not just to indirect speech in the strict sense, but also to REPORTED FEELINGS AND THOUGHTS. In fact, it applies more regularly with verbs such as *know*, *think*, *realise* and *forget* than with verbs such as *say* and *tell*:

I forgot you were listening (rather than 'I forgot you are listening'). | I didn't know he was a teetotaller (rather than 'I didn't know he's a teetotaller').

MEANING AND THE ENGLISH VERB

Strangely, in these conversational examples one cannot easily substitute the Present Tense, even though the situation in the reported clause would normally obtain at the time of reporting. On the other hand, in the case of a general truth, we can say *While still young, I realised that life* IS *a gamble* as well as . . . WAS *a gamble*.

a. It is important to realise that in an example like *I forgot you were listening* above, the reported clause *you were listening* is most likely to extend its reference to the present moment. Here, in following the sequence of tenses ordained by backshift, the Past Tense reported speech differs in one particular way from the characterisation of the Past Tense in §61. Normally the Past Tense indicates that the state of affairs referred to does not extend up to the present moment; but in indirect speech, that constraint does not apply.

Auxiliary verbs and indirect speech

156 In determining backshift, a modal auxiliary followed by a Perfect Infinitive can IN REPORTING CLAUSES, as in other contexts, be counted as the equivalent of a Past Tense form:

'What's wrong?' → You *should have asked* the mechanic what was wrong.

'They're bluffing' → You *must have realised* that they were bluffing.

'I'm guilty' → He *may have admitted* he was guilty.

If we paraphrase this last example 'It is possible that he admitted he was guilty', we use the Past Tense *admitted*, and show that in terms of meaning, this is no exception to the backshift rule.

157 In REPORTED CLAUSES, the backshifting of a primary auxiliary *can, may, will*, etc. results in the use of the secondary form *could, might, would*, etc. Whereas these secondary forms are not always usable for past time reference in direct speech (e.g. **It might rain yesterday* is not the direct Past Tense equivalent of *It may rain today* – see §141), in indirect speech the following backshifts are available without exception: *can* → *could, may* → *might, will* → *would*.

'You *may* stay as long as you like.' → She said they *might* stay as long as they liked.

'It *may* rain tomorrow' → We were afraid it *might* rain the next day.

'I *can* meet you there in an hour' → She said that she *could* meet us there in an hour.

'You *will* keep interrupting me' → He complained that I *would* keep interrupting him.

'The plan *will* fail' → I felt sure that the plan *would* fail.

In the first example, the backshifted *might* (= 'permission') is now rare, and *could* would be a more natural form to use here. At the other extreme of frequency, the last example shows the backshift of future *will* to a 'reported past future' *would*. This *would* is one of the most common uses of *would* – many times more common than the direct future-in-the-past *would* described in §84.

> *a.* The backshift of *shall* to *should* is not so systematically observed, although we meet it occasionally in an example such as the following: *'Shall I open the window?'* → *She asked whether she* SHOULD *open the window.* Here, however, *should* could alternatively be interpreted in the much more common sense of 'weak obligation' (equivalent to *ought to*).
>
> *b.* The backshift of future *shall* to *should* is also possible (though rare) alongside *would* with a first-person subject: *I warned them that we would / should lose the battle unless we tried harder.*
>
> *c.* *Should* is acceptable following verbs such as *promised, decided, insisted* and *intended*, even where the corresponding direct speech use of *shall* would be unusual and rather declamatory: *He promised we should have our reward. We decided that the house should be built of stone.* However, these are best seen as examples of weak-obligation *should* (see §145) or (in the latter case) 'putative *should*' (see §§164, 165), rather than of backshift of *shall*.

158 *Must, ought to, should* (= 'ought to'), *need(n't)* and *(had) better* have no Past Tense forms (see §§140, 145, 146, 150), but in indirect speech they may themselves be used as if they were Past Tense forms. In this sense, these modal forms are tenseless. We can say that *must* is backshifted to *must, ought to* to *ought to*, etc.:

> 'You *must / needn't* take the written exam' → She was told she *must / needn't* take the written exam.
>
> 'You *ought to / should* be ashamed of yourself' → He told me I *ought to / should* be ashamed of myself.
>
> 'You*'d better* hurry up' → He warned her she*'d better* hurry up.

Although it can be said that *must* backshifts to *must* and *need(n't)* backshifts to *need(n't)*, these forms are infrequent in indirect speech, and it is more natural to backshift by switching to the Past Tense forms of *have to* and *need to*: *She was told she* HAD TO *take a written exam. She was told she* DIDN'T NEED TO *take a written exam.*

159 The auxiliaries *may, must, shall* and *ought to* (as we have seen in §§116B, 117A, 127B, and 146) can involve the speaker as the person who exerts his/her will or authority. In indirect speech, the same principle holds good, both for these auxiliaries and their backshifted variants *might* and *should*, so long as we remember that it is THE SPEAKER OF THE REPORTED SPEECH whose will or authority is in question. A sentence like *John has told her she may stay*, in other words, is a true translation into indirect speech of *John has told her 'You may stay'*. If *may, must*, etc. are applicable in direct

MEANING AND THE ENGLISH VERB

speech, they are also (if without backshift) applicable in indirect speech. Ordinarily the speaker of the reported speech is also the subject of the main or reporting clause:

> Jenkins said you *must* pay before you go. (*must* = 'obligation')
>
> Jenkins said they *ought to* be ashamed of themselves. (*ought to* = 'obligation')
>
> Jenkins promised we *should* have our reward. (backshift of *shall* = 'speaker's volition')

In each of these cases it is Jenkins (subject of the reporting clause) whose authority or will is invoked by the modal auxiliary.

Free indirect speech

160 FREE INDIRECT SPEECH, a very common device of narrative writing, consists in the indirect-speech reporting of what someone said or thought by backshifting the verb while omitting (or parenthesising) the reporting clauses (*he said . . .*, etc.) which are the conventional signals of indirect speech.

> DIRECT SPEECH: *Agnes*: 'Why do they always have to pick on me?'
>
> INDIRECT SPEECH: Agnes asked why they always had to pick on her.
>
> FREE INDIRECT SPEECH:
>
> Why did they always have to pick on her (thought Agnes)?
>
> *or simply*: Why did they always have to pick on her?

Free indirect speech is a more flexible medium for reporting than normal indirect speech; it also aids brevity by allowing a writer to retell someone's words in indirect speech and at length without having to keep inserting expressions like *He said* or *She exclaimed*.

Free indirect speech, unlike ordinary indirect speech, can incorporate the question and exclamation structures of direct speech:

> Would they ever meet again? (Anna wondered) | Here was home at last (thought John) | How many years had he and his sister dreamed of this moment! | So that was their plan, was it!

It can also, as these sentences show, include words such as *here* and *this*, which tend to be replaced by *there* and *that* in indirect speech proper.

The use of free indirect speech for describing 'interior monologue' has become a very widespread practice in modern fiction. Instead of *She said . . .* we have to imagine an omitted reporting clause such as *She thought . . .*, *She said to herself . . .*, *She reflected . . . .* Here is a more extended example:

> Well, it *was* no matter now. The dead *couldn't* come back to demand an accounting from the living, and there *was* very little point in dwelling upon her

INDIRECT SPEECH

friend's lack of feeling for a man who'*d been* chosen from complete strangers to be her spouse. Of course, he *wouldn't be* her spouse now. Which nearly *made* one thing.... But no. Rachel forced all speculation from her mind.

(From Elizabeth George, *Deception on his Mind*, Chapter 2.)

The Past Tense verbs in italics in this passage are clearly in indirect speech; they narrate the train of thought in Rachel's mind, which could be otherwise represented in direct speech as 'Well, it's no matter now. The dead can't come back...', etc.

In addition to direct question and exclamation forms, other characteristics of direct speech, such as the *Well* which begins the passage, are telltale signs of free indirect speech. But sometimes the only indicators are backshifted verbs in the Past Tense – including the Past Perfect. For example, *would* in main clauses often invites interpretation as the backshifted equivalent of future *will*, none of the other senses of *will* (volitional, conditional, direct future-in-the-past) being suitable to the context: *That evening he* WOULD *be seeing Sylvie again.*

CHAPTER 8

Mood: Theoretical and Hypothetical Meaning

161 mood: factual, theoretical and hypothetical meaning. THE SUBJUNCTIVE: *162* Present and Past Subjunctive. THEORETICAL MEANING: *163* factual and theoretical meaning, truth-commitment and truth-neutrality; *164* grammatical markers of factual and theoretical meaning; *165* putative *should* and the mandative subjunctive. CONDITIONAL SENTENCES: *166* real and unreal conditions; *167* real conditions; *168* constructions expressing theoretical meaning in *if*-clauses; *169* unreal conditions. HYPOTHETICAL MEANING: *170*; *171* hypothetical meaning in dependent clauses; *172* in main clauses (implied conditions); *173* grammatical markers of hypothetical meaning; *174* relation between real and unreal conditions; *175* negative truth-commitment ('contrary to assumption' and 'contrary to expectation'). HYPOTHETICAL USE OF MODAL AUXILIARIES: *176* indicated by Past Tense form; *177* regularities and exceptions; *178* past hypothetical meaning; *179* signs of fluctuating usage. SPECIAL HYPOTHETICAL USES OF MODAL AUXILIARIES: *180–83*; *181* permission; *182* volition; *183* possibility; *184* three uses of *might have*; *185* 'pure hypothesis'; *186* seven meanings of *could*.

161 Historically, the verbal category of Mood was once important in the English language, as it still is today in many European languages. By distinct forms of the verb, older English was able to discriminate between the Indicative Mood – expressing an event or state as a FACT, and the Subjunctive – expressing it as a SUPPOSITION. Further, the Present Subjunctive – conveying a REAL supposition (such as a plan for the future), was distinct from the Past Subjunctive – conveying an UNREAL supposition (referring to an imaginary or hypothetical state of affairs). Nowadays the Indicative Mood has become all-important, and the Subjunctive Mood is little more than a footnote in the description of the language.

While the contrast between the Subjunctive and Indicative Moods has largely disappeared from present-day English grammar, the distinctions of

THEORETICAL AND HYPOTHETICAL MEANING

meaning which Mood used to express are still important within the language. Modern English has a threefold distinction between FACTUAL, THEORETICAL and HYPOTHETICAL meanings, corresponding to the Mood distinctions mentioned above, and in the title of this chapter I use the term 'mood' loosely to refer to these meanings.

The Subjunctive

162 The Subjunctive Mood survives to a limited degree, in modern English, in both Present Tense and Past Tense forms.

> It is proposed that the Assembly *elect* a new Committee. | William insisted that Sarah *go* to his doctor in Harley Street. | If an Association member *be* found guilty of misconduct, his membership will be suspended and appropriate dues refunded.

Present Subjunctive Mood is here shown by the absence of *-s* from the third-person singular Present Tense verb, and by the use of *be* in place of the Indicative *am / is / are*. Whether it occurs in conditional, concessive, or *that* clauses, the Present Subjunctive is an indicator of non-factual or THEORETICAL meaning (see §§163–4). However, it is in *that*-clauses, illustrated in the first example above, that the Present Subjunctive occurs most. This construction, called the MANDATIVE SUBJUNCTIVE, is more common in AmE than in BrE.

The Past Subjunctive, on the other hand, expresses HYPOTHETICAL MEANING. It survives as a form distinct from the ordinary Indicative Past Tense only in the use of *were*, the Past Tense form of the verb *to be*, with a singular subject: *She looks as if she* WERE *accusing me of fraud*. Like the Present Subjunctive, this is nowadays fairly infrequent, and is often replaced by the Past Indicative *was*: *as if she* WAS *accusing me . . .* especially in informal English.

a. The Subjunctive singular *were*, however, still prevails in more formal style, and in the familiar phrase *If I were you . . . .*

b. In addition to its occurrence in subordinate clauses, the Present Subjunctive (here called the 'formulaic subjunctive') lives on in set exclamatory wishes such as *God* BE *praised! God* SAVE *the Queen! Long* LIVE *the bride and groom! Lord* HAVE *mercy upon us! Heaven* HELP *us all! If the rich countries have to raise taxes, so* BE *it. Far* BE *it from me to spoil the fun.* But here again there is often an alternative construction, the construction beginning with *may* mentioned in §116c: *May God be praised!* (Sometimes *Let*, as a quasi-imperative verb, has a similar function: *Let God be praised.*)

Theoretical meaning

163 The contrast between factual and theoretical meaning was introduced in §121, where it was pointed out that as auxiliaries of possibility, *may* is 'factual', whereas *can* is 'theoretical'. It was noted, by way of exemplification, that while *This illness can be fatal* (= 'It is possible for this illness to be fatal') treats death as an IDEA, *This illness may be fatal* ('It is possible that this illness will be fatal') treats a death as a possible FACT, and to that extent has a stronger and more threatening meaning.

The factual/theoretical contrast is by no means confined to the area of possibility and necessity, as further examples show:

(a) It's a pity to refuse such an offer (IDEA).

(b) It's a pity (that) you refused such an offer (FACT).

(c) It's nice to live high up above the town (IDEA).

(d) It's nice living high up above the town (FACT).

First, notice that the theoretical examples (a) and (c) contain Infinitive constructions, whereas the factual sentences (b) and (d) contain a *that*-clause and a Verb-*ing* construction respectively.

Second, with regard to meaning, notice that the factual sentences assume the truth of the statements they contain, whereas the theoretical sentences do not. Thus sentence (b) lets us know that you *did in fact* refuse the offer; sentence (a) does not tell us whether the offer was refused or not. The factual sentence, we may say, is TRUTH-COMMITTED, whereas the theoretical sentence is TRUTH-NEUTRAL (that is, leaves the question of truth and falsehood open).

164 These observations about sentences (a)–(d) cannot, unfortunately, be generalised to apply to all cases of factual and theoretical meaning. They are useful clues, not infallible tests.

The best I can do, with regard to grammatical form, is to give the following list of constructions *normally* expressing one meaning rather than another:

FACTUAL MEANING:	Indicative mood in dependent clauses
	Verb-*ing* construction
THEORETICAL MEANING:	*to* + Infinitive construction
	should + Infinitive in dependent clauses ('putative' *should*) – especially in British English
	Present Subjunctive – especially in American English

All these constructions are illustrated now with the same phrase (*It*)*'s an excellent thing*:

FACTUAL MEANING:

(1) It's an excellent thing (*that*) *she learns to sing properly*.

(2) *Learning to sing properly* is an excellent thing.

THEORETICAL MEANING:

(3) It's an excellent thing *to learn to sing properly.*

(4) It's an excellent thing *(that) she should learn to sing properly.*

(5) It's an excellent thing *that she learn to sing properly* (rare, possibly archaic).

But these correlations should not be pressed too far. After some verbs of reporting, for example, the *to* + Infinitive construction is factual:

We know Keating to be in town = We know that Keating is in town.

Further, whether a sentence is truth-neutral or truth-committed often depends on factors other than the choice of verbal construction. In *I'm surprised that your wife should object*, the effect of the main verb is to cancel out the neutrality of the *should* + Infinitive construction, with the result that we clearly understand from this sentence that the wife does object. There is hence no logical difference, in many cases, between *should* + Infinitive and the simple Indicative form *objects*. This is not to say, however, that there is no difference in feeling. In *I'm surprised that your wife should object*, it is the 'very idea of it' that surprises me; in *I'm surprised that your wife objects*, I am surprised by the objection itself, which I take to be a known 'fact'.

The meaning swings in the opposite direction (from truth-commitment to truth-neutrality) through the influence of verbs such as *believe* and *suppose*:

I believe (that) his mother is dead. | I suppose (that) you're waiting for my autograph.

Because of the essential element of uncertainty in the meanings of these verbs, a *that*-clause that would elsewhere be truth-committed becomes truth-neutral. The same applies to adjectives such as *possible* and *likely*.

We could go on to note that the primary modals (e.g. *can, may, will*) also express an element of uncertainty, and so belong to the truth-neutral category. However, they express more specific meanings, such as 'possibility' and 'obligation', whereas the forms with 'theoretical' meaning discussed here – the Infinitive, the Subjunctive and 'putative' *should* – express truth-neutrality in its most generalised form.

a. Notice that the differences between *can* ('theoretical possibility') and *may* ('factual possibility') lies not in the modal meaning itself, but (recalling the terminology of §§136 and 142) in the main verb statement that follows the modal. (The modality 'possibility' is by its very nature non-factual.)

b. In support of the distinction drawn here between factual *that*-clauses and theoretical *that*-clauses (with *should*), note the different choice of construction in these sentences: *This fact – that the human race destroys its environment – worries us deeply; This idea – that the human race should destroy its environment – worries us deeply.* It would not be possible here to change the positions of the nouns *idea* and *fact*.

c. Similarly, note that of the following four sentences, the fourth is unacceptable: *I like to see you; I'd like to see you; I like seeing you; *I'd like seeing you*. No doubt this is because the strong element of doubt in the hypothetical construction *I'd like* (§§169–70, 180–2) conflicts with the truth-commitment of the Verb-*ing* construction *seeing you*.

165 PUTATIVE *SHOULD* and the MANDATIVE SUBJUNCTIVE. These terms are used for *should* + Infinitive and the corresponding Present Subjunctive in *that*-clauses. As we would expect from the above discussion, *that*-clauses with the Subjunctive can be converted into *that*-clauses with *should* without any change of meaning:

> The judges have decided / decreed / insisted / voted that the existing law (*should*) *be* maintained.

In this sense, the putative *should* might be called, historically speaking, a 'subjunctive substitute'. Note, however, that the putative *should* construction is usable in many *that*-clauses where the Subjunctive is impossible: *It is interesting that the play should be such a huge success*. The Subjunctive is restricted to *that*-clauses expressing some element of wish, intention or command. This is why it is called the mandative Subjunctive.

Putative *should* has to be carefully distinguished from *should* = 'ought to'; and yet in many instances it is difficult to tell from the context which meaning is meant to apply. Do we interpret *They agree that the rules should be changed* as 'They agree that the rules be changed' or 'They agree that the rules ought to be changed'? In practice, there is little difference between these, although the second interpretation brings out an element of 'obligation'.

There are a number of special uses of putative *should* in exclamations and questions, e.g.:

> Dyson was stunned by the vulgarity of it. That poor old Eddy *should come* to this!
> (= 'the very idea')
> We were having a great time, when who *should come* along but the managing director.
> ('Who do you imagine came along . . . ?')
> How *should* I *know?* | Why *should* we *bother* about that?

a. Fifty years ago the Present Subjunctive appeared to be on its deathbed in BrE. But since then, the mandative Subjunctive has undergone a mild revival, probably under the influence of the more robust survival of the same construction in AmE. However, the mandative Subjunctive remains rare in BrE, and it is not particularly common in AmE either. There is a tendency, particularly in BrE, to avoid both the Subjunctive and the *should* constructions by using a third option, the Indicative: *It's important that the expedition* REACHES *its destination by the end of the month*. Although the factual Indicative form is used, the clause is truth-neutral: the speaker does not claim to know whether the destination will be reached. This use of the Indicative is sometimes felt to be 'incorrect'.

b. May / might + Infinitive, like *should* + Infinitive, can be regarded as a 'subjunctive substitute' in clauses of purpose and concession: *Let us fight on, that every future generation may bless our memory* (= '... that every future generation bless our memory'); *Our cause is just, though the world may be against us* (= '... though the world be against us'). Nowadays, this usage is confined to an elevated, rhetorical style. (See also §116C.)

Conditional sentences

166 In CONDITIONAL SENTENCES, the statement expressed by the main clause is qualified by a condition expressed by an *if*-clause or some equivalent construction (e.g. a conditional clause introduced by *unless, lest* or *whether*). Conditional sentences can express either a REAL CONDITION (also called an 'open condition') or an UNREAL CONDITION:

If you want a dessert, it will cost more money.   (REAL CONDITION)
If you wanted a dessert, it would cost more money. (UNREAL CONDITION)

167 In REAL CONDITIONS, both the main clause and the dependent clause are truth-neutral: hearing the remark *If he asks me, I'll marry him*, we are not in a position to judge whether either the proposal or the marriage will take place. Nevertheless, it is normal, in contemporary English, to use the factual Indicative form of the verb in both clauses. (For future conditions, the Simple Present is used rather than *will* + Infinitive in the dependent clause – see §102). Although a very common type of real condition, as in the above example, refers to the future, there are no special restrictions on the time reference of conditions, or on the tense forms used to express them. The following examples illustrate something of the variety and mixture of times and tense forms permitted for real conditions:

If you're happy, you make others happy.
   (Simple Present + Simple Present)
If James told you that last night, he was lying.
   (Simple Past + Past Progressive)
If my son is a genius, I've underestimated him.
   (Simple Present + Present Perfect)
If they left at nine, they will certainly be home by midnight.
   (Simple Past + *will* 'future').

168 The truth-neutrality of an *if*-clause is reflected in the possibility of using constructions expressing theoretical meaning (Present Subjunctive and *should* + Infinitive) in place of the Simple Present:

PRESENT SUBJUNCTIVE: If the server *serve* a fault twice, he shall lose a point (archaic, legalistic).

should + INFINITIVE: If you *should hear* news of them, please let me know.

The effect of the putative *should* is to make the condition slightly more tentative and 'theoretical' than it would be with the ordinary Present Tense.

a. Another expression of a tentative real condition is achieved by omitting *if* and inverting the subject and auxiliary *should*: *Should you want to return anything for any reason, it's no problem* (cf. §173a).

169 UNREAL CONDITIONS are normally formed by the use of the Past Tense – Indicative or Subjunctive – in the conditional clause, and *would* + Infinitive in the main clause. (Another 'past' modal – *could*, *might* or *should* – can be used instead of *would*.) Thus it is possible to derive unreal conditions from the examples of real conditions in §167 by a process of 'backshift' somewhat similar to that employed in indirect speech:

> If you *were* happy, you *would make* others happy. | If John *had told* you that last night, he *would have been* lying. | If my son *were* a genius, I'd *have underestimated* him. | If they *had left* at nine, they *would* certainly be home by midnight.

The precise grammatical and semantic nature of this switch from real to unreal conditions is discussed in the following account of hypothetical meaning (§§170–3).

Hypothetical meaning

170 When a verbal construction expresses HYPOTHETICAL MEANING, this means that the happening described is assumed to take place not in the real world, but in an imaginary world. For example, someone who says *I wish I* WAS clever, implies '... but I am *not* clever'. Someone who says *Just suppose I* HADN'T APPLIED *for the job*, suggests that '... but I *have* applied for the job'. In effect, this implication is considerably weakened in some contexts (see §§175, 181–3, 185); but it is this NEGATIVE TRUTH-COMMITMENT of hypothetical meaning that distinguishes it both from factual meaning (positive truth-commitment) and from theoretical meaning (truth-neutrality).

The difference between the three meanings is registered in a simple way, in the three sentences:

> *Factual:*
> It's laughable that Septimus is in love ('Yes, it's a fact that he is in love').
>
> *Theoretical:*
> It's laughable that Septimus should be in love ('Whether he *is* in love or not is a different matter').
>
> *Hypothetical:*
> It would be laughable if Septimus were in love ('But actually, he's *not* in love').

THEORETICAL AND HYPOTHETICAL MEANING

Of the three attitudes to Septimus' being in love, we can say the first and the third are opposites, while the second is on neutral territory between them.

a. The negative feeling of the hypothetical construction is demonstrated by the approximate equivalence between *I wish she loved me* (positive, hypothetical) and *It's a pity she doesn't love me* (negative, factual).

171 Apart from unreal conditions such as *If you were happy, you'd make others happy* (§166), hypothetical meaning is found in DEPENDENT CLAUSES in a number of less important sentence-types:

It's time you were in bed ('... I see you're not').

He behaves *as if* he owned the place ('... but he doesn't').

It's not *as though* we were poor ('... we are not').

Suppose / imagine you and I were living on a desert island ('... but of course we aren't').

If only I had listened to my English teacher! ('... but I didn't').

Even though he were my brother, I would refuse to help him (archaic) ('... but he is not').

I wish I were young again ('... but I'm not').

I'd rather you were listening to me ('... you're not listening at the moment').

Of these constructions, those with *it's time*, *if only*, and *wish* require hypothetical verb forms, while those with *as if*, *as though*, *suppose / imagine*, *even though* and *would rather* permit a choice between hypothetical and non-hypothetical forms. The difference between the second sentence above and *He behaves as if he owns the place* is that the sentence with *owns* leaves the question of whether he owns the place open, whereas the sentence with *owned* presupposes that he does not. (However, context may suggest a negative presupposition also where *owns* is used.)

172 In MAIN CLAUSES, a hypothetical verb form often requires the presence of an accompanying conditional clause. **The Eiffel Tower would fall down* standing alone as a main clause is not a self-sufficient English sentence. Unless we add a condition to it, the listener is left baffled, consciously or unconsciously asking the question 'If what?' There are, however, various circumstances in which a hypothetical main clause stands on its own, and we can often explain such cases by positing an IMPLIED (or suppressed) CONDITION. For example:

(1) I'd be inclined to trade that car in for a new one (*suppressed condition*: '... if I were you').

(2) Would you like some peas? ('... if I offered you some').

(3) No, I'd prefer beans / I'd rather have beans, please ('... if you wouldn't mind').

(4) I'd hate to live in a house like that ('... if I had to').

(5) Would you help Robbie change his shirt? ('... if I asked you to').

It is probably an exaggeration to suggest that speakers reconstruct such 'ifs' when producing these somewhat conventionalised utterances, but the ellipsis helps to explain why the hypothetical form is used. As examples (2)–(4) show, we commonly make use of a suppressed hypothetical condition in expressing or alluding to a wish. Apparently this is because there is a certain indelicacy or rudeness in expressing one's wishes bluntly, as a statement of volition can often seem like an imperative. *I'd like beans* is therefore more polite than *I want beans*. It removes from reality the whole question of whether I am going to get the beans or not, or even makes the diplomatic assumption that I am *not* going to receive any.

The most important cases of implied conditions involve the secondary modal auxiliaries *could, might, would* and *should*, and will be dealt with later in §§181–5.

a. Notice that *I'd like beans* is the hypothetical equivalent of *I want beans*. With hypothetical meaning, *would want*... is unidiomatic, and *would like* is substituted for it.

173 The GRAMMATICAL MARKERS of hypothetical meaning are:

1 *Would* + Infinitive
  (a) in main clauses
  (b) in reported speech clauses which would be main clauses if converted into direct speech
  (c) but not in any clause (main or dependent) containing another modal auxiliary, as modals cannot combine with one another. (Instead, other secondary modals can be used: *could, might, should* – see §§176–85.)

2 Past Tense (Indicative or Subjunctive)
  (d) in other dependent clauses.

3 The Past Tense construction *was / were to* + Infinitive (Indicative) or *were to* + Infinitive (Subjunctive) as an alternative to the plain Past Tense
  (e) in conditional clauses (and clauses introduced by *suppose* or *imagine*)
  (f) only in reference to future time, and mainly with 'event' verbs.

Examples:

(1a) I*'d love* to live abroad (if I had the money).

(1b) She says she*'d love* to live abroad.

(1c) If I owned a car, I *could* teach you how to drive. (*could* = 'would be able to')

THEORETICAL AND HYPOTHETICAL MEANING

(2d) He talks as if he *was / were* my rich uncle.

(3e) { Perhaps it would be helpful if I *were to* say something.
Just suppose that crocodile *were to escape*! }

(3f) { *If you *were to know* Spanish, you might get a better job.
If we *were to win* the lottery, we'd go on a world tour. }

It is clear that the Past Tense cannot be used twice in the same verb phrase, so where the Past Tense or *would / should / could / might* + Infinitive is used to signal hypothetical meaning, pastness of time has to be conveyed by the Perfect Aspect. Once again (see §§67, 142) the Perfect acts as a past time indicator where the Past Tense is not available for that function. The hypothetical version of the past real condition *If I said that, I was lying* [*If* ... Past, ... Past] is therefore *If I had said that, I'd have been lying* [*If* ... Past Perfect, ... *would* + Perfect]. (Here the single underlining shows the marker of hypothetical meaning, and the wavy underlining shows the marker of past time meaning.)

a. In a rather formal style of English, a conditional clause with inversion of subject and auxiliary verb (or *be*) is sometimes used instead of a hypothetical *if*-clause: *Had I known* (= 'If I had known'); *Were he to return* (= 'If he were to return ...'); *Were they alive* (= 'If they were alive ...'). *Had* and *were* are the auxiliaries most commonly involved. *Was* is rarely preposed because in the rather elevated style in which this inversion occurs, the Subjunctive is preferred to the Indicative form. Inversion is just possible with *could* and *might*, but not with *would*: *Could / might I but see my child once more* ... (= 'If only I could / might see my child once more ...'). Here the inversion, which has a decidedly archaic, rhetorical flavour, has to be supported by the intensifying word *but*. Comparison can be made between such inversions and the similar inversion of *should* in real-conditional sentences (§168a). Incidentally, *should* is sometimes used as a marker of unreal conditions, as well as of tentative real conditions: *Should the container explode, there would almost certainly be widespread damage.*

b. Examples such as *I wish it would rain* appear to be exceptions to the rule that in dependent clauses, hypothetical meaning is conveyed by the Past Tense rather than *would / should* + Infinitive. Arguably they are not exceptions, however, since *it would rain* in this context is the hypothetical equivalent of future *it will rain* rather than of present *it rains*. Hence the difference between *I wish this clock worked* and *I wish this clock would work* is that the former is a wish about the present, and the latter a wish about the future. In practice, to refer to the hypothetical future we can use the future *would* for 'event verbs', but can only use the non-past hypothetical Past Tense for 'state verbs'. For example, we could not say **I wish that book would belong to me*, but we might say *I wish that bus would arrive soon*. *Would* in this position can have volitional colouring: *We wish you would come and stay with us. I wish you wouldn't drink so much.* Such remarks often have the force of requests or commands.

174 The tables below plot past, present and future time against real and unreal conditional sentences, (1), (2) and (3) being the three grammatical markers of hypothetical meaning listed in §173.

MEANING AND THE ENGLISH VERB

Verbal indicators of real and unreal conditions

	PAST TIME	PRESENT TIME	FUTURE TIME
REAL	Past Tense Present Perfect Tense Past Perfect Tense	non-perfect Present Tense	*will* + Infinitive, etc. non-perfect Present Tense

	PAST TIME	PRESENT TIME	FUTURE TIME
UNREAL	(1) *would* (etc.) + Perfect Infinitive (2) Past Perfect Tense	(1) *would* (etc.) + Infinitive (2) non-perfect Past Tense	(1) *would* (etc.) + Infinitive, etc. (2) non-perfect Past Tense (3) *was / were to* + Infinitive

From the second table it is evident that there is little difference, in unreal conditions, between the expression of present and of future time. This means that a sentence like *If it were my birthday, I'd be celebrating* refers indifferently to the present or the future. We could insert either a future or a present adverbial to make the time-span explicit:

If it were my birthday today, I'd be celebrating.

If it were my birthday tomorrow, I'd be celebrating.

(Incidentally there is no conflict, here, in the co-occurrence of a Past Tense verb with a future adverbial.) It might be appropriate with hypothetical, as with modal verb forms (see §139), to distinguish primarily 'past' from 'non-past' time, rather than 'past' from 'present'.

a. *Was / were to* can be used to single out hypothetical future reference in *if*-clauses, as is seen in examples (3e) and (3f) in §173. But in *if*-clauses *would* cannot be used with this function, but can only be a hypothetical volitional auxiliary, except in the idiomatic sequences *if you would like* . . . and *if you wouldn't mind* . . . . Thus in *If the building were to collapse, there could be catastrophic loss of life, were to* cannot be replaced by *would*: *?*If the building would collapse* . . . . However, the ordinary Past Tense would be an acceptable substitute: *If the building collapsed* . . . (bear in mind, though, that *collapsed* here is 'non-past' in meaning, and so could just as well refer to the present time as to the future).

175 It is now time to think further about the MEANING OF HYPOTHETICAL CONSTRUCTIONS.

I pointed out earlier that the distinguishing mark of hypothetical meaning is its implication of NEGATIVE TRUTH-COMMITMENT. The exact interpretation, however, varies in accordance with past, present and future time.

In referring to imaginary past events, the hypothetical forms in dependent clauses (in practice mostly *if*-clauses) normally have the categorical sense of 'CONTRARY TO FACT', since it is not difficult to have definite knowledge of past events:

> If your father *had caught* us, he *would have* been furious ('... but in fact he didn't').
>
> What if we*'d lost* our way! ('... but in fact we didn't').
>
> I wish I *hadn't swallowed* that last glass of whisky ('... but in fact I did').

Non-past imaginary happenings do not usually have such uncompromising implications. In the present, the sense is not so much 'contrary to fact' as 'CONTRARY TO ASSUMPTION', and in the future, it is weakened further to 'CONTRARY TO EXPECTATION':

> If you really *cared* for your children, you*'d look* after them properly ('... but I assume you don't care for them').
>
> If it *were to snow* tomorrow, the match *would have to be* cancelled ('... but I expect it will not snow').

The second sentence does not rule out the possibility of snow but, on the other hand, its sentiment is more disbelieving (and less pessimistic) than the real condition of: *If it snows tomorrow, the match will have to be cancelled.*

a. The MAIN clause of an unreal condition, unlike the DEPENDENT clause, is not necessarily contrary to fact or to expectation. E.g.:

> I won't tell Susan about my problems: (even) if she were my closest friend, I (still) wouldn't want her to know.

Clearly the implication of the *if*-clause is that 'Susan is not my closest friend'. But the independent clause does not carry the implication that 'I want to tell her about my problems' – in fact it has rather the opposite implication. So the main clause here is not 'contrary to fact / expectation'.

b. The negative truth-commitment of the hypothetical Past is additionally weakened in sentences which indirectly recommend or request a course of action: e.g. *Would you mind if I taped this conversation, Mrs Darcy?* It is a tactful tentativeness, rather than lack of expectation, which leads a speaker to use the hypothetical form in such cases. (Compare the tentative use of *could, might,* etc. – §§181–5.)

c. A more extreme example of weakening is seen in a tendency to use the *it's time* construction in circumstances where the implication of negative truth-commitment is quite inapplicable. You might hear, for example, the following snatch of dialogue: A: *Tiny's cooking the breakfast this morning.* B: *Oh good – it's about time he helped out with the cooking.* Now it is quite evident that here the hypothetical verb *helped* refers to what Tiny is doing, rather than what he is not doing. The hypothetical Past seems anomalous in this construction: the meaning is one of truth-neutrality (or even positive truth-commitment) rather than of negative truth-commitment.

Hypothetical use of modal auxiliaries

176 Modals, if we except semi-modals like *have to*, cannot follow other modals, and therefore cannot combine with *would* according to the rule

(rule 1(a), §173) for expressing hypothetical meaning in main clauses. Instead, in main as in dependent clauses, THE HYPOTHETICAL MEANING OF A MODAL IS INDICATED BY THE PAST TENSE FORM ALONE. Another way to express this is to say that all the secondary modals *would, could, might* and *should* can express, in both independent and dependent clauses, hypothetical meanings corresponding to the meanings of the primary modals *will, can, may* and *shall*. The difference about *would* (see §173) is that, besides expressing *will*'s meanings of prediction and volition in the hypothetical mood, it can also express pure hypothetical meaning in main clauses. Compare:

> If you *could* drive, you *could* teach me.
>
> If you *were* able to drive, you *would* be able to teach me.

Notice that here the first *could* is replaceable by *were able to*, the second with *would be able to*.

> *a. Have to*, being a modal auxiliary only for purposes of meaning, has the infinitive form *have to*, and so in main clauses combines with *would* to form the regular hypothetical form *would have to*: *If the diagnosis should be confirmed, she* WOULD HAVE TO *stay in the hospital*.

177 Difficulties arise because of gaps in the Past Tense paradigm of modal auxiliaries. First, here are straightforward examples of unreal conditions expressed by means of the hypothetical Past Tense:

> *Could*: (a) If you got a job in Sydney, you *could* come to see us more often (= '... it would be possible for ...').
> (b) If I had a visa, I *could* visit the country for as long as I wanted (= '... I would be permitted to ...').
>
> *Might*: (c) If Holmes were playing, Scotland *might* win (= '... it's possible that Scotland would win.').
>
> *Would*: (d) If you were a real friend, you'*d* do anything I asked (= '... you would be willing to ...').

Against these must be placed the following gaps and exceptions:

1 *Might* and *could* rarely occur in unreal conditions with the sense of hypothetical permission (except – rarely in the case of *might* – in polite requests – see §181).

2 The hypothetical forms of *will* (= 'strong volition', 'predictability') and *shall* (= 'volition') are rare or non-existent.

3 As *must* has no Past Tense form, *would have to* is the only verbal expression available for hypothetical obligation, requirement or necessity. Contrast:

> REAL CONDITION: If it's that serious, we *must* act at once.
>
> UNREAL CONDITION: If it were that serious, we'*d* have to act at once.

THEORETICAL AND HYPOTHETICAL MEANING

a. Examples (a) and (c) above associate *could* with 'theoretical possibility' and *might* with 'factual possibility' (§121), as one would expect, seeing that they are the Past Tense forms of *may* and *can* respectively. These are their most common hypothetical meanings. However, both modals can be used in both 'factual' and 'theoretical' senses. Here is *could* in the 'factual' sense: *If the astronaut momentarily lost radio contact with earth, the whole mission could be ruined*; and here is *might* in the 'theoretical sense': *The whole exercise might be described as a self-training process.* (*Might* and *could* are interchangeable in both examples.) If we paraphrase the modal auxiliaries in these examples, an interesting difference between 'hypothetical factual possibility' and 'hypothetical theoretical possibility' emerges. *The whole mission could be ruined* = 'It is possible that the whole mission would be ruined'. *The whole exercise might be described* . . . = 'It would be possible to describe the exercise . . .'. Notice that in the 'factual' case, the hypothetical *would* applies to the main verb, whereas in the 'theoretical' case, it applies to the modal meaning of possibility. This is analogous to the contrast between the main verb negation of *may* (= 'factual possibility'), and the auxiliary negation of *can* (= 'theoretical possibility'), as illustrated in §§136–7.

b. Could in the 'ability' sense does not occur in a hypothetical main clause when the main verb is a 'state verb', referring to a permanent accomplishment: **If you'd had proper lessons, you could speak English.* Instead, *would be able to* or *would know how to* can be used.

c. There is a possible occurrence of the hypothetical form of *will* (= 'predictability') in exclamations like *You 'WOULD make a mess of it! He 'WOULD interfere like that.* These remarks do not have the negative truth-commitment one expects with hypothetical forms, but their sardonic flavour can be brought out by a gloss of this kind: 'This is just the sort of (wilful) behaviour you would predict from such a person'. The hypothetical predictability meaning of *would* is shown in this dialogue: *'The leaders of the nuclear power industry claim that their safety standards are the best in the world.' 'Well, they WOULD (say that), wouldn't they?'* The implication is: 'This is the sort of behaviour we would predict, even if we did not know about it'.

178 With modal auxiliaries, as already noted, past hypothetical meaning can be expressed by the Perfect Infinitive:

If Holmes had been playing, Scotland *might have won* ('. . . it is possible that Scotland would have won'). | Had you come to me sooner, I *could have cured* you. | If he'd asked me politely, I *would / should have given* him a lift.

Would have had to can be used for past hypothetical necessity or obligation: *If fire had taken hold of the building, he would have had to clamber out on to the roof.*

a. In spoken English, utterances like this last example could occur with 'double marking' of the Perfect Aspect (see §179 below): *If the police had caught us, we'd have had to have made a clean breast of it.* In such an utterance, the *have* is invariably reduced to the weak syllable /əv/, so that it could be more realistically rewritten *'ve: . . . we'd've had to've made a clean breast of it.*

179 Past hypothetical meaning and the use of the modals is one of the most difficult areas of English not only for non-native speakers, but also for native speakers. It may be partly as a result of this that the language shows signs of confused and fluctuating usage, especially in the area of 'hypothetical past time'. We have noted that the hypothetical past expressed by a Past Perfect in a dependent clause is strongly associated with 'contrary to fact' meaning. Also 'contrary to fact' are some secondary modals + Perfect in main clauses: we notice this with *shouldn't* (§146a), *needn't* (§147b), and *might* (§183b) + Perfect. (With negatives like *shouldn't have*, of course, it is the negative statement that is assumed to be false, and the positive statement to be true: *You shouldn't have stolen it* implies *You stole it*.) There seems to be a growing tendency, in fact, to associate the Perfect after a secondary modal purely with 'contrary to fact' meaning, rather than past time. On this basis, we can suggest why speakers sometimes produce sentences like this:

> I *would have enjoyed* meeting you and Maria next Thursday, but I'm afraid I'll be away.

In this case, the imaginary event of meeting 'you and Maria' is located in the future, rather than in the past, so it is only the 'contrary to fact' meaning that is applicable: the past meaning of the Perfect seems to have been lost.

Another area of confusion, in spoken English, is in the 'double marking' of hypothetical meaning in examples such as these:

> If they*'d have arrived* yesterday, they*'d have seen* the place at its best.

By 'double marking', I mean that the *if*-clause has two forms signalling the same meaning. The expected construction is *If they'd arrived*, expandable into *If they had arrived* (Past indicating hypothesis, and Perfect indicating pastness). However, the dependent clause in this example matches the main clause, in containing *'d + have* + Past Participle. It seems possible here that the reduced auxiliary *'d* in the dependent clause has been reinterpreted as *would*. This is supported by the occasional (growing?) occurrence of 'pure' hypothetical *would* in dependent clauses – a construction generally supposed to be 'unEnglish':

> ?*I'd feel happier if somebody *would have said* something.

However, the idea that *'d* is reinterpreted as *would* is belied by the negative form *hadn't have* which can occur in the *if*-clause:

> If they *hadn't have arrived* yesterday, they would have missed the gala performance.

In practice the form written *have* here always occurs in its contracted form (*'ve*, pronounced /əv/), so conceivably a new 'contrary to fact' morpheme /dəv/ + Past Participle is entering the spoken language. In any case, it appears that past hypothetical usage in spoken English is in a state of some uncertainty, both semantically and syntactically, and is probably undergoing change.

Special hypothetical uses of modal auxiliaries

180 We turn finally to special hypothetical uses of modal auxiliaries in main clauses where there is no expressed condition. The four main areas of meaning concerned are permission, volition, possibility and 'pure hypothesis'. These special uses can best be explained in terms of psychological factors such as diffidence and tact. Hypothetical forms are substituted in order to tone down the meaning of the non-hypothetical auxiliary where it might be thought too bold or blunt.

181 HYPOTHETICAL PERMISSION. *Could* and *might* are sometimes used as more polite alternatives to *can* and *may* in first-person requests:

> *Could* I see your driving licence? | I wonder if we *could* borrow some tea? | *Might* I ask you for your opinion? | Do you happen to have a brochure I *might* look at?

The strict force of the hypothetical form here is that the speaker does not expect his/her plea to be granted, the negative inference being '... but I don't suppose I can/may'. But this is a further instance of the weakening of hypothetical meaning: people will choose *could* and *might* out of a habit of politeness, even when they expect their requests to be complied with. If one should want to supply an 'implied condition' here, it might be '... if I were bold enough to ask you'.

Here *could* and *might* are parallel to *can* and *may* (= 'permission'), in that *might* is more polite-sounding, and also less common, especially in AmE, than *could*.

a. One of the many ways of making a polite request in English is by the phrase *I don't suppose* followed by a clause containing hypothetical *could*: *I don't suppose I could borrow some wine glasses, could I?* In this case, the negative truth-commitment of the hypothetical form is made explicit in *don't suppose*.

182 HYPOTHETICAL VOLITION. The polite use of *would* instead of *will* (= 'willingness') in second- and third-person requests provides a further example of the absolute use of a hypothetical clause with verbs expressing desire:

> *Would* you lend me fifty pence? | I wonder if someone *would* help me pitch this tent.

We can account for the air of politeness of these requests by postulating again some such unexpressed condition as '... if I were to ask you'. Compared with a direct imperative, the *will* question is itself, of course, a step in the direction of politeness: it issues a directive in the form of a question rather than a command. But through habit, it has acquired strong imperative overtones, especially when delivered in a tone of command:

Will you sit down! It is therefore not surprising that a still more indirect form of imperative, with hypothetical *would*, has come into use.

a. This *would* – the hypothetical form of weak-volitional *will* – needs to be carefully distinguished from *would* used purely as a marker of hypothetical meaning in main clauses. The former differs from the latter in that (a) it can be replaced by *will*; and (b) it can be paraphrased by *would be willing to*. On the other hand, the *would* which precedes *mind* and *like* (*Would you mind . . . ? Would you like . . . ?*) is the pure hypothetical one. In these cases it is the main verb (*mind, like*) that conveys volition.

b. Significantly, the answer to a hypothetical request often contains the corresponding non-hypothetical auxiliary:

'Would you hold the gate open?' 'Of course I will.'
'Could I ask your opinion?' 'Certainly you can.'

The answerer here is granting a favour, and so has no reason to be politely indirect or evasive.

183 HYPOTHETICAL POSSIBILITY. Used hypothetically, *could* and *might* are substitutes for *may* in expressing factual possibility (see §121):

There *could* be trouble at the World Cup match tomorrow. | The door *might* be locked already. | Our team *might* still win the race.

The effect of the hypothetical auxiliary, with its implication 'contrary to expectation', is to make the expression of possibility more tentative and guarded. *Our team might still win the race* can be paraphrased 'It is barely possible that . . .' or 'It is possible, though unlikely, that . . .'.

A possible event in the past can be described by means of the construction *could / might* + Perfect Infinitive: '*Could you have left your umbrella at the bus-station?*' '*I could have.*' In this respect, *could* + Perfect is a slightly more tentative variant of *may* + Perfect (which could not, however, be used in the question form – see §§131, 142). *Might*, on the other hand, seems to be used almost as a variant of *may* (= 'factual possibility') with little implication of reduced likelihood.

Another difference between *could* and *might* is that *couldn't* is an instance of auxiliary negation, and *mightn't* is an instance of main verb negation:

He *couldn't* have made that mistake!
(= 'It is not even barely possible that he made that mistake').

He *might not* have made that mistake
(= 'It is just possible that he did not make that mistake').

In this contrast, *couldn't* and *might not* are parallel to *can't* and *may not* respectively. On the other hand, *might* (= 'possibility'), unlike *may* (= 'possibility'), is very occasionally used in questions: *Might it have been left at the bus station?*

a. Both *could* and *might* are commonly used in suggestions for future action, in a way analogous to the 'democratic imperative' *can* (see §115Aa): *You could answer*

THEORETICAL AND HYPOTHETICAL MEANING

these letters for me. We might meet again after New Year, if you're agreeable. Predictably, the hypothetical forms *could* and *might* are more polite, in their directive force, than *can*, since they make the expression of possibility more tentative. Once again, the contrast between *can* and *may* seems to be smoothed away in the hypothetical forms: there is little to choose between *could* and *might* here, although in the non-hypothetical 'democratic imperative', only *can* is possible (see §115A*a*).

b. In familiar speech, *could* and *might* are used more forcefully, in a tone of rebuke, in such remarks as *You 'could try and be a bit more civilised! You 'might stop grumbling at me for a change!* The negative hypothetical implication is clearly present here: 'It would be possible for you to do these things, but you don't in fact do them'. Notice also the use of *could / might have* in complaints about past omissions: *You might have let me know the boss was in a foul temper! You could have given me some notice!* ('It would have been possible for you to do these things, but you didn't').

184 Note that there are three distinct meanings of *might* + Perfect, all involving possibility:

(1) You might have told me! (§183*b*)
('It would have been possible for you to tell me').

(2) You might have dropped it somewhere (§183)
('It is just possible that you (have) dropped it somewhere').

(3) You might have met him if you'd been there (§177)
('It is possible that you would have met him . . .').

In all three of these examples, *could* can replace *might* without any appreciable change of meaning. In the third, however, *could* would be more likely to convey the somewhat different meaning of theoretical rather than factual possibility: 'It would have been possible for you to meet him if you'd been there'.

a. Note a difference between the main statements in the three examples above: (1) is 'contrary to fact', implying 'but you didn't'; (2) is not 'contrary to fact', as the speaker entertains the possibility that 'it has been dropped'; (3) is not absolutely 'contrary to fact', although as the *if*-clause is, the main clause is also likely to imply that 'you did not meet him'.

185 A fourth special category of the use of hypothetical modals without an overt condition is here called 'pure hypothesis', because it shows the modal *would* used in main clauses in its pure hypothetical sense (§173) – that is, without any additional meaning, such as 'permission', associated with the primary modal:

It *would seem* that much of the furore over drug costs has been misplaced. | The self-teacher *would seem* to be a contradiction. | By the time Felix turned up it was early afternoon, which, *I would think*, would be late enough. | Intuitively one *would expect* that this parameter should be very close to zero.

In such examples, hypothetical *would* + Infinitive could be replaced by the plain Indicative form of the verb: *would seem* can be replaced by *seems*, etc.

MEANING AND THE ENGLISH VERB

There appears to be no suppressed 'if' that could explain the hypothetical form, so the avoidance of the Indicative seems to be just an evasive or defensive strategy on the part of the writer. (This is mainly a feature of written English, strongly represented in academic prose.) The main verb belongs to a category of cognitive state verbs implying lack of knowledge, and so the effect of hypothetical *would* is to distance the writer's claim even further from reality. I say 'even further' because there is a double tentativeness: *it seems* already shows a lack of confidence, and *it would seem* takes an additional step in the same direction.

186 The last three chapters have shown the variability of meanings (past time, past time in indirect speech, and hypothetical) associated with the secondary modals. To conclude, the following sentences illustrate this multiplicity with examples of seven different meanings of *could*. (Past time examples are of direct rather than indirect speech.)

    1 Past time equivalent of *can* (= 'possibility') (cf. §140)
      Nothing *could* be done to stop the water flooding into the house.

    2 Past time equivalent of *can* (= 'ability') (cf. §140)
      Like every self-respecting young Victorian lady, Charlotte *could* paint and play the piano; but she *couldn't* peel a potato to save her life.

    3 Past time equivalent of *can* (= 'permission') (cf. §140)
      After the 1920 Act, women *could* vote, but they still *couldn't* become Members of Parliament.

    4 Hypothetical equivalent of *can* (= 'possibility') (cf. §176)
      The house is one of the most beautiful that *could* be imagined.

    5 Hypothetical equivalent of *can* (= 'ability') (cf. §176)
      Do you know anyone who *could* repair this clock for me?

    6 Hypothetical equivalent of *can* (= 'permission') (cf. §176)
      I'd be grateful if I *could* borrow your electric drill.

    7 Tentative equivalent of *may* (= 'factual possibility') (cf. §183)
      The weather has been terrible up there in the mountains. You *could* find climbing very difficult.

The last meaning is rather more anomalous than the others, as it shows *could* extending its range of meaning into the epistemic territory of 'factual possibility' which is the domain of *may*, not *can*.

Further Reading

Aarts, B. and A. McMahon (eds) (forthcoming) *The Handbook of English Linguistics*, Cambridge: Cambridge University Press

Aarts, B. and C.F. Meyer (eds) (1995) *The Verb in Contemporary English: Theory and Description*, Cambridge: Cambridge University Press

Aarts, F. (1969) 'On the Use of the Progressive and Non-Progressive Present with Future Reference in Present-Day English', *English Studies*, 50, 565–79

Adamczewski, H. (1978) BE + ING *dans la Grammaire de l'Anglais Contemporain*, Lille: Atelier Reproduction des Thèses

Allen, R.L. (1966) *The Verb System of Present-Day American English*, The Hague: Mouton

Bache, C. (1982) 'Aspect and Aktionsart: Towards a Semantic Distinction', *Journal of Linguistics*, 18, 57–72

Bache, C. (1983) *Verbal Aspect: A General Theory and its Application to Present-Day English*, Odense: University Press

Bache, C. and N. Davidsen-Nielsen (1997) *Mastering English: An Advanced Grammar for Non-native and Native Speakers*, Berlin: Mouton de Gruyter (Chapter 9)

Behre, F. (1955) *Meditative-Polemic* SHOULD *in Modern English* THAT-*Clauses* (Gothenburg Studies in English, 4), Göteborg: Acta Universitatis Gothoburgensis

Berglund, Y. (1997) 'Future in present-day English: Corpus-based evidence on the rivalry of expressions', *ICAME Journal*, 21, 7–19

Berglund, Y. (2000) 'Utilising Present-day English Corpora: A Case Study concerning Expressions of Future', *ICAME Journal*, 24, 25–63

Biber, D., S. Johansson, G. Leech, S. Conrad and E. Finegan (1999) *Longman Grammar of Spoken and Written English*, London: Longman (esp. Chapter 6)

Binnick, R. (forthcoming) 'Aspect and Aspectuality', in Aarts and McMahon

Binnick, R.I. (1991) *Time and the Verb*, Oxford: Oxford University Press

Bybee, J. and S. Fleischman (eds) (1995) *Modality in Grammar and Discourse*, Amsterdam: Benjamins

Bybee, J., W. Pagliuca and R.D. Perkins (1994) *The Evolution of Grammar: Tense, Aspect and Modality in the Languages of the World*, Chicago: University of Chicago Press

Close, R.A. (1977) 'Some Observations on the Meaning and Function of Verb Phrases having Future Reference', in W.-D. Bald and R. Ilson (eds) *Studies in English Usage, The Resources of a Present-Day English Corpus for Linguistic Analysis*, Frankfurt: Lang, 125–56

Close, R.A. (1980) '*Will* in *if*-clauses', in Greenbaum *et al.*, 100–09

Close, R.A. (1981) *English as a Foreign Language: its Constant Grammatical Problems* (3rd edn), London: Allen & Unwin

Coates, J. (1980) 'On the Non-equivalence of MAY and CAN', *Lingua*, 50, 209–20

FURTHER READING

Coates, J. (1983) *The Semantics of the Modal Auxiliaries*, London: Croom Helm

Coates, J. (1995) 'The Expression of Root and Epistemic Possibility in English', in Aarts and Meyer, 145-56

Coates, J. and G. Leech (1980) 'The Meanings of the Modals in Modern British and American English', *York Papers in Linguistics*, 8, 23-33

Collins, P. (1987) '*Will* and *shall* in Australian English', in W. Bahner, J. Schildt and D. Viehweger (eds) *Proceedings of the Fourteenth International Congress of Linguistics II*, Berlin: Akademie-Verlag, 181-99

Collins, P. (1991) 'The Modals of Obligation and Necessity in Australian English', in K. Aijmer and B. Altenberg (eds) *English Corpus Linguistics: Studies in Honour of Jan Svartvik*, London: Longman, 145-65

Comrie, B. (1976) *Aspect*, Cambridge: Cambridge University Press

Comrie, B. (1985) *Tense*, Cambridge: Cambridge University Press

Cowper, E. (1998) 'The simple present tense in English: A unified treatment, *Studia Linguistica*, 52, 1-18

Cruse, D.A. (1973) 'Some Thoughts on Agentivity', *Journal of Linguistics*, 9, 11-23

Crystal, D. (1966) 'Specification and English Tenses', *Journal of Linguistics*, 2, 1-34

Davidsen-Nielsen, N. (1983) 'Tense in Modern English and Danish', *Papers and Studies in Contrastive Linguistics* (Poznan: Adam Mickiewicz University Press), 20, 73-84

Declerck, R. (1979) 'Tense and Modality in English *Before*-Clauses', *English Studies*, 60, 720-44

Declerck, R. (1991a) *Tense in English: its Structure and Use in Discourse*, London: Routledge

Declerck, R. (1991b) *A Comprehensive Descriptive Grammar of English*, Tokyo: Kaitakusha

Declerck, R. (forthcoming) 'Time and Tense', in Aarts and McMahon

Denison, D. (1998) 'Syntax', in S. Romaine (ed.) *Cambridge History of the English Language, Vol. 4 (1776-1997)*, Cambridge: Cambridge University Press

Depraetere, I. and S. Reed (forthcoming) 'Mood and Modality', in Aarts and McMahon

Dušková, L. (1999) *Studies in the English Language*, Prague: Karolinum (Charles University)

Ehrman, M. (1966) *The Meanings of the Modals in Present-Day American English*, The Hague: Mouton

Elsness, J. (1997) *The Perfect and the Preterite in Contemporary and Earlier English*, Berlin: Mouton de Gruyter

Facchinetti, R. (2002) 'CAN and COULD in Contemporary British English: A Study of the ICE-GB Corpus', in P. Peters, P. Collins and A. Smith (eds) *New Frontiers of Corpus Research: Proceedings of the 21st ICAME Conference*, Amsterdam: Rodopi, 229-46

Facchinetti, R. (2003) 'Pragmatic and sociological constraints on the functions of *may* in contemporary English', in Facchinetti *et al.*, 301-27

Facchinetti, R., M. Krug and F.R. Palmer (eds) (2003) *Modality in Contemporary English*, Berlin: Mouton de Gruyter

Fenn, P. (1987) *A Semantic and Pragmatic Examination of the English Perfect*, Tübingen: Narr

Gachelin, J.-M. (1997) 'The Progressive and Habitual Aspects in Non-standard Englishes', in E.W. Schneider (ed.) *Englishes around the World I: General Studies, British Isles, North America; II: Caribbean, Africa, Asia, Australasia: Studies in Honour of Manfred Gorlach*, Amsterdam: John Benjamins, 33-46

Givón, T. (1993) *English Grammar: A Function-Based Introduction*, Amsterdam: Benjamins (Chapter 4)

Goldsmith, J. and E. Woisetschlaeger (1982) 'The Logic of the English Progressive', *Linguistic Inquiry*, 13, 79-89

Greenbaum, S. (1974) 'Problems in the Negation of Modals', *Moderna Språk*, 68, 244-55

FURTHER READING

Greenbaum, S., G. Leech and J. Svartvik (1980) (eds) *Studies in English Linguistics for Randolph Quirk*, London: Longman

Haegeman, L. (1980) 'Have To and Progressive Aspect', *Journal of English Linguistics*, 14, 1–5

Haegeman, L. (1981) 'Modal *Shall* and Speaker's Control', *Journal of English Linguistics*, 15, 4–9

Haegeman, L. (1982) 'The Futurate Progressive in Present-Day English', *Journal of Linguistic Research*, 13–19

Haegeman, L. (1983) *The Semantics of* WILL *in Present-Day British English: A Unified Account*, Koninklijke Academie, Turnhout: Brepols

Haegeman, L. and H. Wekker (1984) 'The Syntax and Interpretation of Future Conditionals in English', *Journal of Linguistics*, 20, 45–55

Halliday, M.A.K. (1969) 'Functional Diversity in Language, as seen from a Consideration of Modality and Mood in English', *Foundations of Language*, 6, 322–61

Harsh, W. (1968) *The Subjunctive in English*, Alabama: University Press

Hermerén, L. (1978) *On Modality in English* (Lund Studies in English, 53), Lund: Gleerup/Liber

Hirtle, W.H. (1967) *The Simple and Progressive Forms: An Analytical Approach* (Cahiers de psychoméchanique du langage, 8), Québec: Les Presses de l'Université Laval

Hirtle, W.H. (1995) 'The Simple Form Again: An Analysis of Direction-giving and Related Uses', *Journal of Pragmatics*, 24: 265–81

Huddleston, R.D. (1980) 'Criteria for Auxiliaries and Modals', in Greenbaum *et al.*, 65–78

Huddleston, R.D. (1995) 'The English Perfect as a Secondary Past Tense', in Aarts and Meyer, 102–22

Huddleston, R.D. and G. Pullum (2002) *Cambridge Grammar of the English Language*, Cambridge: Cambridge University Press (esp. Chapter 3)

Jacobson, S. (1980) 'Some English Verbs and the Contrast Incompletion/Completion', in Greenbaum *et al.*, 50–60

Jacobsson, B. (1974) 'The Auxiliary *Need*', *English Studies*, 55, 56–63

Jacobsson, B. (1975) 'How Dead is the English Subjunctive?' *Moderna Språk*, 69, 218–31

Jacobsson, B. (1977) 'Modality and the Modals of Necessity *Must* and *Have to*', *English Studies*, 60, 296–312

Jacobsson, B. (1980) 'On the Syntax and Semantics of the Modal Auxiliary *Had Better*', *Studia Neophilologica*, 52, 47–53

Jespersen, O. (1917) 'Negation in English and Other Languages', *Historisk-filologiske Meddeleser*, 75; reprinted in *Selected Writings of Otto Jespersen*, London: Allen & Unwin, 1962, 3–151

Jespersen, O. (1931) *A Modern English Grammar on Historical Principles*, Part IV, Copenhagen: Munksgaard

Johannesson, N.-L. (1976) *The English Modal Auxiliaries: A Stratificational Account* (Stockholm Studies in English, 36), Stockholm: Almqvist and Wiksell

Klein, W. (1992) 'The Present Perfect puzzle', *Language*, 68, 525–52

Klein, W. (1994) *Time in Language*, London: Routledge

König, E. (1980) 'On the context-dependence of the progressive in English', in C. Rohrer (ed.) *Time, Tense, and Quantifiers: Proceedings of the Stuttgart Conference on the Logic of Tense and Quantification*, Tübingen: Niemeyer, 269–91

König, E. (1995) 'He is being Obscure: Non-verbal Predication and the Progressive', in Bertinetto *et al.* (eds) *Temporal Reference, Aspect and Actionality*, 2 vols, Torino: Rosenberg and Sellier, 155–68

FURTHER READING

Krug, M. (2000) *Emerging English Modals: A Corpus-based Study of Grammaticalization*, Berlin/New York: Mouton de Gruyter

Langacker, R. (2001) 'The English Present Tense', *English Language and Linguistics*, 5, 251–72.

Leech, G. (1969) *Towards a Semantic Description of English*, London: Longman (esp. Chapters 7 and 9)

Leech, G. (2003) 'Modality on the Move: The English Modal Auxiliaries 1961–1992', in Facchinetti *et al.*, 223–40

Leech, G. and J. Coates (1980) 'Semantic Indeterminacy and the Modals', in Greenbaum *et al.*, 79–90

Ljung, M. (1980) *Reflections on the English Progressive* (Gothenburg Studies in English, 46), Göteborg: Acta Universitatis Gothoburgensis

Lyons, J. (1977) *Semantics*, Vol. 2, Cambridge: Cambridge University Press

Mair, C. and M. Hundt (1995) 'Why is the Progressive becoming more Frequent in English? A Corpus-based Investigation into Language Change in Progress', *Zeitschrift für Anglistik und Amerikanistik*, 43, 111–22

McCarthy, M. (1998) *Spoken Language and Applied Linguistics*, Cambridge: Cambridge University Press (Chapter 5)

McCoard, R.W. (1978) *The English Perfect: Tense-choice and Pragmatic Inferences*, Amsterdam: North-Holland

Miller, J. (2000) 'The Perfect in Spoken and Written English', *Transactions of the Philological Society*, 98: 2, 323–52

Mitchell, K. (2003) '*Had better* and *might as well*: On the margins of modality?' in Facchinetti *et al.*, 129–49

Mindt, D. (1995) *An Empirical Grammar of the English Verb: Modal Verbs*, Berlin: Cornelsen

Mindt, D. (2000) *An Empirical Grammar of the English Verb System*, Berlin: Cornelsen

Mourelatos, A.P.D. (1978) 'Events, Processes, States', *Linguistics and Philosophy*, 2, 5–34

Myhill, J. (1995) 'Change and Continuity in the Functions of the American English Modals', *Linguistics*, 33, 157–211

Nehls, D. (1975) 'The System of Tense and Aspect in English', *International Review of Applied Linguistics in Language*, 13, 275–92

Nehls, D. (1978, 1986) *Semantik und Syntax des Englischen Verbs* (Parts I and II), Heidelberg: Julius Groos

Ota, A. (1963) *Tense and Aspect of Present-Day American English*, Tokyo: Kenkyusha

Palmer, F.R. (1977) 'Modals and Actuality', *Journal of Linguistics*, 13, 1–23

Palmer, F.R. (1988 [1974]) *The English Verb*, 2nd edn, London: Longman

Palmer, F.R. (1990) *Modality and the English Modals*, 2nd edn, London: Longman

Palmer, F.R. (2001) *Mood and Modality*, 2nd edn, Cambridge: Cambridge University Press

Palmer, F.R. (2003) 'Modality in English: Theoretical, Descriptive and Typological issues', in Facchinetti *et al.*, 1–17

Perkins, M.R. (1982) 'The Core Meanings of the English Modals', *Journal of Linguistics*, 18, 245–74

Perkins, M.R. (1983) *Modal Expressions in English*, London: Frances Pinter

Quirk, R., S. Greenbaum, G. Leech and J. Svartvik (1985) *A Comprehensive Grammar of the English Language*, London: Longman (esp. Chapter 4)

Scheffer, J. (1975) *The Progressive in English*, Amsterdam: North-Holland

Schopf, A. (1984) *Das Verzeitungssystem des Englischen und seine Textfunktion*, Tübingen: Niemeyer

Schlüter, N. (2002) *Present Perfect: Eine Korpuslinguistische Analyse des Englischen Perfekts mit Vermittlungsvorschlägen für den Sprachunterricht*, Tübingen: Naar

Serpollet, N. (2001) 'The Mandative Subjunctive in British English seems to be Alive and Kicking... Is this due to the Influence of American English?' in P. Rayson, A. Wilson, A. Hardie and S. Khoja (eds) *Proceedings of the Corpus Linguistics 2001 Conference*, Lancaster University: UCREL, 531–42

Smith, C. (1997 [1991]) *The Parameter of Aspect*, 2nd edn, Dordrecht: Kluwer

Smith, N. (2001) 'Ever Moving On? The Progressive in Recent British English', in P. Peters and P. Collins (eds) *New Frontiers of Corpus Linguistics*, Amsterdam: Rodopi, 317–30

Smith, N. (2003) 'Changes in the Modals and Semi-modals of Strong Obligation and Epistemic Necessity in Recent British English', in Facchinetti *et al.*, 241–66

Smitterberg, E., S. Reich and A. Hahn (2000) 'The Present Progressive in Political and Academic Language in the 19th and 20th Centuries', *ICAME Journal*, 23, 99–118

Swan, M. (1997) *Practical English Usage*, Oxford: Oxford University Press

Sweetser, E.E. (1990) *From Etymology to Pragmatics: Metaphorical and Cultural Aspects of Semantic Structure*, Cambridge: Cambridge University Press

Takahashi, T. (2002) 'Use Differences between *will* and *going to*: Effects of Grammaticalization', *International Journal of Pragmatics*, 12, 27–38

van der Auwera, J. (1999) 'On the Semantic and Pragmatic Polyfunctionality of Modal Verbs', in K. Turner (ed.) *The Semantics/Pragmatics Interface from Different Points of View*, Amsterdam: Elsevier, 50–64

Vendler, Z. (1957) 'Verbs and Times', *Philosophical Review*, 56, 143–60

Verkuyl, H. (1993) *A Theory of Aspectuality*, Cambridge: Cambridge University Press

Wekker, H.C. (1976) *The Expression of Future Time in Contemporary British English*, Amsterdam: North-Holland

Williams, C. (2002a) 'Non-progressive Aspect in English in Commentaries and Demonstrations using the Present Tense', *Journal of Pragmatics*, 34, 1235–56

Williams, C. (2002b) *Non-progressive and Progressive Aspect in English*, Fasano, Italy: Schena Editore

Index

References are to *section numbers*, NOT *page numbers*. Sometimes reference is made to subsections (e.g. 37A, 37B) or to notes within sections (e.g. 77*a*, 77*b*). A **bold face** number refers to the chief place where the topic in question is explained or discussed.

'activity verbs', **36**C, 40, 42, 44, 78
adverbials in relation to tense and aspect, 68ff
—, with Past Tenses, 69
—, with Present Perfect, 70
—, with either Perfect or Past, 71–2
after, 74
already, 72
always, 52, 64*d*, 71
am / is / are to, 149

backshift, 153ff
be able to, 115B*c*, 140*d*
be about to, 112
be bound to, 151
be going to, 86, **92**ff, 110, 111, 126B*a*
—, 'future outcome of present', 92
—, 'future fulfilment of present intention', 93
—, 'future of present cause', 94
—, 'imminent future', 94*a*, 96
—, in conditional sentences, 95
—, often interchangeable with *will*, 96
—, Past Tense of, 83, 97
—, Present Perfect Tense of, 97
be supposed to, 151
be to + Infinitive, *see am / is / are to*; *was / were to*
bounded events, 31*a*

can, 114, **115**, 119ff
—, with verbs of perception, 40, 115B*a*
—, 'ability', 115B
—, 'permission', 115C, 122
—, 'possibility', **115**A, 121, 132, 142f
—, 'strong recommendation', 115C*b*
—, tactful imperative, 115A*a*
—, negation of, 136

can't, 136
can't help, 151*a*
conditional sentences, 166ff
continually, 52
continuous, *see* Progressive Aspect
could, Past Tense of *can*, 140f
—, in questions, 132
—, Past Tense in indirect speech, 157
—, hypothetical Past Tense, 177
—, 'polite permission', 181
—, 'tentative possibility', 183
—, 'tentative suggestion', 183*a*, 183*b*
—, seven uses of, 186

definite and indefinite meaning, **64**, 73, 89*a*
direct and indirect speech, 152ff
'double marking', 178*a*, 179

epistemic modality, **125**, 151
'eternal truths', 8, 13
'event verbs', **12**, 54, 78, 139. *See also*
   'momentary verbs', 'transitional event
   verbs', 'activity verbs', 'process verbs'
ever, 71

factual and theoretical meaning, 121, 138, **161**ff
factual and theoretical possibility, 121, 177*a*
for, 31*a*
forever, 52
formulaic Subjunctive, 116
free indirect speech, 160
futurate Present, 14, **103**ff, 111
futurate Progressive, 15, 98f
future in the past, 83f

INDEX

future time, expression of, 86ff
—, and modal auxiliaries, 139

gerund, *see* Verb-*ing*
go, 59*b*. See also *be going to*

(had) better, 150
have got to, 118Cc, **148**
have to, **118**, 119ff
—, 'obligation', **118**A, 123, 125
—, 'requirement', **118**B, 125
—, '(logical) necessity', **118**C, 124, 143
—, in questions, 133, 135
—, negation of, 136
—, Past Tense of, 140
—, hypothetical form of, 176*a*, 177
hypothetical meaning, 161f, **170**ff
—, in dependent clauses, 171
—, in main clauses, 172
—, grammatical markers of, 173f
—, semantic implications of, 175

if-clauses, 102, 131. See also conditional sentences
imaginary time, past, 22, 66
—, present, 24ff
—, future, 89*b*
in, 31*a*
Indicative Mood, 162, 164
indirect speech, 152ff
Infinitive construction, 164
inverseness, **120**, 138

just, 71
just now, 71

lately, latterly, 70

mandative Subjunctive, 162, 165
may, **116**, 119ff
—, 'permission', **116**B, 122
—, 'possibility', **116**A, 121, 142f
—, 'exclamatory wish', 116C
—, in *if*-clauses, 115C*a*, 131f
—, in questions, 129
—, negation of, 136ff
—, in indirect speech, 159
—, 'quasi-subjunctive', 116C, 165*b*
may as well, 151*a*
might, Past Tense of *may*, 140f
—, Past Tense in indirect speech, 157
—, as 'subjunctive substitute', 165*b*
—, hypothetical Past Tense, 177
—, 'polite permission', 181

—, 'possibility', 183, 184
—, 'tentative suggestion', 183*a*
might as well, 151*a*
modal auxiliaries, **114**ff
—, primary, 114ff
—, in questions and *if*-clauses, 129ff
—, negation of, 136ff
—, future use of, 139
—, Past Tense or secondary, 114, 140f
—, with Perfect Aspect, 142f
—, with Progressive Aspect, 143
—, and indirect speech, 156ff
—, hypothetical use of, 176ff
'momentary verbs', 35A
mood, 161ff
must, **117**, 119ff
—, 'obligation', **117**A, 123
—, 'requirement', 117B
—, in questions, 129, 134, 135
—, in *if*-clauses, 117A*a*, 135*a*
—, '(logical) necessity', **117**C, 124, 137*b*, 139*b*, 143
—, weakened to 'reasonable assumption', 117C*a*
—, negation of, 136ff
—, in indirect speech, 158f
mustn't, 136f

need (modal auxiliary), in questions, 133, 135
—, negation of, 136, 137
—, compared with *need to*, 147
—, in indirect speech, 158
need to (full verb, semi-modal), 147
needn't, 137, 147
negation, 'double', 136*a*
—, auxiliary and main verb, 136ff
never, 64, 71
next, 69
non-finite verb, 67
non-perfect, 3
non-progressive, 3
now, 72

once, 72
ought to, 144, **146**
—, in indirect speech, 158f

past in future, 90
past participles, resultative use of, 59*a*
Past Perfect Progressive Tense, 3, **82**
Past Perfect Tense, 3, **73**f
—, in indirect speech, 153, 154*c*
—, with past hypothetical meaning, 173f
Past Progressive Tense, 3, 31ff
—, tentative use of, 43*a*

139

INDEX

—, referring to fairly recent communicative happenings, 46
—, referring to future in the past, 83
Past Tense, 3, 18ff, 60ff
—, in indirect speech, 153
—, as marker of hypothetical meaning, 21, 170ff. *See also* Simple Past Tense; Past Perfect Tense; Past Progressive Tense; Past Perfect Progressive Tense
Perfect Aspect, 3, **53**ff
—, in non-finite constructions, 67
—, with modal auxiliaries, 142f
—, in hypothetical constructions, 173f, 178
See also Present Perfect Tense; Past Perfect Tense; Perfect Progressive, Past Perfect Progressive Tense
Perfect Progressive, 75ff
—, 'temporary situation leading up to present moment', 76
—, rarity in passive of, 77*b*
—, 'potential incompleteness of activity', 78
—, 'effects of activity still apparent', 79
—, summary of main meaning of, 80
—, habitual use, 81
performative verb, 11
point of reference, 63, 73
Present Perfect Progressive Tense, 3, **75**ff
Present Perfect Tense, 3, **54**ff
—, with *since*, 7*a*
—, 'state-up-to-the-present', 55
—, 'indefinite past', 56, 63, 64
—, 'recent indefinite past', 57
—, 'habit-in-a-period-leading-up-to-the-present', 58
—, 'resultative past', 59, 62
—, indicating 'completeness', 59*c*
—, compared with Simple Past, 60ff
See also Present Perfect Progressive Tense
Present Progressive Tense, 3
—, compared with Simple Present, 10, 11
—, with future meaning, 86, **98**ff, 110, 111
—, compared with be *going to*, 99
See also Present Perfect Progressive Tense; Progressive Aspect
Present Tense, 3
See also Simple Present Tense; Present Progressive Tense; Present Perfect Tense
'process verbs', 36D, 41, 45, 78
Progressive Aspect, 4, **27**ff
—, referring to temporary happenings, 28ff
—, 'limited duration', 28, 30, 33
—, 'actual' rather than 'potential', 30
—, 'activity not necessarily complete', 31
—, with 'temporal frame' effect, 32f

—, classes of verb occurring with, 34ff
—, classes of verb normally incompatible with, 37ff, 55*a*, 77*c*, 101*b*
—, apparent exceptions to incompatibility of certain verbs with, 39ff
—, indicating tentativeness, 43
—, habitual use of, 48ff
—, referring to future or future in the past, 51, **98**ff
—, 'persistent or continuous activity', 52
—, with modal auxiliaries, 143
—, 'interpretive' use with speech act verbs, 32*b*
proverbs, 8, 13, 126A*a*

real and unreal conditions, 166ff
recently, 71
relative clauses, 102
root modality, 125, **151**

semi-modals, 143*b*, **147**ff, **151**
shall, future use (prediction), 87f, 91
—, 'intention', 127B
—, other volitional meanings, 127C
—, rules and regulations, 127D
—, in questions, 130
—, negation of, 136ff
shan't, 137*c*, 138*g*
should, as Past Tense of *shall*, 140f
—, = 'ought to', **145**, 165
—, Past Tense in indirect speech, 157*a*, 158f
—, putative, 165
—, in conditional clauses, 168, 173*a*
Simple Past Tense, 3, **18**ff, 53, 57*a*
—, habitual, 19
—, in relation to sequence, 20
—, hypothetical, 21, 171, 173f
—, in narrative, 22
—, in evasive reference to present, 23
—, compared with Present Perfect, 60ff
Simple Present Tense, 3, 6ff
—, 'state (or unrestrictive)', 7f
—, 'event (or instantaneous)', 9ff, 13
—, 'habitual', 13
—, referring to future, 14, 86, **102**ff
—, 'historic present', 15
—, with verbs of communication, 16
—, in reference to works of art, 17
—, in newspaper headlines, 17*b*
—, imaginary uses, 24ff
—, in fiction, 25
—, in stage directions, 25*a*
—, in travelogues and instructions, 26
—, in conditional and temporal clauses, 102
since, 7*a*, 77*d*
so far, 70

soon, 69
sports commentaries, 9
'state verbs', **12**, 37H, 54, 55
still, 72
Subjunctive, 161, **162**, 164, 168
—, mandative, 162, 165
subordinate future use of Present, 102
suppressed condition, **172**, 180ff

that-clauses, 102, 164
then, 69
today, tonight, 71
'transitional event verbs', 35B
truth-neutrality and truth-commitment, **163**f, 168, 170, 175

unbounded events, 31*a*
unreal conditions, 169ff
used to, 85

verb classes, 12, 34ff
  See also 'event verbs', 'state verbs', 'activity verbs', 'momentary verbs', 'process verbs', 'transitional event verbs', 'verbs of attitude', 'verbs of inert perception', 'verbs of inert cognition', 'verbs of having and being', 'verbs of bodily sensation'
Verb-*ing*, 164
'verbs of attitude', 37G
'verbs of bodily sensation', **38**J
'verbs of having and being', **37**H, 44
'verbs of inert cognition', 37F, 42
'verbs of inert perception', 37E, 40f

want to, wanna, 151
was / were to, 84, 149*a*

—, future in the past, 84
—, as marker of hypothetical meaning, 173f
will, **126**, 139f
—, future use ('prediction'), 86, **87**ff, 110, 111, 127
—, 'characteristic behaviour', 126A
—, 'willingness', 126C
—, in *if*-clauses, 102*b*
—, in requests, 126C*a*
—, 'insistence', 126D
—, 'intention', 126B
—, prediction, 'predictability', 126A, 143
—, 'disposition', 126A*d*
—, negation of, 136ff
—, quasi-imperative, 89*d*, 126D*a*
—, with Progressive Infinitive, 86, **106**ff, 110, 111
—, in conditional sentences, 89, 102*b*
—, with Perfect Infinitive, 90
won't, 136, 137
would, future in the past, 84
—, Past Tense of *will*, 140
—, 'predictability', hence 'characteristic behaviour', 140
—, 'insistence, strong volition', 140*b*
—, Past Tense in indirect speech, 157
—, hypothetical meaning in main clauses, 169, 185
—, hypothetical meaning in dependent clauses, 173*b*
—, hypothetical Past Tense of *will*, 177, 177*c*
—, 'polite volition', 182
—, 'pure hypothesis', 185
would rather, 171

yesterday, 69
yet, 72

研究課題

§10a 'Up we go!'（＝瞬間的現在）の状況としては、子供を抱っこして高く持ち上げる時とか、アンデルセンの童話「空飛ぶかばん」に出てくる商人の息子が、かばんに乗ってふわっと空高く舞い上がる時に興奮して叫ぶ場面などいろいろ考えられる。実際に上がるのは本人だけであっても、1人称複数代名詞の we が用いられるのはなぜであろうか。

英語の現在時制の瞬間的な用法に対して、日本語では、「る形」と「た形」の2種類の瞬間用法が考えられる。

(1) a.　あ、看板が落ちる！
　　 b.　あ、看板が落ちた！　　　　　　　　　　　　　　　（安藤(1986:182)）

安藤(1986)によれば、(1a)は、看板が落ちてゆくのを見たり、グラグラして落ちそうになっているのを見て、反射的に発せられる表現であるという。看板が実際に落下している途中であるのか(すなわち、まだ地面に達していない)、あるいは、はずれそうになっているのかという違いは、次の例にも現れている。

(2) a.　ビルの屋上からヒラヒラと看板が落ちるのが見えた。
　　 b.　大きな地震だったので、あぶなく看板が落ちるところだった。

「ヒラヒラと」という修飾語句から示唆されるように、(2a)では看板はまだ空中にある。すなわち、落下という出来事はまだ完了してはいない。一方、(2b)では看板はまだ壁にくっついている。ただし、(2a)と異なって、(3)では、看板は地面に落ちたことは確実である。

(3)　看板が落ちる音がした。

次の文はどちらも、遠くから村人が話し手に向かって近づいてくる場面を目撃して発話されたものとする。状況は同じなのに、なぜ一方では「る形」を、他方では「た形」を用いるのであろうか。

(4) a. あれ、おかしいな。村人がたくさんやって来る！
    b. あれ、おかしいな。村人がたくさんやって来た！

§11 「遂行動詞」(performative verbs)とは、次の文に見られるように、

(1) I name this ship the Queen Elizabeth.
(2) I give and bequeath my watch to my brother.
(3) I bet you sixpence it will rain tomorrow.　　　　　(Austin(1962: 5))

適切な条件の下でその文を発話することがとりもなおさずその行為(例えば、命名、遺言、賭けなど)を遂行することになるような動詞である。日本語の遂行文(performative sentences)として次の例を見られたい。

(4) ここに第1回町民体育大会の開会を宣言します。
(5) 宣誓。我々はスポーツマンシップにのっとり正々堂々と戦うことを誓います。
(6) このたびの不祥事に対し心からおわび申しあげます。

これらの文を発することはすなわち「開会宣言」、「宣誓」、「謝罪」の行為を遂行することである。なお、上のような遂行文が適切であるためには、通例、遂行動詞は、1人称、単純現在時制でなければならない。次の(7)や(8)は遂行文としては失格である。

(7) (進水式で)*I am naming this ship the Queen Elizabeth.
(8) (開会式で)*宣誓。我々はスポーツマンシップにのっとり正々堂々と戦うことを誓っています。

一体、それはなぜであろうか(Austin(1962)、Searle(1969)など参照)。

§15 日本語の文体の特徴の1つに、同一の文脈の中で、「る形」と「た形」が交代するということがある。例えば、(1)と(2)を比較してみよう。

(1) 踊子は十七くらいに見えた。私には分からない古風の不思議な形に大きく髪を結っていた。それが卵形の凛々しい顔を非常に小さく見せながらも、美しく調和していた。髪を豊かに誇張して描いた、稗史的な娘の絵姿の

ような感じだった。踊子の連れは四十代の女が一人、若い女が二人、ほかに長岡温泉の宿屋の印半纏を着た二十五六の男がいた。

(川端康成『伊豆の踊子』)

（２）　出入りするのは子供ばかりではないとみえて、空地にはところどころにこわれた木箱や、ぼろ切れのようなものが捨ててある。垣根から半分ほど道に顔を出しているその木樽も、近所の者が空地に捨てたのを、子供たちがそこまでひっぱり出して来たらしかった。木槿の垣根も、空地の中の雑草もうっすらと芽吹いている。季節は春のさかりにむかっていて寒くはなかった。

(藤沢周平「贈り物」)

(1)は「た形」が統一的に用いられているが、(2)では「ある」(＝る形)、「来たらしかった」(＝「た形)、「いる」(＝る形)、「なかった」(た形)という具合に交互に変化している。こうした変化はどのように説明できるであろうか。

§31　Leech は、次の例を比較している。

（１）a.　The dog was drowning in the sea.
　　　b.　The dog drowned in the sea.　　　　　　　(Leech (2004³: 21))

(1a)の場合には犬はまだ死んでいなかったので、「誰かが飛び込んで助けた」と言えるのに対して、(1b)の場合には犬は既に死んでいたので、そうは言えないとしている。すなわち、(1a)は「その犬は海中で溺死していた」ではなく、「その犬は海中で溺死しつつあった」を意味している。なぜ、was drowning＝「溺死していた」とならないのであろうか。

　金田一(1976: 10)は、「ている」を付けると「進行中の活動」にはならず、「結果状態」を表すようになるタイプの動詞を「瞬間動詞」と名付けた(Vendler (1967)の動詞分類で言えば「到達動詞」(achievement verb)に相当する)。

（２）　死ぬ、(電灯が)点く、(電灯が)消える、終わる、出発する、到着する、…

「死んでいる」、「点いている」、「消えている」、「終わっている」、「出発している」、「到着している」などの場合、すべてその出来事が終わった後の結果状態を示している。「溺死する」を瞬間動詞とみなすならば、「溺死している」が結果状態を示すことは自然に説明可能である。

　金田一によれば、瞬間動詞の場合、「～している最中だ」とは言えない。よって、

「死んでいる最中だ」、「列車が到着している最中だ」などは不適格である。その代わりに、「〜しつつある」というように、その出来事に接近する途中段階を示すことが可能である。「死につつある」、「到着しつつある」などは適格である。
　さらに、次の文の違いについて、

　　（3）a.　Meg was reading a book that evening.
　　　　b.　Meg read a book that evening.　　　　　　　　　（Leech (2004³: 21)）

Leech は、(3a)(＝過去進行形)と異なって、(3b)(＝単純過去)では、本を読み終えたことになると述べている。しかし、(3b)は本を読み終えたことにしかならないのであろうか(内田(2010)など参照)。
　次の文を比較してみよう。

　　（4）a.　He read a book *in two hours*.
　　　　b.　He read a book *for two hours*.

時間を表す表現として、(4a)には in 句が、(4b)には for 句が生起している。in 句は「2 時間で」というように、目標となるある行為を達成するのにかかった時間を示すのに対し、for 句は「2 時間（の間）」というように、ある出来事が継続した時間を示す。それゆえ、(4a)は「ある本を 2 時間で読みあげた」という意味に、(4b)は「2 時間読書した」という意味になる。すなわち、Vendler (1967)の動詞分類で言えば、(4a)の read は「達成動詞」(accomplishment verb)に、(4b)の read は「行為動詞」(activity verb)にあたる。このように考えるならば、(3b)は多義的ということになろう。
　read を達成動詞にとれば、1 冊の本を最後まで読んだ後でなければ、"read a book" とは言えない。一方、行為動詞にとれば、たとえ途中までしか読まなくても、"read a book" と言える。達成動詞には run a mile とか draw a circle などいろいろあるが、これらも、その行為の途中では(すなわち、まだ 0.5 マイルしか走っていない時点とか、まだ半分しか丸を書いていない時点では) run a mile、draw a circle とは言えない (Vendler (1967: 101–102))。
　では、副詞 almost (＝もう少しで〜するところだ)の観点から見ると、次の(5)の read my diary は「行為」であろうか、それとも「達成」であろうか。

　　（5）　John *almost* read my diary last night.

§32b　Leech は、次のような例の進行形の用法を「解釈的用法」(interpretive use)と称している。

（1） A: Were you lying when you SAID that?
　　　B: No, I was telling the truth.　　　　　　　　　　(Leech (2004³: 22))

この用法は、一般に「行為解説」と称される用法に近い。次のような例を考えてみよう。

（2） A: What happened to the money I lent you last week?
　　　B: You'll have it back by tomorrow.
　　　A: I need the money badly.
　　　B: I am promising to return it by tomorrow.　　　　（高司（1994:18））

高司（1994）に述べられているように、最後の、話し手Bの発話は、お金を返すという約束そのものではなく、自分が言っていることは約束にほかならないという（いらだちを込めて発話された）「行為解説」である。この場合の進行形は、(3)におけるような発語内行為(illocutionary act)の定式に見られる進行形に等しい(Austin (1962))。

（3） In saying x I was doing y.（xと言うことはyという行為をすることにほかならなかった）

(3)は、xという発話がyという発語内行為であったことを述べたものである。例えば、次の(4)は、

（4） In saying I would shoot him I was threatening him.

「私は彼を撃つぞと言ったが、それは彼に対する脅しであった」という意味である。小説などから「行為解説」の進行形の用例を集めて、この用法がどのようなコンテクストで用いられるかを考察してみよう。

§35 B 徐々にそうなるというのではなく、いきなりそうなるような瞬間的現象である場合（言い換えれば、「〜徐々にしつつある」とか「〜しかけている」などと言えないような場合）には、このタイプの進行形は用いられない。国広(1971: 204)は次のようなデータを挙げている。

（1）a.　The candlelight is going out.
　　　b.(*)The electric light is going out.

この違いについて、国広 (1971) は、ろうそくの火はだんだん消えてゆくが、電灯の光はそうではないので、(1a) のようには言えても、(1b) のようには言えないとしている。しかしながら、徐々に停電するような特殊な状況では (1b) は適格になると予想されるが、実際にはどうであろうか。各自、英語の母語話者にチェックしてみよう。さらに、次のような場合はどうであろうか。

(2) a. The campfire is going out.
    b. My cigar is going out.

また、下の (3) は、torch の意味 (「たいまつ」か「懐中電灯」(flashlight)) によって、文法性が変わってくると予測されるが、実際にはどうであろうか。さらに、「懐中電灯」の場合、適格になる場合とならない場合があると考えられるが、適格になる場合とはどのような場合であろうか。

(3) This torch is going out.

§55 ここで挙げられている文の中で、次の例における時間の副詞句 for ages の解釈の違いに注意せよ。

(1) a. That house has been empty for ages.
    b. That house was empty for ages.　　　　　　　　　(Leech (2004³: 37))

(1a) の for ages は過去のある時点から現在までの期間であり、(1b) のそれは過去のある一定の期間である。
　実は、(1a) のような現在完了文に付く for 句は多義的である場合がある。次の例を考えてみよう。

(2) Sam has been in Boston for 20 minutes.　　　　　(Mittwoch (1988: 203))

1 つの解釈は、「サムは 20 分間だけボストンにいたことがある」(=経験) であり、もう 1 つの解釈は、「サムは 20 分前からボストンにいる」(=継続) である。このことを構造的に分析すれば、for 句は、前者の意味では、have been in Boston 全体を修飾し、後者の意味では been in Boston だけを修飾しているとも考えられよう。なお、興味深いことに、for 句を文頭に置くと、後者の意味にしかならないという。

(3) For 20 minutes Sam has been in Boston.　　　　(Mittwoch (1988: 204))

これはどのような理由によるのであろうか、意味の面と構造の面から考察してみよう。

§61　ここに挙っている例では、すでに存在していない人や物が主語になった場合には、現在完了形ではなく過去形が用いられている。例えば、次の例で、

（1）a.　Has Tom Stoppard written any novels?
　　　b.　Did Anton Chekhov write any novels?　　　　（Leech (2004³: 41)）

(1a)ではトム・ストッパーはまだ生きており、(1b)ではロシアの短編作家・劇作家アントン・チェーホフ(1860–1904)はもう亡くなっている。次の例においては、能動文(2a)が不適格となるのは主語のシェイクスピア(1564–1616)がすでに過去の人であるからであり、受身文(2b)が適格となるのは、主語が Shakespeare ではなく、a lot of plays であるからである（Shakespeare は話題化されてはいない）。

（2）a.　*Shakespeare has written a lot of plays.
　　　b.　A lot of plays have been written by Shakespeare.　　（Palmer (1987²: 50)）

では、次の例を考えてみよう。

（3）a.　Even Queen Victoria has visited Brighton.
　　　b.　Shakespeare has written most of the best plays we know.
　　　　　　　　　　　　　　　　　　　　　　　　　　（Palmer (1987²: 50)）

ヴィクトリア女王(1819–1901)もシェイクスピアも明らかに過去の人物である。にもかかわらずこうした例が適格になるのはなぜであろうか（(3a)ではブライトンが、(3b)では「最上の演劇」が話題となっていると考えるべきであろう）。この場合、「主語」ではなく、その文の「話題」は何かという観点が重要である（さらに、(McCawley (1971)など参照)。

§69　on Monday、at 5:00 といった時点副詞類は、通例、単純過去文を修飾することはできるが、現在完了文を修飾することはできない。

（1）a.　He came here on Monday.
　　　b.　*He has come here on Monday.

ところが、(1b)は次のような文脈(=経験)の中に置かれると適格になる(助動詞 have の強調については、§56b、あるいは Palmer (1987[2]: 52) など参照)。

(2) A: He has never come here on Monday.
B: He HAS come here on Monday. (HAS はストレスを示す。)

このような適格性の違いはどこから来るのであろうか。
こうした問題を考察するには、時点副詞類の「特定性」という観点が有効であると思われる。ここで次の条件を仮定してみよう。

(3) 現在完了文において出来事を修飾する時点副詞類は非特定的でなければならない。

以下、条件(3)を支持する証拠を挙げてみよう。
第1に、(4)のような「習慣」を意味する現在完了がある。そこでは、時点副詞類は非特定的に解釈される。

(4) a. Mary has always left the office at 5:00.
b. The news has been broadcast at ten o'clock for as long as I can remember.
(Leech (2004[3]: 39))

(4)で、「メアリーが5時に退社した」とか「ニュースが10時に放送された」といった出来事は、過去から現在に至る期間の中で繰り返し起こったもので、1回きりの特定的なものではない。
第2に、「経験」の意味の現在完了がある。ここでも、時点副詞類は非特定的に解釈される。

(5) Mary has {often/never} left the office at 5:00.

(5)においては、過去から現在に至る期間に「メアリーが5時に退社する」という出来事が繰り返し起こり得たということが前提とされている。結果的に、その出来事が一度しか起こらなくても、あるいは一度も起こらなくても、その前提には変化がない。それゆえ、「経験」の現在完了も(5)と同じ図式化が可能と言えよう。
では、次の例はどうであろうか。

(6) The man has been killed (*on Monday).

(6) の中に on Monday といった時点副詞類を挿入することはできない。ここで注意しなければならないのは同じ人（あるいは物）が殺される（枯れる、生まれる）といった出来事は、いったん終わってまた再び起こるといったことはありえないということである。それは、復元可能な出来事ではなく、1回的な出来事である。したがって、(6) は「経験」の意味を持ち得ない。それゆえ、ここに時点副詞類 on Monday を挿入しても、それは非特定的に解釈されず、条件(3)に違反してしまうのである。

条件(3)の有効性は、例(2)と次の例(7)を比較すればより明瞭になるであろう。「完了」の文脈を持つ(7B)では、at 5:00 を非特定的に解釈することはできない。

(7) A: The taxi hasn't come yet.
　　 B: You are wrong. It HAS come (*at 5:00).

さて、次の例に示されるように、疑問詞 when は、現在完了文には現れないのが普通である。

(8) *When has he come here?

このことに関して、安藤(1969:67–68)は次のような興味深い例を挙げている。

(9) When have I ever had a secret from you?（いつ、ぼくが君に隠し立てをしたことがあるかね）　　(C. Doyle, *The Memoirs of Sherlock Holmes*)

安藤(1969)によれば、このようなタイプの文は修辞疑問であり、実質は強い否定文である。

(10) I have never had a secret from you.

しかしながら、(9)と異なって、次のような習慣文ならば適格となる。

(11) A: When has he always come here, on Tuesday or on Wednesday?
　　 B: (He has always come here) on Tuesday.

これはどのような理由によるのであろうか。on Tuesday という時間副詞の非特定性という観点から考察してみよう（澤田(1992)、中村(2010)参照）。

§70　「最近の出来事」を示唆する lately と recently を比較してみよう。両者は共に現

在完了と共起できるが、次のような文は微妙に意味が異なると言われる（詳しくは、McCoard (1978: 130ff.)参照）。

(1) a.　I've bought a new car *lately*.
    b.　I've bought a new car *recently*.

(1b)と異なって、(1a)は私がこのところ数カ月毎に車を買い換えていることを表すという。すなわち、反復的な読みである。一方、(1b)は、最近車を買い換えたことを表すという。すなわち、1回きりの出来事の読みである。McCoard (1978: 130ff.)の観察はどこまで一般性を持つのであろうか。各自、この2つの副詞の意味の違いについてさらに深く考察してみよう。

§73　ここで、Leech が B (= 'before then')、T (= 'then')、NOW と表示している点は、それぞれ、Reichenbach 流に言えば、事象時 (event time) (= E)、基準時 (reference time) (= R)、発話時 (speech time) (= S)に相当する。p.47 に示されているように、過去完了においては、この3つの時点が時間軸上で異なった位置にある。

　注意しなければならないことは、過去完了文はしばしば多義的であるということである。次の例を考えてみよう。

(1)　The secretary had eaten at 3 p.m.　　　　　　(Hornstein (1990: 39))

Hornstein (1990)が指摘するように、(1)は多義的である。すなわち、次の解釈Ⅰと解釈Ⅱである。

(2) a.　秘書が食事をした時刻は午後3時だった。（解釈Ⅰ）
    b.　午後3時の時点では秘書はそれ以前に食事を終えてしまっていた。（解釈Ⅱ）

過去完了における時点副詞類のこのような多義性はどこからくるのであろうか。考えられることは、こうした多義性は、時点副詞類が指す時（例えば午後3時）が事象時（= E）か、基準時（= R）かということである。

　ここで、過去完了とは現在完了が過去になった場合と単純過去が過去になった場合の両方があると想定してみよう（Salkie (1989)参照）。すると、例(1)の意味構造は(3)のごとく表示できるであろう。

(3) (i)　PAST (the secretary ate at 3 p.m.) (解釈Ⅰ)

(ii) at 3 p.m. (PAST (the secretary has eaten)) (解釈 II)

(3i)の「午後3時」は「秘書が食事をした時間」(＝E)であり、(3ii)の「午後3時」は「秘書はすでに食事を終えてしまっていたことを知った時間」(＝R)である。この場合、いずれの時刻も特定の時刻である。

「時点副詞類の特定性」という観点からすれば、文(1)にはもう1つの解釈が存在することが予測される。すなわち、「午後3時」が現在完了における非特定的な副詞類として解釈される場合である。この解釈は(4)におけるような意味構造で表示されるであろう。

(4) PAST (the secretary has eaten at 3 p.m.)

(4)の意味は、「秘書はそれまでに午後3時に食事をしたことがあった。」(＝経験)、あるいは「秘書はそれまでずっと午後3時に食事をしていた。」(＝習慣)といった意味になる。

次の例を参照されたい。

(5) The secretary had always eaten at 3 p.m.
(6) The secretary had eaten at 3 p.m. {before/once}.

(5)、(6)はそれぞれ「習慣」、「経験」と解釈される。そこでは、「午後3時」は特定の時刻ではない。

さらに、過去完了に現れた時点副詞類がWH疑問文と分裂文の焦点になった場合、すなわち、時点副詞類が話題化されておらず新情報として焦点化されている場合を考察してみよう。

(7) A: What time had she eaten, at 2 p.m. or at 3 p.m.? (＝解釈 I)
    B: (She had eaten) at 3 p.m. (＝解釈I)

(7)では、時点副詞類の解釈としては解釈Iしかない。時点副詞類に対して、このような焦点化に関わる統語的操作を施すと解釈が1つだけになってしまうのはなぜであろうか。

§89 Leech は、(1)におけるような文と比較して、(2)におけるような、時間が不在の文は不自然であるとしている。

(1) ?Tomorrow's weather will be cold and cloudy.
(2) *It will rain. (Leech (2004³: 57))

同様に、Binnick (1972) は、未来の事柄を表現するのに、be going to と異なって、will を用いた文は、それだけだと不完全に響くとした。

では、次の文を比較してみよう。

(3) a. ?The rock'll fall.
    b. The rock is going to fall.

Binnick によれば、(3b) と違って、(3a) が舌足らずに感じられるのは、そこに条件的語句がないからである。(3a) を (4) か (5) のようにすれば問題はない。

(4) The rock'll fall *if you pull the wedge out from under it*.
(5) *Don't pull the wedge out from under that boulder, you nitwit!* The rock'll fall.
(Binnick (1972: 3))

すなわち、(3b) では岩が今にも落ちそうになっているのに対して、(3a) はそのままでは落ちず、楔を抜いたら落ちる。それゆえ、(2) の文がおかしいのは、条件や時間が示されていないからである。

では、こうした観点からすれば、次の文はどのように異なるであろうか (さらに、Haegeman (1989)、吉良 (2010) など参照)。

(6) a. When the sun sets, we'll be frozen.
    b. When the sun sets, we're going to be frozen. (Binnick (1972: 4))

§102b 次の文をもう少し詳しく検討してみよう。

(1) a. If you are alone at the New Year, let us know about it.
    b. If you {will/are going to} be alone at the New Year, let us know about it.
(Leech (2004³: 64))

Leech によれば、上の文はそれぞれ次のように書き換えられる。

(2) a. If, at The New Year, you find yourself alone, let us know about it at that time.
    b. If you can predict now that you {will/are going to} be alone at the New Year,

let us know about it now (or at least before the New Year).

(2a) の if 節は、「お正月に一人ぼっちになったらご連絡下さい」という単純な条件文（P → Q）である。一方、(2b) の if 節は、「お正月に一人ぼっちになりそうだというのなら、前もってご連絡下さい」というように、相手が述べた内容をそのまま引用しつつ、仮定している（詳しくは、Close (1980)、Haegeman and Wekker (1984)、Dancygier (1998)、Dancygier and Sweeter (2005)、澤田 (2006)、長友 (2010) など参照）。後者の場合、「あなたがお正月に一人ぼっちになる」という命題内容は、意味的には、次のような名詞節の形で if 節の中に導入されている。

（3） If [you predict/it is the case] that *you will be alone at the New Year*, ...

このように分析するならば、(2b) の if 節はみかけは副詞節であるが、意味的には、(旧情報を表す) 名詞節として振る舞っていると言えよう (名詞節の中には未来の will は自由に入り得ることに注意)。
　同じく、次の文を比較してみよう。

（4）a.　If it rains tomorrow, the match will be cancelled.
　　 b.　If it will rain tomorrow, we might as well cancel the match now.
(Haegeman and Wekker (1984: 48))

ここでも、(4a) の文は「雨が降ったら試合は中止となる」という未来の事柄に関する単純な条件文（P → Q）である。(4b) の場合は、しかしながら、「（あなたの言うように）明日雨が降るという {の／こと} なら、今のうちに試合を中止した方がましだ」といった意味になる (日本語では、「〜であるという {の／こと} なら」というように、「の」あるいは「こと」という形式名詞によって、相手の言ったことを旧情報の形で名詞節に埋め込んで表現している)。Haegeman and Wekker (1984) は、(4b) のタイプの if 節は cleft 文の焦点の位置には生じないことを指摘した。

（5）a.　It is <u>if it rains tomorrow</u> that the match will be cancelled.
　　 b.　*It is <u>if it will rain tomorrow</u> that we might as well cancell the match now.
(Haegeman and Wekker (1984: 48))

次の例はいずれも溶岩が流れて来る危険性について述べたものである。両者の if 節の違いについて考察せよ (Close (1980) 参照)。

（6）a.　If the lava comes thus far, anyone still here will stand no chance of survival.

b. If the lava will come down as far as this, all these houses must be evacuated at once.

ここでは、条件文を次のように大別し、

（7）　条件文 ⎧ 予測的（＝内容）……………「たら」「ば」
　　　　　　　 ⎩ 非予測的（＝認識的）………「というのなら」

基本的に澤田（1993: 201–202）、Dancygier（1998: 118）、Dancygier and Sweeter（2005: 87–89）などの考察に基づいて、(8)–(12)のような非予測的条件文について、その特徴を(13)のようにまとめておくことにしたい（これらの例は「〜というのなら」で訳される）。

(8) If he is giving the baby a bath, I'll call back later.
(9) If I have met him, I didn't recognize him.
(10) If they left at nine, they have arrived home by now.
(11) If he won't arrive before nine, there is no point in ordering for him.
　　　　　　　　　　　　　　　　　　　　　　　　（Dancygier (1998)）
(12) If he'll get better by tomorrow, I won't cancel our theater tickets.
　　　　　　　　　　　　　　　　　　　（Dancygier and Sweeter (2005: 88)）
(13) 非予測的（＝認識）条件文に関する一般化：
　　(i) if節には相手が述べたこと、もしくは旧情報に属することが示されている。
　　(ii) その動詞形はそれが示しているままの時間を指示している（すなわち、動詞の時制は後転移（backshift）されていない）ので、その内容はif節からそのまま取り出すことが可能である。

例えば、(12)の場合、"he'll get better by tomorrow" という if節の内容は、相手（例えば、医者）が述べたことであり（＝旧情報）、その内容は if節からそのまま取り出すことが可能である。各自、条件文のデータを集めて、それがどのタイプに属するものかを研究してみよう（長友（2010）など参照）。

§108　この節では、日常会話で未来の事象を表す "will/shall be 〜 ing" 構文が、相手に何かを提案したり、持ちかけたりする際の「前置き」表現として使用されることが述べられている。

未来の事象といっても、捉え方が違えば、表現の仕方も違ってくる。例えば、次の文は、両方とも、話し手がこれから郵便局へ行くと述べている。ニュアンスという点では、両文はどのように異なるのであろうか。

（1）a.　I'll go to the post office. Shall I post your letters?
　　　b.　I'll be going to the post office. Shall I post your letters?

(Declerck (1991: 166))

Declerck (1991: 166) によれば、前者は自分の意志を表明しているが、後者はそうではない。後者は意志性を欠いた、なりゆき的・没我的未来文である。前者の場合、「あなたの手紙を出しにわざわざ郵便局へ行く」と言っているように受け取られかねないが、後者の場合、こうした心配は無用である。「どうせこれから郵便局に行くんだから、ついでにあなたの手紙、出しといてあげようか？」といったニュアンスになり、相手に気兼ねをさせることがない。相手との心的距離を保ち、相手の領域に立ち入らないからである。

このように考えると、(1b) のような、なりゆき的・没我的な "will/shall be ～ ing" 構文は、相手に対する気配り・配慮・丁寧さといった語用論的な側面と深く関わっていることが分かるであろう (Leech (2004[3]: 68)、澤田 (2006: 451ff.))。澤田 (2006: 451ff.) では、後者の表現を、Declerck (1991)、Leech (2004[3]) に従って、「ことのなりゆき」(matter of course) と称している (Thomson and Martinet (1986[4]) や Swan (2005[3]) は「通常のなりゆき」(normal course of events) と称している)。

文脈の支えがなければ、"will/shall be ～ ing" 構文は多義的になってしまう。次の文を考えてみよう。

（2）　I will be flying to London at 5 p.m.　　　　(Declerck (1991: 167))

Declerck (1991: 167)、Leech (2004[3]: 68) などで論じられているように、この文は2通りに解釈することができる。1つの解釈は「ある未来時における進行中の状況」である。この意味は「午後5時の時点では、ロンドン行きの飛行機の中だ」であり、午後5時は「基準時」(= R) である。すると、飛行機が空港を飛び立ったのは午後5時以前 (例えば、午後1時) であるということになる。

もう1つの解釈は「ことのなりゆき」である。この意味は「(このままゆくと) 午後5時にロンドンに向けて飛び立つことになる」であり、午後5時は「事象時」(= E) である。この場合、飛行機はちょうど午後5時に空港を飛び立つ。よって、この場合、"at 5 p.m." という前置詞句 (PP) は "flying to London" という動詞句 (VP) を修飾する付加部となっているとみなすことができよう。

興味深いことに、(3) で "at 5 p.m." が話題化されて文頭に置かれると「未来にお

ける進行中の状況」の解釈にしかならないという (Declerck (1991: 167))。

 （3） <u>At 5 p.m.</u> I will be flying to London.

この場合、「午後5時」は基準時であり、この時点は「飛んでいる」という進行中の状況の中の一時点を切り取ったものである。では、それはどのような理由からだろうか。「ことのなりゆき」タイプの典型的な例は次のようなものである。各自、「〜（このままいくと）することになる」という意味で解釈してみよう。

 （4） We'*ll be writing* to you soon.
 （5） When *will* you *be moving* to your new house?
 （6） Next week we'*ll be studying* Byron's narrative poems.
 （7） Ladies and gentlemen, welcome to the Shinkansen. This is the HIKARI superexpress bound for Shin-Osaka. We *will be stopping* at Nagoya and Kyoto stations before arriving at Shin-Osaka terminal.　　　（新幹線の車内放送）
 （8） "Get the car," Michael called down to him. "I'*ll be leaving* in five minutes. Where's Calo?"　　　（M. Puzo, *The Godfather*)（イタリック筆者）

新幹線の車内放送で、停車駅の予告をしていることから考えても、(7)における "be stopping" は進行中の状況を表しているとは考えられない。「新大阪に到着する前に名古屋と京都に停車している」という「未来時における進行中の状況」はあり得ないということに加えて、通例、次のような例は、

 （9） The bus was stopping.

バスが停車していたのではなく、スピードを落として停車しつつあったことを表しているからである (Leech (2004³: 20))。
 最後に、副詞句に注意を払うことも重要である。次の例（クリスティ『そして誰もいなくなった』第1章第4節から）を参照されたい。エミリーは今インディアン島へ向かう途中である。混みあった列車の中で、彼女は、ひと夏の休暇を一緒に過ごしませんかという招待状をくれた人物の名前を思い出そうとするが、どうしても思い出せない。署名の文字がひどく読みにくいのである。

 （10） Emily Brent thought to herself: '*I shall be getting a free holiday at any rate.*' With her income so much reduced and so many dividends not being paid, that was indeed something to take into consideration.
      （A. Christie, *And Then There Were None*)（イタリック筆者）

上の "I shall be getting a free holiday at any rate." は、「どうせ、ただで休暇を過ごすことになるんだし」という意味で、「ことのなりゆき」を表していると解釈される。この解釈の手掛かりとなるのが副詞類 at any rate（＝どうせ）である。この副詞には、「余分なことをしないでなりゆきにまかせる」という、話し手の没我的な態度が潜んでいる。この場合の話し手の論理は、「どうせなるようにしかならないんだから、思い悩むのはやめにしよう」、すなわち、「どうせAなんだから、Bしよう」であり、前件Aは後件の「前置き」となっている。

　副詞 anyway も同じような働きをしている。次の例を見られたい。

(11)　A: Shall I take you to the station?
　　　B: Oh, I don't want to trouble you.
　　　A: That's all right. *I'll be driving past it anyway.*　　（Declerck (1991: 165)）

この場合も、「どうせついでですから」といった「なりゆき性」が感じられる。各自、小説などからこの構文の用例を集めて、この構文がどのようなコンテクストで用いられるかを考察してみよう。

§**114**　1960年代以降、法助動詞の意味は、大きく2体系に分類されてきた。すなわち、「根源的」(root) と「認識的」(epistemic) である（Hofmann (1966)、Jenkins (1972)、Coates (1983)、Davidsen-Nielsen (1990)、Sweetser (1990)、Declerck (1991)、Langacker (1991)、澤田 (1975, 1993, 2006, 2010)）。この場合の「根源的」とは、「語源的」と言うに等しく、「認識的」とは「推量的」と言うに等しい。前者は「義務」、「許可」、「約束」、「可能」、「意志」など、「そうあるべき世界」に関わる意味であり、後者は「そうだと思われる世界」に関わる意味である。こうしたモダリティの2分法が追求されるようになったのは、Hofmann (1966) を嚆矢とする。

　ここで、法助動詞の意味の総体が「モダリティ」という意味的カテゴリーで括られると想定してみよう。「モダリティ」は、以下のように定義され得る（澤田 (2006: 2)）。

（1）　モダリティとは、事柄(すなわち、状況・世界)に関して、たんにそれがある（もしくは真である）と述べるのではなく、どのようにあるのか、あるいは、あるべきなのかということを表したり、その事柄に対する知覚や感情を表したりする意味論的なカテゴリーである。

次の(2)に示されように、「根源的」は、Palmer (2001[2]) の言う「束縛的」(deontic)（義務・必要、許可、約束など）と「力動的」(dynamic)（能力・可能、意志など）を包含する広いカバータームとなっている。認識的／根源的という分類基準に従うと、英語の

法助動詞のほとんどが根源的／認識的という多義性を有していることになる。

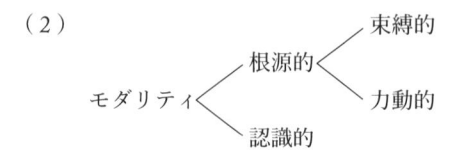

（２）　　　　　　　　　　　　束縛的
　　　　　　　　　　　　根源的＜
　　　　モダリティ＜　　　　　　力動的
　　　　　　　　　　　認識的

　認識的／根源的という体系は、状況を捉える場合の捉え方として、それを判断の産物として捉えるのか、それをあるべきものとして捉えるのか、という２つの捉え方を示している。Sweetser (1990) は、英語法助動詞に別々の意味が２つあるというのではなく、まず「根源的意味」が基にあって、それがメタファーを介して「認識的意味」に拡張されたという見解を提出して、モダリティ分析に大きな影響を与えた。

　Sweetser (1990: 49–50) によれば、根源的／認識的という多義性は、英語だけでなく、様々な言語に見られるという。例えば、フィリピン諸島の諸言語、ドラビダ諸語、マヤ語諸語、フィン・ウゴル諸語などである。

　古代語助動詞の「む」や現代語助動詞の「（よ）う」を考えてみれば、この多義性は日本語にも存在することがわかる。「む」の本義は、「まだ実現していない事柄や不確かな事柄についてそれが実現することを予想したり、不確かな事柄についてそのあり方を想像したりする意を表す」とされるが、主語・述語、あるいは下接語の種類などに応じて、「推量」、「想像」、「意志・決意・希望」、「勧誘・適当・命令」「婉曲・仮定」などの意味に別れるとされる（『日本語文法大辞典』）。例えば、次の例においては、

（３）　居り明かしも今夜(こよひ)は飲ま<u>む</u>ほととぎす明け<u>む</u>朝(あした)は鳴き渡ら<u>む</u>そ
　　　　　　　　　　　　　　　　　　　　　　　　　　（『萬葉集』巻第十八　4068）

3個の「む」が現れている。この歌を、「寝ずに夜を明かしてまでも今夜は飲もう。ホトトギスは夜の明けた朝にはきっと鳴き渡るだろう」（『萬葉集 四（新日本古典文学大系）』p.206）と解釈した場合、最初の「む」は動作動詞「飲む」に後続して話し手の「意志」を表し、2番目の「む」は名詞「朝」にかかる非動作動詞「明ける」に後続して「婉曲」を、そして、3番目の「む」は非動作動詞「鳴き渡る」に後続して「推量」を意味している。すると、最初の「む」は根源的に、後の２つは「認識的」に分類可能である。

　同じく、次の例における「（よ）う」、「まい」においては、

（４）a.　今からその番組を見<u>よう</u>。
　　　b.　午後には雨も上がろ<u>う</u>。
（５）a.　彼は彼女にそれをさせ<u>まい</u>とした。

160

　　　　b.　僕がここにいるとは誰も知る<u>まい</u>。

　(4a)の「よう」は、動作動詞「見る」に後続して話し手の「意志」を表し、(4b)の「う」は、非動作動詞「上がる」に後続して話し手の「推量」を表している。前者は「根源的」であり、後者は「認識的」である。同じく、(5a)の「まい」は動作動詞「させる」に後続して「彼」の「意志」を表し、(5b)の「まい」は非動作動詞「知る」に後続して話し手の「推量」を表している。やはり、前者は「根源的」であり、後者は「認識的」である。
　さらに、根源的と認識的とに両義的に解釈される語句を挙げて、各々の特徴を調べてみよう（例：be going to）。

§115a　ここで、Leech は、知覚動詞を従える法助動詞 can は知覚状態を表すとしている（すなわち、「能力」の can とは別物である）。このことについてもう少し検討を加えてみよう。§37E で挙げられている次の例を見られたい。

（1）a.　I *heard* a door slam.
　　 b.　(At that moment) I *heard* a door slamming.
　　 c.　?*I *could hear* a door slam.
　　 d.　I *could hear* a door slamming (all night).　　(Cf. Leech (2004³: 25–26))

　この場合、動詞 slam は瞬間動詞なので、進行形にしない限り、could と共に用いることはできない。なぜなら、slam の瞬間性と could の状態性とが衝突してしまうからである。すなわち、heard は完結的・瞬間的な知覚を、could hear は非完結的・状態的な知覚を表している。
　澤田（2006: 384ff.）は、主語に自然に知覚される感情・感覚・意識を表す動詞を「自発動詞」、それを表す文を「自発文」と称している。

（2）　自発文とは、概念化主体に、ある心理的作用（感情・知覚・思考など）が自
　　　然に生じる状態を表す構文の集合である。

自発動詞には、次の原則が成立すると考えられる（澤田（2006: 384）参照）。

（3）　自発動詞の原則：
　　　自発動詞は、現在時制形（日本語においては「る」形）の場合には非完結的（imperfective）（すなわち、状態的（stative））な解釈が、過去時制形（日本語においては「た」形）の場合には完結的（perfective）（すなわち、非状態的

(nonstative))な解釈が無標である。

　英語の自発文の１つに、法助動詞 can を用いる場合がある。すなわち、自発動詞として、後に、see, hear, smell, feel, taste などの知覚動詞や remember, understand, believe, think, imagine などの認識・思考動詞（いわゆる「私的動詞」(private verbs)（Palmer (1990[2]: 86–88)）を従えて、全体として自発文を形作る用法である（アメリカ英語では、この意味では、can see/hear などの代わりに、see/hear がよく用いられる（Swan (2005[3]: 102)）。

(４) a.　I can see the house.
　　 b.　We could hear singing.
　　 c.　I could feel vibrations.
　　 d.　Can you smell the soap?
　　 e.　I could taste the garlic in the soup.　　　　(Quirk, et al. (1985: 203))

例えば、(4a) では、話し手にその家を見る能力があるとか、話し手がその家を見ることが可能であるといったことが述べられているのではなく、話し手に自然にその家が見える状態が述べられている（詳しくは、Boyd and Thorne (1969: 72)、Lakoff (1972: 242)、Leech (2004[3]: 25–26)、Palmer (1990[2]: 86–88)、Declerck (1991: 167–168)、柏野 (2002: 60ff.)、Swan (2005[3]: 102)、安藤 (2005: 275–276)、澤田 (2006) など参照）。Boyd and Thorne (1969: 72) や Coates (1983: 90) は、この can が「アスペクト的」(aspectual) であるとし、(4a) の can see は (5) の進行形 *am seeing の代用であるとしている。換言すれば、can（＝自発）は知覚の非完結性（＝状態性）を表している。

(５)　*I am seeing the house.

Palmer (1990[2]: 86–87) では、次の例が比較されている。

(６)　I can see the moon.
(７) a.　He has marvellous eyes; he can see the tiniest detail.
　　 b.　From the top you can see the whole of the city.

Palmer によれば、(6) の can（＝自発）には「能力」という意味はほとんどないので、(6) は次の (8) とほとんど変わらない。

(８)　I see the moon.

一方、(7) では、(7a) の can は「能力」を、(7b) の can は「可能」を意味しているので、can see を sees や see に変えることはできない。Palmer の立場は、(4) や (6) の can/could は慣用的な用法であり、(7) の「能力」や「可能(性)」の can とは独立した用法であるというものである。

ここで、(1c)–(1d) や (4) における can (=「自発」) は「自発文」の集合を形成すると想定する。自発においては、対象の存在を自然に知覚するという知覚主体の心的経験が叙述されている。こうした想定によるならば、次の例における could は、「自発」ではなく、「可能」と解釈されることになる。
can (=自発) と can (=能力・可能) は安藤 (2005: 276) でも峻別されている。

(9) I can see the moon tonight.
(10) Cats can see in the dark. 　　　　　　　　　　　(安藤 (2005: 276))

安藤では、前者の can は「顕在的能力」を、後者の can は「潜在的能力」を表すとされ、特定的な主語についての叙述では、通例、潜在的能力の読みが得られ、総称文の主語についてのそれでは、潜在的能力の読みが得られると述べられている。

以下、自発動詞 hear を用いた自発文において、過去時制形 heard は完結的・瞬間的知覚を表すが、「can (=自発) + hear」形式は非完結的・状態的知覚を表すことを、実例を通して実証してみよう。

第1に、次の例 (ドイル「まだらの紐」から) を考えてみよう。ホームズとワトソンがロイロット家の屋敷の中の一室で灯りを消したまま寝ずの番をしている場面である。ホームズは、ふと、蒸気が吹き出るようなかすかな音を耳にした。その音を聞くやいなや、ホームズはベッドから立ち上がり、マッチを擦って、呼び鈴の綱めがけてステッキを振り下ろした。

(11) *The instant* that we *heard* it, Holmes sprang from the bed, struck a match, and lashed furiously with his cane at the bell-pull.
"You *see* it, Watson?" he yelled. "You *see* it?"
But I *saw* nothing. At *the moment* when Holmes struck the light I *heard* a low, clear whistle, but the sudden glare flashing into my weary eyes made it impossible for me to tell what it was at which my friend lashed so savagely.
　　　　　　　　　　(C. Doyle, "The Speckled Band") (イタリック筆者)

ここでは、heard が瞬間性を表す the instant/moment 節と共に用いられている。それゆえ、heard が完結的であることは明らかである。この場面では、heard を could hear に置き換えることはできない。

(12) *The instant that we *could hear* it, Holmes...

興味深いことに、(11)では"You see it, Watson?"のように、現在時制の see が用いられている。この場合の see は、「見えたか？」に相当する有標の"dramatic"な言いまわしであり、完結的な用法であると見られる(Leech (2004³: 26) 参照)。この表現はこの文脈にぴったりである。

第2に、次の例(クリスティ『そして誰もいなくなった』第5章第5節から)における could hear について考えてみよう。ここでは、退役した老将軍マッカーサー(Macarthur)の内面における意識の流れが描写されている。夜中、開け放たれた窓から、波が岩に打ち寄せる音が聞こえる。風も強くなってきたようだ。

(13) Through the open window he *could hear* the waves breaking on the rocks — a little louder *now* than earlier in the evening. Wind was getting up, too.
(A. Christie, *And Then There Were None*)(イタリック筆者)

この場面では知覚主体(この場合はマッカーサー)の意識の流れが描写されている。このことは、文全体が過去時制であるにもかかわらず"now"(「今は」)が用いられていることからも明らかである。上の could hear は、知覚主体が聴覚によって、「波が岩に打ち寄せている」という事象の存在を知覚している状態を表している。仮に(13)で heard が用いられていたならば、知覚主体はその事象を短時間しか知覚しなかったという可能性が生じる。しかし、この文脈では知覚対象は潮騒であり、瞬時に消え去ってしまう性質のものではない。それゆえ、heard は適切とは言えない。

では、(3)の「自発動詞の原則」は日本語においてはどのように適用できるであろうか。次の例を考えてみよう。

(14) a. ?突然、隣の部屋の窓ガラスの割れる音が聞こえる。
    b. 突然、隣の部屋の窓ガラスの割れる音が聞こえた。
(15) a. あそこに {?稲妻／車／富士山} が見える。
    b. あそこに(ちらっと){稲妻／車／富士山} が見えた。

興味深いことに、「聞こえる」、「見える」は「聞こえた」、「見えた」と異なって、「非完結性」(あるいは「状態性」)を有している。(14a)は副詞「突然」があるために、その文は瞬間的となり、不適格となる。同じく、(15a)は「見える」が状態的であるために、その知覚対象として、「稲妻」を選ぶと不自然になる。稲妻は瞬間的であるからである。

§116a ここで、Leech は次のような例を may（=「譲歩」(concessive)）と称している。

(1) The buildings *may* be old, *but* it's an excellent school. （Leech (2004³: 76)）

以下、澤田（2006: 351ff.）に従って、may（=「是認」）と名付け、may（=「可能性」）と区別すべきことを述べてみたい。

はじめに、次の(2)と(3)の例を比較してみよう。

(2) a. I *may* be almost 50, *but* there's not a lot of things I've forgotten.
   (*COBUILD*³)
   b. There *may* be some evidence to suggest that the man is guilty, *but* it's hardly conclusive.
(3) a. You *may* laugh, *but* just check it out for me, will you? (*COBUILD*¹)
   b. We *may* not have class the last week of February, *but* I'll let you know for sure as the time approaches. (*LAAD*)

(2a)は「なるほど私はもう少しで 50 に手が届くが、物忘れはそれほどひどくはない」と、(2b)は「なるほどその男が有罪であるという証拠はかなりあるが、決定的な証拠とはとても言えない」と解釈される。

一方、(3a)は「もしかすると君は笑うかもしれないが、念のためにちょっとそれを調べてくれないかね」と、(3b)は「もしかすると 2 月の最後の週は授業はないかもしれないが、その時期が近づいたらはっきりしたことを知らせてあげよう」と解釈される。(3a)の場合も(3b)の場合も、話し手が前半の命題 p を是認しているという構図ではない。

Sweetser (1990) は may（=「是認」）の用法を「言語行為(speech act)的」であるとする。

(4) a. He *may* be a university professor, *but* he sure is dumb.
   b. There *may* be a six-pack in the fridge, *but* we have work to do.
   （Sweetser (1990: 70)）

(4a)は、「私は、彼が大学教授であることは認めるが、にもかかわらず彼が愚鈍であることは確かだ」、(4b)は、「冷蔵庫にビールの 6 缶入りがあるんだけど」とビールをすすめられてたようなコンテクストでは、「ビールは有り難いですが、仕事があるので飲めません」といった読みになる。この場合、may は「私は認める」(I admit)に、接続詞 but は「にもかかわらず私は〜と主張する」(I nonetheless insist)に相当し、いずれも言語行為レベルの用法である。言いかえれば、may は、それぞれ、（私たちの）会話世界において、「彼が教授である」という相手の「言明」を「妨げない」、「ビー

ルを飲みませんか」という相手の「申し出」を「妨げない」ということを表している (Sweetser (1990: 71))。

　上の例で、言語行為的 may (=「是認」) の命題内容「彼が大学教授であること」、「冷蔵庫にビールがあること」は、いずれも話し手によって「事実」であると認められている (すなわち、話し手はそのことを知っている) ということが重要である。この点で、言語行為的 may (=「是認」) は、次の認識的 may (=「可能性」) とは決定的に異なっている。

　　（5）a.　He *may* be a university professor, *but* I doubt it because he's so dumb.
　　　　b.　There *may* be a six-pack in the fridge, *but* I'm not sure because Joe had friends over last night.　　　　　　　　　　(Sweetser (1990: 70))

but に続く "I doubt it" や "I'm not sure" から分かるように、それぞれの文で、認識的 may (=「可能性」) の命題内容は話し手によって「事実」と認められているのではない。話し手は、「彼が大学教授であること」、「冷蔵庫にビールの6缶入りがあること」に確証が持てないでいるのである。

　では、語行為的 may (=「是認」) と認識的 may (=「可能性」) はどのようにして区別できるであろうか。以下、言語行為的 may/might (=「是認」) と認識的 may/might (=「可能性」) とを識別するために、次の診断法を導入する (澤田 (2006: 364))。

　　（6）A：言語行為的 may/might (=「是認」) は認識副詞 perhaps と共起することは不可能であるが、認識的 may/might (=「可能性」) はそれが可能である。
　　　　B：言語行為的 may/might (=「是認」) は could に置き換わることは不可能であるが、認識的 may/might (=「可能性」) はそれが可能である。

これら2つの診断法は、言語行為的 may/might (=「是認」) と認識的 may/might (=「可能性」) とが別物であることを証明する働きを持っており、法助動詞の「単義性」分析に疑問を投げかけるものである。以下、テクストの中に見出される "may/might 〜 but" 文がどのように解釈されるのかについて実例を通して考えてみよう。

　次の例 (クリスティ『そして誰もいなくなった』第7章第2節から) では、アームストロング医師は、誰か相談できる相手を探している。彼は判事のウォーグレイヴ氏に目をつけた。しかし、彼はウォーグレイヴ氏をあきらめる。彼はもっと行動力のある人間を必要としたのである。

　　（7）　As before, the doctor hesitated for a moment. His eyes rested speculatively on Mr. Justice Wargrave. He wanted to consult with someone. He was conscious of the judge's acute, logical brain. But nevertheless he wavered. Mr.

Justice Wargrave *might* have a good brain *but* he was an elderly man. At this juncture, Armstrong felt what was needed was a man of action.
　　　　　　（A. Christie, *And Then There Were None*）（イタリック筆者）

ここでは、may ではなく、might が用いられているが、それは、この文が話し手であるアームストロングの意識の流れが描出話法で表されているためである（すなわち、この文はアームストロングの独白である）。それゆえ、"might ～ but"文を直接話法で書き換えるならば、次のように "may ～ but"文となる。

(8)　Mr. Justice Wargrave *may* have a good brain *but* he is an elderly man.

この "may ～ but"文は次のような3つの命題の相互作用で表示されよう。

(9)　文A：判事は鋭敏で論理的な頭脳を持ち合わせている。（既存命題）
　　　　↑‥‥‥是認
　　　文B：確かにウォーグレイヴ判事は頭がいい。（前半命題）
　　　　↑‥‥‥反論
　　　文C：しかし、彼は老人だ。（後半命題）

以下、(7) の may が言語行為的 may（＝「是認」）と解釈されることを検証してみよう。(6) の2つの診断法によれば、(7) の "may ～ but"文においては、(i) perhaps を挿入することも、(ii) may を could で置き換えることも不可能であると予測されるが、事実は予測通りである（以下、＊印は意味を変えることなく書き換えることは不可能であることを示す）。

(10)　*Perhaps*, Mr. Wargrave {*may*/*could*} have a good brain but he is an elderly man.

一方、次の例（クリスティ『そして誰もいなくなった』第3章第3節から）はどうであろうか。この場面では、元警部のブロアが正体不明の人物から来た手紙を調べつつ、つぶやいている。「新品のコロネーションのタイプで打たれている。紙はエンサインで、特別な製品ではない。指紋が残っているかもしれないが、望み薄だ。」

(11)　He twitched it out of the other's hand, and ran his eye over it. He murmured: 'Coronation machine. Quite new — no defects. Ensign paper — the most widely used make. You won't get anything out of that. *Might* be finger prints, *but* I doubt it.'　　（A. Christie, *And Then There Were None*）（イタリック筆者）

この場面では、話し手は、might の命題内容 "there are finger prints" を是認しているのではなく、ただその可能性を推量しているにすぎない。"I doubt it" がこの解釈を裏づけている ((5a) 参照)。さらに、上の2つの診断法も、(11) の might が認識的 might (=「可能性」) であることを示している。

 (12) *Perhaps*, there {*might / could*} be finger prints, but I doubt it.

「是認―反論」の定型的表現は日本語にも見出される。次のような「なるほど〜が、しかし〜」の構文である。

 (13) 「<u>なるほど</u>、万葉歌は主情で構成されている。それに、いろいろと文学的な修辞がほどこされているから、こういうもので考古学をやろうとするのは、乱暴かもしれない。いや、危険かもしれないね。<u>だがね</u>、たとえば、ここにぼくが一つの題を出してみよう。君たちは、巻十三に収められている、淳名河（ぬなかわ）の、というのを知ってるかい？」

（松本清張「万葉翡翠」）（下線筆者）

この例では、「なるほど」という副詞によって、前半命題である「万葉歌は主情で構成されている」是認されており、その後、「だがね」によって反論が加えられている。

§121 ここで、Leech は、can の表す「理論的可能性」は不定詞で書き換えられ、may の表す「現実的可能性」は that 節または独立文で書き換えられると述べ、両者の違いを明確にしている。

 (1) a. The road *can* be blocked.
  b. It is possible *for the road to be blocked*.
  c. It is possible *to block the road*.
 (2) a. The road *may* be blocked.
  b. It is possible *that the road is blocked*.
  c. Perhaps *the road is blocked*.   (Leech (2004^3: 82))

Leech によると、can の表す「可能性」は「理論的」なので、例えば、警部が同僚の警部に「その道路は封鎖しようと思えばできる。封鎖すれば、犯人を逮捕できる」と言ったような状況で用いられる。一方、may の表す「可能性」は「現実的」なので、例えば、お客の到着を今か今かと待ちわびている夫婦が「もしかしたら道路が洪水で通れなくなっているのかもしれないね」と顔を見合わせて案じているような状況で用

いられる。Leech の言う 'factual'(「現実的」)を、ここでは、「ある事柄が現実にある、あるいはあると考えられる」という意味に理解することにする。

(1)の「理論的可能性」の can は「～できる」を意味し、can(=「可能」)とみなせるが、他方、次の例を見られたい。

(3) *Even* expert drivers *can* make mistakes. (Leech (2004[3]: 74))

(3)は、熟練の運転手でも事故を起こすこともあると述べている。ここで尺度副詞 even が用いられていることが重要である。この副詞は、可能性の度合いから言って、その事柄(=熟練の運転手が事故を起こすこと)が生じる確率は本来低いことを含意しているからである。

このタイプの can の意味について、Poutsma (1926) は「再発的」(recurrent)、Boyd and Thorne (1969) は「散発的」(sporadic)、Thomson and Martinet (1986[4]) は「偶発的」(occasional) としている。また、モダリティの種類としては、Palmer (1987[2], 1990[2]: 107–109) は、von Wright (1951: 1–2) に従って、「存在的モダリティ」(existential modality) に属するとし、Brennan (1997) は、「量化的モダリティ」(quantificational modality) に属するとしている。というのは、some–all と possibility–necessity との間には平行性が見られるからである。ここでは、can (=「散発性」) と称することにする。

以下の例から分かるように、can (=「散発性」) は、その状況の存在の仕方がまばらであることを表している。それゆえ、その状況は、数が少なくて、間があいた状態で分布していることになる。

(4) a. Measles *can* be quite dangerous.
 b. This road *can* be slippery. (Brennan (1993: 294))
 c. Sonny turned to Tessio. The Brooklyn *caporegime* shrugged.
  "Any man can turn traitor…"
   (M. Puzo, *The Godfather*)(イタリック原文、下線筆者)
 d. Women *can* be awful, can't they? You know what she did to poor Alex Roscoff. (A. Christie, *Mrs McGinty's Dead*)(イタリック筆者)
 e. "Well," I said, When I heard about it, "it does show that she ought never to have been alone in the house — that niece of hers ought to have been with her. A man in drink *can* be like a ravening wolf, …"
   (A. Christie, *The ABC Murders*)(イタリック筆者)
 f. Roses *can* be mauve. (Palmer (1990[2]: 107))

(4a)は、はしかといえど油断大敵である。(肺炎を併発して)死亡することもあると述べている。(4b)は、この道路は時には(凍結などのため)滑りやすくなることもあると

169

述べている。滑りやすくなる期間は冬の一時期であろう。(4c)は、「どんな男でも裏切り者になることがある」と述べている。すなわち、裏切り者になるということがあり得ないような男はいない。(4d)は、女もひどいことをすることがあるというように、女は一般にやさしいとみなされているが、それも人によりけりであると述べている。(4e)は、男は酒が入ると飢えたオオカミのようになることがあると述べている。最後に、(4f)は、バラにも藤色のものもあると述べている。

ここで語用論的に興味深いことは、(4f)で、バラの色を表すのに"mauve"が用いられ、"blue"は用いられてはいないことである。"blue roses"(＝「青いバラ」)とは「不可能なもの」の代名詞である。ただし、最近、バイオテクノロジーの発達によって、ついに「青いバラ」が開発された。

次の例(クリスティ『アクロイド殺人事件』第4章第1節から)を見られたい。殺されたロジャーの義理の妹の娘にフロラ・アクロイドがいる。彼女は皆から好かれてはいないが、もてることは確かである。

（4） Quite a lot of people do not like Flora Ackroyd, but nobody can help admiring her. And *to her friends she can be very charming.*
    (A. Christie, *The Murder of Roger Ackroyd*)(イタリック筆者)

イタリック部は、「友達に対しては、彼女はとても魅力的に振る舞うことがある」と解釈されよう。ここで彼女は自分の友達にはいつでも魅力的に振る舞うというわけではないことが分かる。その文の前で、「彼女は嫌われている」とあることがその証左である。

ここで、can(＝「散在性」)とmay(＝「可能性」)(＝～かもしれない)の違いに関して、以下のような区別をしてみよう。

（5） can(＝「散発性」)は「存在的モダリティ」に属し、その事柄・状況の存在の仕方がまばらであるという客観的状態を表すが、may/might/could(＝「可能性」)は「認識的モダリティ」に属し、その事柄・状況の可能性は高くないという、概念主体の主観的推量を表す。

こうした区別に基づくならば、例えば、次の2つの文の真理条件は同じではあり得ない。

（6）a. Lions *can* be dangerous.
    b. Lions {*may/might/could*} be dangerous.

なぜなら、canは「ライオンは時と場合によっては、危険なこともある」、ないし

は、「危険なライオンもいる」という具合に、ライオンの種類を表しているが、may/might/could は「ライオンは危険かもしれない」という話し手の推量を表しているからである。

　以下、can (=「散在性」) と may/might/could (=「可能性」) の違いについて考えてみよう。違いの1つは「過去の意味になるかどうか」である。過去の意味になれば、それは命題内容の一部であり、したがって客観的な表現であるとみなすことが可能である。ここで、次の原則を立ててみよう。

　　(7)　客観的助動詞は過去の意味になり得るが、主観的助動詞は過去の意味になり得ない。

この原則を考慮に入れて、次の文を考えてみよう。

　　(8)　My uncle had a feeble-minded boy, and he *could* go very nasty *sometimes* — as he grew up, that was.　(A. Christie, *Mrs McGinty's Dead*) (イタリック筆者)
　　(9)　In those days, a transatlantic voyage *could* be dangerous.　(Leech (2004³: 97))

　まず、(8)の例(クリスティ『マギンティ夫人は死んだ』第7章第2節から)では、叔父さんの息子は、成長するにつれて手に負えなくなることがあったという、過去の状況について述べられている(頻度副詞 sometimes に注意)。

　一方、(9)では、かっての航海の状況について述べられている。すぐに連想されるのは、世界最大の海難事故と言われるタイタニック号の遭難である。1912年4月14日の夜、タイタニック号はサザンプトンからニューヨークに向かう途中、ニューファンドランド島沖で氷山に衝突して翌日沈没し、約1,500人の犠牲者を出したとされる。しかし、こうした過去の状況を次の文で表すことはできない。この might には過去の意味はないからである。

　　(10)　*In those days, a transatlantic voyage *might* be dangerous.

　最後に、can (=「散在性」) と may (=「可能性」) が表す状況の「深刻さ」の違いについて考えてみよう。

　　(11) a.　This illness *can* be fatal.
　　　　b.　This illness *may* be fatal.　　　　　　　　　(Leech (2004³: 82))

Leech (2004³: 82) は、患者にとって、「実際的可能性」を表す(11b)の方が「理論的可能性」を表す(11a)よりもずっと不安であり、深刻であると述べている。

これに対して、柏野（1993）は、下のような例（シーガル『家族の問題』から）を挙げて反論している。子供が腹膜炎（peritonitis）にかかって入院した。父親のボブは気が気でない。心配のあまり、彼は待合室で担当のインターンをつかまえて尋ねる。

  （12） "How serious is peritonitis?"
     "Well, in young children *it can be a pretty dicey thing*."
     "Meaning what? *Can* it be fatal?"
     "Well, sometimes in children…"
     "Jesus!"   （E. Segal, Man, *Woman and Child*）（イタリック筆者）

ボブが「なんですって！」と驚いたのは、腹膜炎といえども、子供の場合には命にかかわることがあると聞かされたからである。いくら腕の良い医者に手術されようと、愛する子供が死んでしまう可能性が少しでもあれば、親の不安ははかり知れない。can（=「散在性」）と may（=「可能性」）のどちらが不安を呼ぶかは、結局、文脈によるのである（(12) の例の資料を提供していただいた柏野氏に感謝したい）。

§137b ここで、Leech は、認識的な can't と must not（あるいは mustn't）を比較している。

 一般に、認識的 must の否定形は、アメリカ英語ではしだいに許容されつつあるが、イギリス英語ではそれほど一般的ではないとされている（Halliday (1970)、Lyons (1977)、Jacobsson (1979: 298)、Coates (1983: 19)、Tottie (1985)、Quirk et al. (1985: 225)、Palmer (1990[2], 2003: 10)、Declerck (1991: 407)、柏野 (2002: 75)、Leech (2004[3]: 137)、Swan (2005[3]: 337)）。次の例を見られたい。

  （1） His absence *must not* have been noticed. （Quirk et al. (1985: 225)）
  （2） He *mustn't* be there after all.   （Palmer (1990[2]: 61)）

(1) は「彼がいなかったことはばれなかったに違いない」を、(2) は「（いろいろ考えた結果）、彼はそこにはいないとしか結論できない」を意味している。

 Tottie (1985) は、認識的法助動詞と否定の関係を調べるために、イギリス英語の母語話者 37 人とアメリカ英語の母語話者 45 人（いずれも学生）にアンケート調査をした。Tottie の仮説は、「明示的否認」か「暗示的否認」の違いが、認識的な can't と must not の適格性を決定しているというものである。Tottie の言う「明示的否認」、「暗示的否認」とは、それぞれ、(3)、(4) のようなケースである。

  （3） 明示的否認：

　　　　A: John must have read the instruction booklet.
　　　　B: He *can't* have read it. He is making so many mistakes.
（ 4 ）　暗示的否認：
　　　　John *must not* have read the instruction booklet. He is making so many mistakes.　　　　　　　　　　　　　　　　　　　(Tottie (1985: 95))

　(3)の対話では、話し手Bは、「ジョンは説明書を読んだに違いない」という話し手Aの発話に対して、「そんなはずはない」あるいは「そうとは思えない」と明示的に「否認」している。一方、(4)では、話し手は、ジョンがたくさん間違いを犯しているという証拠に基づいて、「ジョンは説明書を読まなかったに違いない」あるいは「ジョンはきっと説明書を読まなかったのだ」と「断定」している。
　Tottie の調査結果の一端を検討してみよう。はじめに、「明示的否認」のケースを挙げる。例えば、ジョンとピーターがおしゃべりをしているとき、ジョンが次のように言ったとする。

（ 5 ）　John: Have you seen Bill today? He's not at work. I think he's ill.

ジョンの発言に対するピーターの答えについての調査結果は次の通りである ((6)はアメリカ英語、(7)はイギリス英語。無視すべき回答数は省略)。

（ 6 ）　Peter: Oh, no. He {*can't* (71%) /*couldn't* (20%) /*mustn't* (0%) /*must not* (0%)} be ill. I saw him on the bus this morning. (アメリカ英語)
（ 7 ）　Peter: Oh, no. He {*can't* (76%) /*couldn't* (11%) /*mustn't* (0%) /*must not* (0%)} be ill. I saw him on the bus this morning. (イギリス英語)

　括弧の中の統計から分かるように、アメリカ英語であれ、イギリス英語であれ、「彼は病気だ」という「既存」(もしくは「既知」)(given)の命題を明示的に否認する場合、can't/couldn't しか用いられていない。(6)と(7)が明示的否認であることは、"Oh, no." という間投詞からも分かる。
　次に、「暗示的否認」のケースを挙げる。例えば、テッドが車を運転しながら道に迷っている様子を見て、同乗者が「彼はここに来たことがないに違いない」と判断したとしよう。下の例では、まず、否定的な断定がなされ、ついで、そう断定する根拠が示されている ((8)はアメリカ英語、(9)はイギリス英語。無視すべき回答数は省略)。

（ 8 ）　Ted {*can't* (4%) /*couldn't* (49%) /*mustn't* (2%) /*must not* (27%)} have driven this way before. He seems absolutely lost! (アメリカ英語)

(9)　Ted {*can't*(78%)/*couldn't*(11%)/*mustn't*(0%)/*must not*(0%)} have driven this way before. He seems absolutely lost!（イギリス英語）

　(8)から分かるように、アメリカ英語では、couldn't が全体の約半数を占め、must not が 27% で続いている。can't はごくわずかであり、must not と mustn't とでは、前者の方がはるかに一般的である。
　次に、(9)から分かるように、イギリス英語では、can't と couldn't だけしか用いられず、can't の方が圧倒的に多い。ただし、Tottie の調査を拠りどころにして、イギリス英語では mustn't が全く用いられないと即断することはできない。
　Tottie の調査結果で興味深いことは、いわゆる「明示的否認」のケースでは、（アメリカ英語でもイギリス英語でも）命題否定である must not（あるいは mustn't）は用いられないのに、「暗示的否認」のケースとなると、アメリカ英語では、couldn't と並んで、must not（あるいは mustn't）も用いられるということであり、イギリス英語では、専ら、can't が用いられ、must not（あるいは、mustn't）は用いられないということである。
　なぜ、Tottie の言う「暗示的否認」の場合には、（アメリカ英語では）モダリティ否定（＝ couldn't）と命題否定（＝ must not）とが共存できるのであろうか。両者には、どのような捉え方の違いがあるのであろうか。
　まず最初に、次の条件を提出する。

(10)　既存命題否認の条件：
　　　話し手は、モダリティ否定の認識的法助動詞を用いる際には、証拠 q に基づいて、既存の命題（もしくは、主張・想定）p（又は、〜 p）を否認したり、p（又は、〜 p）とは思えないと主張したりしている。

ここで言う「既存の命題」には、(i)百科事典的知識（常識）に基づくもの、(ii)先行文脈で述べられたもの、あるいは(iii)自らの心中に想定したもの、などがあると想定する。以下、幾つかの例に基づいて、「既存命題否認の条件」を検証してみよう。
　第 1 に、次のやりとりを考えてみよう。

(11)　A: John didn't come to class today; *maybe* he is ill.
　　　B: He *can't* be ill; I heard him play the bagpipes this morning.
　　　　　　　　　　　　　　　　　　　　　　（Johannesson (1976: 63)）

このやりとりでは、話し手 A が maybe を用いてなした（弱い）主張（＝「彼は病気かもしれない」）を、話し手 B が can't を用いて否認している。証拠 q は、彼がバグパイプを演奏していたという事実である。

Johannesson (1976) が述べているように、ここでは、「ジョンが病気かどうか」が話題となっているので、"He must be well." ではなく、"He can't be ill." の方が適切である。なぜなら、前者では、新たな主張をすることになり、談話の流れが切れてしまう。
　一方、認識的な must not (あるいは mustn't) に対して、以下の条件を提出する。

(12) 否定命題断定の条件：
話し手は、命題否定の認識的法助動詞を用いる際には、「命題 p ならば、証拠 q ということはないはずだ。しかし、実際には、q だ。それゆえ、p ではない」と断定している。

　この推論プロセスによれば、話し手が must not (あるいは mustn't) を用いて否定的な必然性を述べる場合には、単純に、証拠 q に基づいて、p でないと (弱く) 断言するのではなく、背後で、「p ならば、q ということはないはずだ」という論理が働いているということになる。以下、幾つかのデータによって「否定命題断定の条件」を検証してみたい。
　次の例を考えてみよう。

(13) Brian said he would definitely be here before 9:30. It's 10:00 now, and he's never late. He *must not* be coming.
(14) She walked past me without speaking. She *must not* have seen me.
(15) Tom walked straight into a wall. He *must not* have been looking where she was going. (Murphy (2000^2: 54))

　まず、(13) においては、「p (＝ブライアンは来る) ならば、q (＝ブライアンは遅刻する) ということはないはずだ」という推論が働き、こうした推論に基づいて、「実際には、q (＝ブライアンは遅刻している) だ。それゆえ、p (＝ブライアンは来る) ではないに違いない」と断定している。
　次に、(14) においては、「p (＝彼女が私を見た) ならば、q (＝彼女は私に声をかけずに通り過ぎた) ということはないはずだ」という推論が働き、こうした推論に基づいて、「実際には、q (＝彼女は私に声をかけずに通り過ぎた) だ。それゆえ、p (＝彼女が私を見た) ではないに違いない」と断定している。
　最後に、(15) においては、「p (＝トムが前をよく見ていた) ならば、q (＝トムは壁にぶつかった) ということはないはずだ」という推論が働き、こうした推論に基づいて、「実際には q (＝トムは壁にぶつかった) だ。それゆえ、p (＝トムが前をよく見ていた) ではないに違いない」と断定している。
　第2に、次の例を考えてみよう。

(16) I couldn't understand what these people were doing, playing badminton and golf. They *mustn't* be really sick at all, to do that.

(S. Plath, *The Bell Jar*)（イタリック筆者）

　この場合、話し手は、q（＝患者たちはバドミントンやゴルフをしている）を根拠にして、p（＝患者たちは病気である）ではないと断定している。こうした断定に至るのは、背後に、p（＝病気である）ならばq（＝バドミントンやゴルフをする）ということはないはずだ、という推論が働き、こうした推論に基づいて、「実際には、q（＝患者たちはバドミントンやゴルフをしている）だ。それゆえ、p（＝病気である）ではないに違いない」と断定している。
　(16)では、mustn'tの代わりにcan'tを用いることも可能である。

(17) They *can't* be really sick at all, to do that.

なぜなら、人が入院しているというコンテクストから考えて、p＝「患者たちは病気である」ということは（話し手の心中の）既存の想定となり得るからである。話し手は、彼らがスポーツをするのを見て、「本当はpなんかじゃない」というように、pという既存の命題を否定することもできるのである。
　第3に、次の例を考えてみよう。

(18) 'Ma'am, you *must not* be feeling good,' one of the guards said good-naturedly.

(P. Cornwell, *Point of Origin*)（イタリック筆者）

　この例でも、話し手は、q（＝薬をどっさり持っている）ということを根拠に、p（＝気分が良い）ではないと断定している。こうした断定に至るのは、背後に、p（＝気分が良い）ならばq（＝薬をどっさり持っている）ということはないはずだという推論が働き、こうした推論に基づいて、「実際には、q（＝薬をどっさり持っている）だ。それゆえ、p（＝気分が良い）ではないに違いない」と断定している。
　(18)では、must notの代わりにcan'tを用いることは不自然である。

(19) ??You *can't* be feeling good.

「既存命題否認の条件」によれば、このことは次のように説明される。すなわち、治安官と彼女は入り口で会ったばかりであり、当然のことながら、治安官は彼女が気分が良いかどうかを問題にはしない（するとすれば、非礼であろう）。すなわち、p（＝あなたは気分が良い）は既存命題とはなりにくい。各自、小説から認識的なmust notの実例を集めてみよう。

§**139b**　must の意味は、一般に、「義務・必要」と「論理的必然性・推量」とに大別される(Sweetser (1990)、Swan (2005³: 334–335))。モダリティのタイプからすると、前者は「束縛的」、後者は「認識的」に相当する。

　Leech はここで、次の例の両義性について述べている。

（1）　The building *must* be demolished.　　　　　　　(Leech (2004³: 96))

1つは「その建物は取り壊されなければならない」(＝束縛的)であり、もう1つは「その建物は取り壊されているに違いない」(＝認識的)である。注意すべきは動詞句が示す命題内容の時間である。前者の場合、その時間は未来であるが、後者の場合、その時間は現在である。

　次の例を考えてみよう。

（2）　The picture to the left of the fireplace *must* be a Chagall.
　　　　　　　　　　　　　　　　　　　　　　　　　　(Johannesson (1976: 51))

Johannesson (1976: 51)が指摘するように、(2)の must は多義的である。1つの意味は(3a)であり、もう1つの意味は(3b)である。

（3）a.　暖炉の左に絵を飾るとすれば、シャガールでなければならない(＝シャガールしか飾ってはならない)。(＝束縛的)
　　　b.　暖炉の左に飾ってある絵はシャガールに違いない(＝きっとシャガールだ)。(＝認識的)

Johannesson によれば、(3a)の解釈の場合、絵はまだ飾られてはおらず、どの絵にしたものかと壁を見ながら思案している状況である。一方、(3b)の場合、「暖炉の左に飾ってある絵」とは、発話時点で既に壁に飾ってある絵に他ならない。

　must の多義性を解釈するうえで、must が指し表している「事柄」(すなわち、状況・世界)が「これからあろうとする事柄」(＝未然)なのか「既にある(あった)事柄」(＝已然)なのかは決定的に重要である。なぜなら、認識的 must に対しては、通例、次のような命題内容条件が課されるからである(詳しくは、Rivière (1981)、Lakoff (1972)、Johannesson (1976: 52)、Langacker (1991)、澤田(2001, 2006, 2010)など参照)。

（4）　非未来性の条件(現代英語)：
　　　　その命題内容は((単純)未来の will で表されるような)未来の状況であってはならない。

例えば、次の例を考えてみよう。この例は、命題内容（＝ジョンの病気の回復）（＝(John) be better）の時間に関するかぎり、「これから回復する」（＝未来）のか、「既に回復している」（＝現在）のかで多義的であるが、

（5） John *must* be better.　　　　　　　　　　　　（Johannesson (1976: 52)）

(5)の文全体は、must が束縛的の場合には「ジョンにこれから回復して欲しい」（＝未来）といった解釈を、must が認識的の場合には「ジョンは既に回復しているのに違いない」（＝現在）といった解釈を受ける（Johannesson (1976: 52)）。

では、次の例(6)（オー・ヘンリー「賢者の贈り物」から）における must は「束縛的」であろうか、それとも「認識的」であろうか。

明日はクリスマスだというのに、デラにはわずか1ドルと87セントしかなかった。これでは、とうてい愛する夫ジムのためのクリスマスプレゼントは買えない。若い二人には大切な宝物が2つあった。ジムの金時計とデラの髪である。デラはジムのためのクリスマスプレゼントを買うために自分の大切な髪を売って20ドルを手にした。幸せいっぱいの彼女は、店から店へとプレゼントを探し歩き、やっとすばらしい鎖を見つけ出した。それは夫の時計にぴったりの品であった。

（6） As soon as she saw it she knew that *it must be Jim's*. It was like him. Quietness and value —— the description applied to both.
　　　　　　　　　　　　（O. Henry, "The Gift of the Magi"）（イタリック筆者）

(6)の斜体部の文を、次のように単独で取り出すならば、

（7） It must be Jim's.

must は認識的にも束縛的にも解釈され得る。しかしながら、(i) その場のコンテクスト、(ii) 命題内容の未来性、(iii) 話し手の意志、といった点を考慮に入れるならば、「束縛的」にしか解釈されない。なぜなら、(i) 鎖は店に陳列してあり、(ii) デラはこれからそれを購入しようとしており、(iii) それをジムの所有物にしようというのが話し手のデラの意志であるからである。それゆえ、(6)の斜体部は「なにがなんでもこれをジムに買ってあげないといけない」といった彼女の固い決意を表していると解釈される。しかしながら、仮に彼女が道ばたでジムのものとおぼしき時計鎖を拾ったようなコンテクストでは、(7)は「きっとこれはジムのものに違いない」といった彼女の確信（＝認識的）を表していると解釈せざるを得ない。

「非未来性の条件（現代英語）」によれば、認識的法助動詞のうち、may, might, could などと異なって、認識的 must の場合には、一般に、その命題内容は未来の状況であっ

てはならない。このことを以下の例によって確かめてみよう。

(8) You {*may/might/could/*must*} feel better after a good night's sleep.
(9) Don't go near the lion. It {*may/might/could/*must*} bite you.
(10) They {*may/might/could/*must*} miss the train unless they take a taxi.

(8)–(10)で言及されている状況は、すべて未来の状況である。これらの例で、認識的 may/might/could と異なって、認識的 must が不適格になることは、認識的 must に対して「非未来性条件」が適用されることを示唆している (Rivière (1981: 189)、澤田 (2006: 255))。

　上の例で興味深いことは、(8)が、実は多義的であるということである。この例は、「今夜一晩ぐっすり眠れば、あなたはきっと気分が良くなるでしょう」というように、未来の状況に言及している場合には不適格となるが、「昨夜ぐっすり眠ったので、今あなたはさぞかし気分がいいでしょう」というように、現在の状況に言及している場合には適格となる。後者の状況は、(8)を次のように書き換えることよってはっきりする。

(11) You *must* feel better after having had a good night's sleep.

こうした事実も、非未来性条件によって自然に説明可能である。以上のことを実際に母語話者に確かめてみよう。

　上で挙げた(4)の「非未来性の条件」は、この段階ではたんに現代英語の認識的 must だけに適用される個別的な条件にとどまっている。しかしながら、例えば、日本語における古語の推量助動詞「らし」、「らむ」などの事例も併せて分析するならば、(4)はより高いレベルの一般性を獲得する可能性がある。

　以下、「らむ」「らし」について考えてみよう。周知のように、「らし」、「らむ」は、それぞれ、「確実な根拠(多くの場合明示される)に基づいて現在の事態を確信的に推量する意を表す」、「眼前にない現在の事柄を推量する意を表す」(『古語大辞典』)ので、これらの助動詞に対しては、次のような(命題内容)条件が課される。

(12) 非未来性の条件(古代日本語)：
　　 その命題内容は、(「む」で表されるような)未来の状況であってはならない。

　次の例(以下、『萬葉集』の例は佐竹昭広・山田英雄・工藤力男・大谷雅夫・山崎福之校注『新日本古典文学大系』岩波書店(1999–2003)による)では、

(13) 春過ぎて夏来たるらし白たへの衣干したり天の香具山　　（巻第一　28）
(14) あみの浦に船乗りすらむ娘子らが玉裳の裾に潮満つらむか　（巻第一　40）

「らし」は、香具山に白い衣が干してあるのを見て、春が過ぎて今や夏がやって来たのだと、概念化主体が推定しているさまを表している。一方、「らむ」は、伊勢の海辺で官女が今頃は船遊びをしており、彼女たちの美しい裳裾に潮が満ちていることだろうと、概念化主体（この場合は柿本人麿）が都にいながら想像し、その光景に対してあこがれているさまを表している。

　英語の場合、「非未来性の条件」が認識的 may, might, should などには適用されず、認識的 must だけに適用されるのは、なぜであろうか。

§144　ここで、Leech は、should は must の「弱い」形であると述べているが、はたしてそのように考えるだけでいいであろうか。両者の根本的な違いがあるのではなかろうか。
　ここでは、基本的に澤田 (2006: 192ff.) に基づいて、(1) に示すように、認識的法助動詞が表す推論には、「説明」(explanation) と「予測」(prediction) という2つのパタンがあるという仮説を提出し、

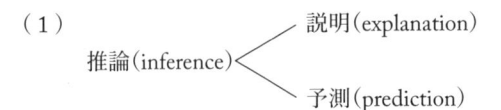

(1)　　推論 (inference) ＜ 説明 (explanation)
　　　　　　　　　　　　　予測 (prediction)

この仮説に基づいて、次の2点を実証する。

(2) 認識的 must は、意識主体が、現時点で入手可能な直接的証拠に基づいて、（その原因は）p に違いないと「説明」することを表す。
(3) 認識的 should は、意識主体が、抽象的知識（道理、法則、公式、過去の経験など）に基づいて、（そうだとすると）p となるはずだと「予測」することを表す。

　下の例（クリスティ『そして誰もいなくなった』第7章第1節から）における認識的 must（＝「推量・論理的必然性」）の意味解釈について考えてみよう。ヴェラはエミリーと、インディアン島の大邸宅の裏山から海を眺めつつ、急死した召使のロジャーズ夫人のことを話している。「あんなにおびえている女の人は見たことがないわ」とヴェラが言う。

（４） Vera said:
　　　'The way she looked — scared of her own shadow! I've never seen a woman look so frightened... *She must have been always haunted by it...*'
　　　　　　　　　　　　　(A. Christie, *And Then There Were None*)（イタリック筆者）

　イタリック部で、ヴェラは、「彼女はずっと恐怖にとらわれていたに違いない」と説明している。ヴェラがそう説明した証拠は、彼女が自分の影におびえていたからである。恐怖にとらわれていなかったらあんなにおびえるはずがない。証拠と説明の関係は、認識レベルにおける原因と結果である。
　では、事象レベルにおける因果性から見るとどうなるであろうか。彼女がおびえていたのは、恐怖にとらわれていたからである。おびえたことは「結果」に、恐怖にとらわれていたことは「原因」に相当する。
　ヴェラの推論を、認識レベルにおける因果性と事象レベルにおける因果性から整理すれば、「結果を証拠として、原因を説明している」ということになろう。興味深いことに、こうした場合、認識的 must の代わりに認識的 should を用いることはできない。一体、それはなぜなのであろうか。
　従来、認識的な must と should の違いは、「should よりも must の方が可能性が高い」(Hornby (1956: 223))などと説明されてきた。こうした分析に従えば、上の例で must のかわりに should が用いられないのは、should は must よりも可能性の度合いが低いからだということになるかもしれない。must, should, may の可能性の度合いは次図で示されるようなものである。

（５）　低 ←── could ── may/might ── should ── must ──→ 高

　しかし、可能性の度合いの高低による説明は十分な説得力を持たない。なぜなら、上の例で、should よりも可能性の度合いが低い may や might が適格になるからである。

（６）　She {must/*should/may/might} have been always haunted by it ...

(2)–(3)の分析法によるならば、(4)で must は使えても should は使えないのは、結果を証拠として、その原因を説明しているからだということになる。
　Lakoff (1972) は法助動詞の語用論に関する古典として評価が高い。それは、コンテクストを取り込むことによって法助動詞の微妙な意味を浮き彫りにしたからである。彼女は、次の文を用いて、認識的な must と should を比較した。

（７）　John *must* be easy to talk to.
（８）　John *should* be easy to talk to.　　　　　　　　(Lakoff (1972: 233))

コンテクストは次のようなものである。今、話し手と聞き手はジョンの研究室の前の廊下に立っている。聞き手はジョンとアポイントメントを取って、自分の順番を待っている。聞き手はジョンがどのような人物なのか不安である。こうした場合、話し手は聞き手に安心感を与えるために、(7)と(8)のどちらを用いてもよいが、Lakoff によれば、「ジョンは話しやすい」と推論する証拠の種類は、must と should では異なっている。must の場合は次のようなものである。話し手はジョンの研究室のドアの近くに立っている。中からジョンの闊達な笑い声が聞こえてくる。笑い声は話しやすさの現れである。そこで、話し手は「ジョンは話しやすいに違いない」と推論する。一方、should の場合、話し手にはジョンの話し声は聞こえない。しかし、話し手はジョンの性格を知っている。彼は学生時代に教授からいじめを受けたので、自分は決して学生をそんな目に遭わせないと誓ったという。こうした情報に基づいて、話し手は「ジョンは話しやすいはずだ」と推論する。

ここで、事象レベルでの因果性という観点から、(7)と(8)の例を捉え直してみよう。一般に、話しやすい性格の人はよく笑う。してみると、話しやすさと笑い声は、原因と結果の関係である。すると、(7)の must の場合、結果を証拠として原因を推論していることになる（＝「笑っているのは話しやすいからに違いない」）。一方、(8)の should の場合には、こうした事象レベルでの因果性はない。

以上の分析を実例に基づいて検証してみたい。第1に、次の例（クリスティ『アクロイド殺人事件』の第7章から）における認識的 must について考えてみよう。殺害されたアクロイドの部屋で、ポアロはドアの近くに置いてあった安楽椅子の位置を問題にし、椅子を元の位置に戻したのは誰かと、「私」やパーカーに質問する。

(9) 　Poirot looked at me.
　　　'Did you, doctor?'
　　　I shook my head.
　　　'It was back in position when I arrived with the olice, sir,' put in Parker. 'I'm sure of that.'
　　　'Curious,' said Poirot again.
　　　'*Raymond or Blunt must have pushed it back,*' I suggested. 'Surely it isn't important?'
　　　　　　　　　(A. Christie, *The Murder of Roger Ackroyd*)（イタリック筆者）

イタリック部で、「私」は「きっとレイモンドかブラントが元に戻したんでしょう」と答えているが、この場合、認識的 must の用法は「原因説明」であり、安楽椅子が元の位置に戻っているのは、レイモンドかブラントが元に戻したことが原因であることを表している。

では、上のイタリック部の must は他の法助動詞に置き換わるであろうか。予想通

り、may, might に置き換わることはできるが、should に置き換わることはできない。

(10) Raymond or Blunt {*must*/*should/*may*/*might*} have pushed it back, I suggested...

このデータは、認識的な may, might にも「原因説明」の用法があることを示している。各自、(4) や (10) のデータについて、母語話者にチェックしてみよう。

§147a, b need に (i) 本動詞用法と (ii) 法助動詞用法があることはよく知られている（Palmer (1990[2]: 41)）。

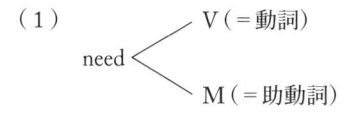

(1) need ＜ V (＝動詞)
       　　　 M (＝助動詞)

本動詞と法助動詞の特徴はそれぞれ次のようにまとめられる。

(2) 本動詞用法
　　a. 3人称単数現在時制標識の -s や過去時制標識の -ed が付く。
　　b. 否定文や疑問文を形成するとき、do による支えを必要とする。
　　c. 補部に to 不定詞、名詞句、ing 形などいろいろな文法カテゴリーを取る。
　　d. 非定形の形（不定詞、分詞、動名詞など）になり得る。
(3) 法助動詞用法
　　a. 3人称単数現在時制標識の -s や過去時制標識の -ed が付かない。
　　b. 否定文や疑問文を形成するとき、do による支えを必要としない。
　　c. はだか不定詞を従える。
　　d. 非定形の形（不定詞、分詞、動名詞など）になり得ない。

need にこうした全く異なる形態的・文法的振る舞いがあるということは、英語において「本動詞」と「法助動詞」が互いに独立したカテゴリーであることの証しであるように思われる。では、なぜ、need は、こうした2つのカテゴリーに分化しているのであろうか。まず、両者の比較をしてみよう。

　上述したように、本動詞の need の場合、肯定文も否定文も適格であり、現在時制形だけでなく、過去時制形もある。また、後にはいろいろなカテゴリーの目的語が現れ得る。

(4) a. He desperately *needed* money.
　　b. The building *needs* quite a few repairs.
　　c. The taste of vitamins is not too nice, so the flavour sometimes *needs* to be disguised.
　　d. I *need* you to do something for me. 　　　　　　　　　　(*COBUILD*²)
　　e. Do you *need* a new telephone? 　　　　　　　　　　　　(*COBUILD*¹)

いずれの例においても、need の目的語となっているもの（あるいは行為）が得られなかったら、その主語指示物の存在が危ぶまれ、本来の機能が果たせないということが述べられている。単に、主語指示物が目的語指示物を欲しているということではない。(4a) では、彼はその時無一文の状態であった。(4b) では、建物は壊れていてこのままでは住めない。(4c) では、ビタミン剤は味付けしないと服用できないことがある。(4d) では、私はあなたに助けてもらわないとどうにもならない。(4e) では、聞き手が使っている電話機は使い物にならない（決して、贅沢を言っているのではない）。

一方、法助動詞の need は、主として否定文、疑問文、あるいは if 節の中など、いわゆる「非断言的」(non-assertive) な環境でしか用いられない（Quirk et al. (1985:138)、Palmer (1990²)、Swan (2005³)、安藤 (2005: 306)、澤田 (2006)）。以下の (a)–(d) と (f)–(g) が「非断言的」な環境である。

(5) a. You *needn't* fill in a form.
　　b. *Need* I fill in a form?
　　c. I wonder if I *need* fill in a form.
　　d. This is the only form you *need* fill in.
　　e. *You *need* fill in a form. 　　　　　　　　　　　　　(Swan (2005³: 342))
　　f. That is all you *need* know.
　　g. Her field isn't one that we *need* go for. 　　　　　　　(Palmer (1990: 41))

注意すべきことは、(a)–(d) と (f)–(g) には、一様に「そんなことはしなくてもいい」、「そのことはするには及ばない」という否定的な含意があることである。(5a) は相手から用紙に記入すべきかと聞かれたような場合に用いられ、(5b–c) では「私は用紙に記入しなくてもいいように思うのだが」といったニュアンスが感じられる。(5d) にも「これ以外の用紙には記入しなくていい」という含意がある。(5f) は「それ以上のことはあなたは知る必要がない」と相手を牽制している。(5g) の that 節は統語論的には肯定であるが、「彼女の畑は我々がわざわざ手に入れようとしなくてもいいものだ」というように、否定的含意が含まれている。ところが、(5e) の場合、こうした否定的な含意は存在しないので、不適格になってしまう。

なぜ、法助動詞の need は、こうした「非断言的」な環境でしか用いられないので

あろうか。この問題を考える基盤として、次のような意味記述を想定しておきたい（*COBUILD*[2] 参照）。

- （6） 本動詞の need は、その人・物（＝主語）にとって、ある対象物が欠かせない（必要不可欠である）という状態を叙述する。
- （7） 法助動詞の need は、(i)「そんなことはしなくていい」（＝束縛的意味）、(ii)「必ずしもそうとは限らない」（＝認識的意味）というふうに、既に言及された行為を実行する義務を免除したり、命題の妥当性・真実性を「否認」する。

(7)を発話と発話、概念と概念の「相互作用」の観点から言うならば、法助動詞としての need は先行文（先行発話、あるいは、前提・共通知識などの既存概念）を否認しているということになろう。

以下の例で、(8B)、(9B)は、それぞれ、法助動詞としての need の束縛的、認識的な例である。

- （8） A: *Must* I pay for this?
  B: No, you *needn't*.
- （9） A: He's a captain, so he *must* be in the Navy.
  B: No, he *needn't* be in the Navy: he *might* be in the Army.

(Tredidgo (1982: 83))

まず、(8)の対話では、Aから「私、弁償しなきゃいけない？」と聞かれて、Bは「いや、そんなことはしなくてもいいよ」と弁償の義務を「免除」している。また、(9)の対話では、Aから「彼は海軍にいるに違いない」と言われて、Bは「海軍にいるとは限らない」と反論している。こうした認識的な needn't も先行文でなされた判断の妥当性を否認している。

では、Leech が挙げている次の例を考えてみよう。

- (10) a. The hedges *needn't* be trimmed this week, John.
  b. The hedges *don't need* to be trimmed this week, John.

(Leech (2004[3]: 103))

Leech によれば、(10a)では「ジョン、今週は、生け垣は刈らなくていいからね」と、話し手は聞き手（＝庭師のジョン）に労務を免除してやっている（聞き手をいたわっているか、他の仕事をやって欲しいと思っている）。この文の話し手（＝P夫人）の頭の中には、当然、ジョンズが今週も普段どおり生け垣の手入れをするという想定があ

185

ろう。一方、(10b)は「ジョン、(このぶんでは)今週は生け垣はまだ刈る必要がないわね」と生け垣の伸び具合を叙述している。(10b)の場合、芝生でお茶でも飲みながら、生け垣を眺めているのかもしれない。Sweetser (1990)流に言うならば、法助動詞の need は「言語行為領域」で、本動詞の need は「現実世界領域」で用いられているということになろう。(10)の両文の違いは「言語行為論」から言えば、以下のように分析し得る。

(10a)の発話は雇用者(=例えばP夫人)と被雇用者(=庭師)との間の力関係を反映している。この文を発話することは世界を変えることである(庭師は生け垣を刈らず、他の行為をする)。Searle (1979)による、言語行為の分類基準としての「合致の方向性」から言えば、「庭師が生け垣を刈らない」という世界は、話し手の言葉に合うように創出されるものであるがゆえに、「世界から言葉への合致」である。しかし、(10b)には、こうした力関係は関与していない。この文を発話しても世界が変わるとは限らない(生け垣の伸び具合に影響はない)。「合致の方向性」から言えば、「今週は生け垣はまだ刈る必要がない」という(現実の)世界の状況は、話し手の言葉によって描出されたものである。よって、「言葉から世界への合致」である。

では、この問題を、実例を通して考えてみよう。次の例(クリスティ『オリエント急行殺人事件』第2部第6章から)における法助動詞 need について考えてみよう。種々の国籍の乗客を乗せたオリエント急行はユーゴスラヴィアとチェコの国境の山中で大雪のため立ち往生してしまった。深夜、密室状態のコンパートメントの寝台で一人のアメリカ人の富豪が全身を刺されて死んでいた。ポワロとブック氏はすべての乗客の話を聞くことにした。ここは、ドラゴミロフ侯爵婦人の話を聞こうとしている場面である。

(11) She cut short a flowery phrase of apology from M. Bouc.
'You need not offer apologies, Messieurs. I understand a murder has taken place. Naturally, you must interview all the passengers. I shall be glad to give all the assistance in my power.'

(A. Christie, *Murder on the Orient Express*)(イタリック筆者)

侯爵婦人はブック氏の美辞麗句をつらねた謝罪の言葉を途中でさえぎり、「謝らなくて結構」と答えている。ここには明らかに「否認」の言語行為がある。すなわち、相手が謝罪をしているので、話し手は「謝ることはない」と、それをさえぎったからである。

各自、英米の小説などから助動詞 need が用いられたデータを集めて、分析してみよう。

§148 ここで、Leech は have (got) to の如く、got を括弧にくくっているが、興味深いのは have to と have got to の文法的・意味的な相違である。すなわち、have got to の have は、(have to の have と異なって) 次の特徴を備えているので、法助動詞のメンバーに入れることができよう (詳しくは、LeSourd (1976)、Battistella (1987)、Coates (1983) など参照)。

(1) a. 直接否定の not を従える (haven't got to ～)。
　　b. 倒置可能である (Have we got to ～ ?)。
　　c. 非定形 (= 不定詞や ing 形) はない (*to have got to ～ /*Having got to ～)。
　　d. 法助動詞と共起しない (may have got to~)。

こうした点では、have got to の have は be to の be に類似している (§149 参照)。
意味的には、have got to は習慣的な意味でなく一回的な意味を持っている。次の例を比較せよ。

(2) a. I *have to* take these pills *every day*.
　　b. *I *have got to* take these pills *every day*.
　　　　　　　　　　　　　　(Cf. Coates (1983: 54), Declerck (1991: 383))
(3) a. Do you *have to* be at your office by 8 o'clock *every day*?
　　b. *Have you *got to* be at your office by 8 o'clock *every day*?
　　　　　　　　　　　　　　　　　　　　　　　(Declerck (1991: 377))

すなわち、過去から現在にわたる習慣的な意味の「毎日」に言及している場合には、have to は適格であるが、have got to は不適格となる。それゆえ、often, usually, always, never といった、過去に始まり現在も継続している習慣に言及する副詞がある場合には、have to は適格であるが、have got to は不適格となる。

(4) a. I *usually* have to get to work at eight.
　　b. *I *usually* have got to get to work at eight.

最後に、次の例における「金曜の晩」の解釈に注目されたい。

(5) 　I've got to work *on Friday evenings* next term. But Betty hasn't got to.
　　　　　　　　　　　　　　　　　　　　　　　(Chalker (1984: 85))

next term という時間副詞類によって示唆されるように、この例における「金曜の晩」はこれからスタートする定期的な義務としてしか解釈できない。

ここで、日本語に視点を移してみたい。下の例に見られるように、「ねばならない」を縮めた口語的な言い方に「ねば」とか「なきゃ」という言い方がある。

（6）――とにかく<u>急がねば</u>。
　　　というのが、秀吉の最大課題であった。
　　　　　　　　　　　　　　　　　　　　　　（司馬遼太郎『新史太閤記』）（下線筆者）
（7）――おつぎちゃんに<u>会わなきゃ</u>……。
　　　と思いながら千吉は歩き出し、足音をしのばせて店の前を通りすぎると三丁目にむかった。　　　　　　　　　　（藤沢周平『本所しぐれ町物語』）（下線筆者）

次の例に見られるように、一見すると、「ねば」、「なきゃ」はそれぞれ、「ねばならない」、「なきゃいけない」と意味は変わらないかのように見える。

（8）a.　急が<u>ねばならない</u>。
　　 b.　急が<u>ねば</u>。
（9）a.　おつぎちゃんに会わ<u>なきゃならない</u>。
　　 b.　おつぎちゃんに会わ<u>なきゃ</u>。

しかし、次の例から、必ずしもそうではないことが分かる。

（10）a.　毎晩この薬を飲ま<u>ねばならない</u>。
　　　b.　毎晩この薬を飲ま<u>ねば</u>。
（11）a.　学生には毎週レポートを出させ<u>ないといけない</u>。
　　　b.　学生には毎週レポートを出させ<u>ないと</u>。

これらの例で、a文の「毎晩」や「毎週」は、以前から続いている習慣としての毎晩や毎週とも、これからスタートする日課としての毎晩や毎週とも解釈できるが、b文の「毎晩」や「毎週」は後者の意味での毎晩や毎週としか解釈できない。この観察が正しいことは、次の例で、b文が非文であることからも裏付けられる。

（12）a.　このところ毎晩この薬を飲ま<u>ねばならない</u>。
　　　b.　*このところ毎晩この薬を飲ま<u>ねば</u>。
（13）a.　去年からずっと学生には毎週レポートを出させ<u>ないといけない</u>。
　　　b.　*去年からずっと学生には毎週レポートを出させ<u>ないと</u>。

　こうした「ねばならない」と「ねば」の意味的な違いは、have to と have got to のそれと平行する面があることは極めて興味深い。have got to と have to の違いについて

さらに考察してみよう。

§164–165　Leech は次の例を比較している。

(1) a.　I'm surprised that your wife *should object*.
　　b.　I'm surprised that your wife *objects*.　　　　　　(Leech (2004³: 116))

これらの例においては、両方とも、「驚く」という心的経験をしたのは主文主語（＝「私」）であり、命題内容は「君の奥さんが反対していること」である。
　では、(1a)と(1b)の意味の違いとは何であろうか。Leech によれば、(1a)では「君の奥さんが反対しているという観念(idea)」そのものが、(1b)では「君の奥さんが反対しているという事実(fact)」が(私の)驚きの原因であるとする。しかし、(1b)だけでなく、(1a)においても、「奥さんが反対している」という「事実」は含意されていることに注意しなければならない。より重要なことは、"your wife objects"のように、現在時制を用いた(1b)は、聞き手の奥さんが反対していることを感情をまじえないで述べているということであろう。
　以下の例を考えてみよう。

(2) a.　It's astonishing that she *should* say that to you.　　(Swan (2005⁴: 512))
　　b.　It strikes you as odd that Ackroyd *should* have flown into a rage about so trivial a matter.
　　　　　　(A. Christie, *The Murder of Roger Ackroyd*)（イタリック筆者）
　　c.　"Why the hell *should* he stick his neck out?" Michael asked.
　　　　　　(M. Puzo, *The Godfather*)（イタリック筆者）

(2)の各文の法助動詞 should は、「感情の should ("*emotional should*")」(Jespersen (1949))、「瞑想と論争の should ("*meditative-polemic should*")」(Behre (1955))、「感情の should ("*emotive should*")」(Aijmer (1972))、「推定の should ("*putative should*")」(Quirk et al. (1985))、「想念の should ("*notional should*")」(安藤 (2005: 328)) など、さまざまな名称で呼ばれてきた。ここでは、澤田 (2006: 422ff.) に従って、「評価的 should ("*evaluative should*")」(＝「感情」)と称することにする。
　(2a)の評価的 should (＝「感情」)は、「彼女がそんなことをあなたに言うなんて」(信じ難い)というように、「彼女がそんなことをあなたに言う」という命題内容が、話し手にとって心理的・感情的に受け入れ難いことであることを表している。さらに、(2b)の評価的 should (＝「感情」)は、「アクロイドがそんなささいなことで激怒したなんてあなたにはおかしいと感じられる」というように、「アクロイドがそんなささい

なことで激怒した」という命題内容が聞き手にとって不可思議であることを表している。最後に、(2c)の評価的should(=「感情」)は、「一体なぜ彼は余計なことをして面倒を起こすんだ」というように、「彼が余計なことをして面倒を起こす」という命題内容が話し手にとって理解し難いことを表している。

評価的should(=「感情」)や評価的「なんて」(=「感情」)の現れ方を統一的に説明するために、次の意味的原則を想定してみよう(澤田(2006: 425))。

(3) 「心理的衝突の原則」(Principle of Psychological Conflict)：
評価的should(=「感情」)は、主題として取り立てられた命題内容(すなわち、事柄・状況・世界)が評価主体(すなわち、概念化主体)の想定と心理的に衝突することを表す。

評価的should(=「感情」)が用いられている場合、その命題内容は評価主体によって、受け入れがたいもの、予想しがたいもの、存在しがたいものとして捉えられている。この原則によるならば、評価的should(=「感情」)の適格性は、上位の節の感情表現によって自動的に決められているのではなく、あくまで、命題内容に対する評価主体の捉え方によって決められていることになる。

英語の評価的should(=「感情」)に対応する日本語の表現に、本章で言う評価的「なんて」(=「感情」)がある。

(4) 君の奥さんが反対している<u>なんて</u>僕には信じられない。

この例においても、「驚く」という心的経験をしたのは主文要素(=「僕」)であり、命題内容は「君の奥さんが反対していること」である。

次の例から分かるように、「なんて」と「のは」の違いは、評価主体としての話し手による命題内容の捉え方の違いを反映している。

(5) a.　太郎が反対している<u>なんて</u>{嘘だ／デマだ}。
　　 b.　*太郎が反対している<u>なんて</u>{本当だ／確かだ}。
(6) a.　*太郎が反対している<u>のは</u>{嘘だ／デマだ}。
　　 b.　太郎が反対している<u>のは</u>{本当だ／確かだ}。

筆者の語感では、「なんて」は「嘘だ／デマだ」とは共起できるが、「本当だ／確かだ」とは共起できない。一方、「のは」は「本当だ／確かだ」とは共起できるが、「嘘だ／デマだ」とは共起できない。このことは、「のは」と異なって、「なんて」の場合、その命題内容が話し手の想定と心理的に衝突するものとして捉えられていることを示唆している。

興味深いことに、(5b)は、疑問文に変えられると適格となる。

（６）　太郎が反対しているなんて{本当です／確かです}か？

このことから、「なんて」と「本当だ／確かだ」との共起可能性は、主文述語の種類からだけでは決定できないことが分かる。
　ここで、評価的 should（＝「感情」）と、下の例に見られるような should（＝「仮定法現在代用」）とを比較しておきたい。

（７）a.　Mr. McCarthy was very *anxious* that there *should* be a marriage between us.
　　　　　　　　　　　（C. Doyle, "The Boscombe Valley Mystery"）（イタリック筆者）
　　　b.　'It is very *essential*, Miss Stoner,' said he, 'that you *should* absolutely follow my advice in every respect.'
　　　　　　　　　　　（C. Doyle, "The Speckled Band"）（イタリック筆者）
　　　c.　'It is now *necessary* that we *should* try to throw some light upon this third bullet, which has clearly, from the splintering of the wood, been fired from inside the room...'　（C. Doyle, "The The Dancing Men"）（イタリック筆者）

Declerck (1991: 421)、Leech (2004[3]: 118)、Swan (2005[3]: 512)、澤田 (2006: 429–430) など多くの文献に述べられているように、should（＝仮定法現在代用）は、形式ばったイギリス英語において、提案、勧告、要求、命令などの概念（例えば、動詞 advise, command, insist, suggest など、形容詞 anxious, essential, necessary, vital など）を表す主文の従属節に現れる。アメリカ英語では、should を省き、仮定法現在形（いわゆる「命令の仮定法」(mandative subjunctive)）を用いることが多いとされる（イギリス英語でもこの傾向があるが、イギリス英語ではさらに直説法も用いられる傾向があるという）。
　一方、Leech も注意しているように、should（＝「仮定法現在代用」）と異なって、評価的 should（＝「感情」）の場合には、その従属節の中において、通例、should を省いてその代わりに仮定法現在形を用いることはできない (Leech (2004[3]: 117)、安藤 (2005: 329)、澤田 (2006: 430))。この点はこれら２種類の should を区別するための重要な基準の１つである。

（８）　It's surprising that she {*should say/says/said/* *say} that sort of thing to you.
　　　　　　　　　　　　　　　　　　　　　　　　　　　　　　　（Swan (2005[3]: 522)）
（９）　It is interesting that the play {*should be/* *be} a huge success.
　　　　　　　　　　　　　　　　　　　　　　　　　　　　　　　（Leech (2004[3]: 118)）

(8)においては、従属節の内容、すなわち、「彼女があなたにそんなことを言うこと」

は、省略された主文要素「私」によって事実であると受けとめられており、その事実に対して主文要素「私」は驚いている。また、(9)においても、「その劇が大成功であったこと」は、省略された主文要素「私」によって事実であると受けとめられており、その驚くべき事実に対して主文要素「私」は興味を引かれている。こうした状況においては仮定法現在形は用いにくいと言えよう。なぜなら、仮定法現在形とは、現時点においてはまだ存在していない状況を存在するように希求する表現形式であるからである。

最後に、評価的 should（=「感情」）の注目すべき例を2つ考えてみよう。

(10) Well, now, in considering this case there are two points about young McCarthy's narrative which struck us both instantly, although they impressed me in his favour and you against him. *One was the fact that his father should, according to his account, cry 'Cooee!' before seeing him.*
(C. Doyle, "The Boscombe Valley Mystery")（イタリック筆者）

この例では、ホームズが「マカーシーの供述によると、彼の父親は、まだ彼の姿を見ていないのに、『クーイ』という合図の叫び声をあげたという事実」を問題にしている。この場合の評価的 should（=「感情」）は "fact" という名詞の同格節の中に現れており、この名詞はそれ自体では「評価性・感情性」を持っていない。では、なぜ評価的 should（=「感情」）が現れることができるのであろうか。

これを説明するためには、話し手の認識を考慮に入れなければならない。すなわち、マカーシーの父親が、まだ彼の姿を見ていないのに、『クーイ』という合図の叫び声をあげたという「事実」に対する話し手の驚きである。したがって、問題の文は、次の文とほぼ同値である。

(11) It is strange that his father *should*, according to his account, cry 'Cooee!' before seeing him.

第2に、次の例（クリスティ『アクロイド殺人事件』第1章から）を考えてみよう。

(12) I told her firmly that her whole idea was nonsense. I was all the more firm because I secretly agreed with some part, at least, of what she had said. But *it is all wrong that Caroline should arrive at the truth simply by a kind of inspired guesswork.*　　(A. Christie, *The Murder of Roger Ackroyd*)（イタリック筆者）

主人公である医師の「私」（=シェパード）の姉、キャロラインは直感の鋭い女性である。彼女はファラーズ夫人が自殺したのは、夫を殺したという後悔の念からだという。「私」は断固としてそんな馬鹿な話はないと言って彼女を諫めるが、内心では、

彼女の言っていることの少なくともある部分は当たっていると思っている。斜体部では、評価的 should（＝「感情」）が用いられているが、この場合の評価主体の感情とはどのようなものであろうか。

　主節には "all wrong" という表現が用いられている。コンテクストから言って、ここでは、"all wrong" は「間違っている」とか「悪い、おかしい」といった意味に解釈することはできない。そうではなく、「驚くべきことだ」といったように、話し手の常識を超えていることを意味していると思われる。

　評価的 should（＝「感情」）はイギリス英語に多いとされるが、アメリカ英語ではどうであろうか。アメリカの小説などから例を集めてみよう。

§177　ここでは、いわゆる「仮定法過去形」(subjunctive past) の法助動詞 could, might, would が論じられている。以下、仮定法の概念について見ておきたい。Quirk et al. (1985: 155–158) によれば、仮定法は以下の 3 タイプに限られている。

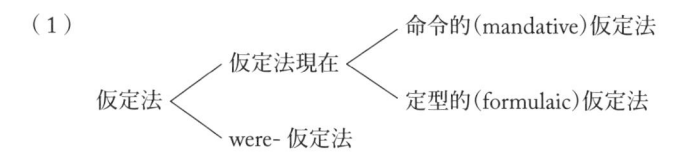

（1）
```
                            ┌─ 命令的(mandative)仮定法
              ┌─ 仮定法現在 ─┤
  仮定法 ─────┤              └─ 定型的(formulaic)仮定法
              └─ were-仮定法
```

この分類によれば、真の意味での「仮定法過去形」は仮定法専用 were に限られる。Quirk et al. (1985) が挙げる「we 仮定法」の例は、以下のようなものである。

　（2）a.　If I *were* rich, I would buy you anything you wanted.
　　　b.　Tim always speaks quietly on the phone, as though he *were* telling a secret.
　　　c.　I wish the journey *were* over.

　Quirk et al. (1985: 1010–1012) は、(were 仮定法を除く) いわゆる「仮定法過去」、「仮定法過去完了」について、それぞれ、「仮想的過去」(hypothetical past)、「仮想的過去完了」(hypothetical past perfect) と称し、Declerck (1991:355ff.) は、それぞれ、「法的過去」(modal past)、「法的過去完了」(modal past perfect) と称している。また、Huddleston and Pullum (2002: 1002–1004) も「仮定法過去」ではなく、「法的過去」(modal preterite) という用語を用いている。こうした考え方によるならば、いわゆる「仮定法過去」、「仮定法過去完了」は、直説法の過去、過去完了が (時間的にではなく)「心理的に」用いられた用法であることになる。ここでは、「仮想的過去」、「仮想的過去完了」という用語を採用することにする。

　以下、(3)、(4)は、それぞれ、仮想的過去、仮想的過去完了の例である。ここでは、

一括して「仮想構文」(hypothetical constructions)と称することにする。

(3) a. If she {*tried*/*were to try*} harder next time, she would pass the examination.
 b. I wish this bus *went* to the university.
 c. He acts as if he *knew* you.
 d. Suppose we *told* her the truth.
 e. Imagine your child *played* truant.
 f. I'd rather we *had* dinner now.
 g. It's time you *were* in bed.

(4) a. If they *had asked* me, I would have had to speak.
 b. I might have married her if she *would have* agreed.
 c. If only I had *listened* to my parents! (Quirk et al. (1985: 1011))

(3)の仮想的過去文の場合には、現在または未来の事柄に言及しており、問題の動詞の形は過去形が用いられている。一方、(4)の仮想的過去完了文の場合には、過去の事柄に言及しており、問題の動詞の形は過去完了形が用いられている。

仮想構文の概念構造を明確にするために、次のように想定してみよう。

(5) 仮想構文の本質は仮想条件文であり、その基本的概念構造は前件(antecedent)(= E_1)と後件(consequent)(= E_2)から成り立っている(「E_1 だったら、E_2 なのに(なあ)」)。ただし、表面上、前件(= E_1)だけから成り立っているものもあれば、後件(= E_2)だけから成り立っているものもある。前件(= E_1)は仮想的過去形もしくは仮想的過去完了形で、後件(= E_2)は仮想標識 would に導かれることを基本とする。

この想定に基づいて、仮想構文を次のタイプに分類してみよう。

(6) (i) 前件(= E_1)と後件(= E_2)から成り立っている(=両件型)
 ((16a), (17a), (18a)–(18b))
(ii) 前件(= E_1)だけから成り立っている(=前件型)
 ((16b), (16c), (17b)–(17g), (18c))
(iii) (表面上)後件(= E_2)だけから成り立っている(=後件型)

前件型に関して言えば、概念構造から考えて、(16b)の as though は as if に等しく、(16c)の I wish は If only に等しい。又、(17d)の Suppose と(17e)の Imagine は If に等しく、(17f)の I'd rather と(17g)の It's time は I wish (= If only)に等しい。

さらに、「後件型」は次のような例(ドイル「赤毛連盟」から)である。

（7）　I could tell you tales of cobbler *which would disgust you with human nature.*
(C. Doyle, "The Red-Headed league")（イタリック筆者）

この例では、(赤毛連盟の事務所の男が、応募してきたウィルソン氏の赤毛を力いっぱい引っ張った後で)「あなたに靴クリームの話をしてあげることもできるが、その話を聞いたらきっとあなたは人間の性(さが)に嫌気がさすだろうよ」と述べている。この例の関係節の would の場合、前件(= E_1)が省略されている。

モダリティという点から注意すべきことは、(4a)の仮想条件文における主節 "I would have had to speak"（=「話さざるをえなかっただろう」）においては仮想標識 would が用いられ、(4b)の仮想的条件文における主節 "I might have married her"（=「彼女と結婚したかもしれないのに」）においては、仮想標識 would ではなく、仮想的な認識的 might が用いられていること、さらには、(4b) の if 節 "if she would have agreed"（=「仮に彼女が同意してくれていたら」）の would have は、概念的には、will（=「意志」）の仮想的過去完了の形式に相当するということである。

(4b) の if 節の would と関連して、次のような制約を立ててみよう。

（8）　前件(= E_1)の中に現れる would は仮想標識の would ではなく、力動的 would（=「意志」）である。

この制約によるならば、以下のような「前件(= E_1)型」の仮想構文の would（= イタリック）は統一的に力動的 would（=「意志」）と解釈することができる。

（9）a.　I wish it *would* stop raining.　　　　　　　(Swan (2005³: 619))
　　b.　If only it *would* stop raining, we could go out.　(Swan (2005³: 241))
　　c.　If you *would* reserve seats, we would be sure of a comfortable journey.
(Graver (1986³: 96–97))

一方、仮想構文の後件(= E_2)には基本的に仮想標識 would が含まれていると想定する。この仮想標識 would の意味は「客観的」であり、その機能を次のように捉えておきたい。

（10）　仮想標識 WOULD の意味的機能：
　　　仮想標識 WOULD（=「〜のに」）は、仮想条件文において、前件の事柄(= E_1)が成立すれば、後件の事柄(= E_2)も必然的に成立することを示す（逆に、E_1 が成立しなければ、E_2 も成立することはない）。

仮想条件文で表わされた仮想世界の事柄は、(11)のように図示される（S =話し手）。

(11)　if　$\boxed{E_1}$　　$\boxed{E_2}$　　仮想世界(hypothetical world)
　　　　　　　↑　　　↑　**would**
　　　　　　　｜　　／
　　……………｜…／………………………………………………………
　　　　　　　｜／　　　　　　　　現実世界(real world)
　　　　　　　Ｓ

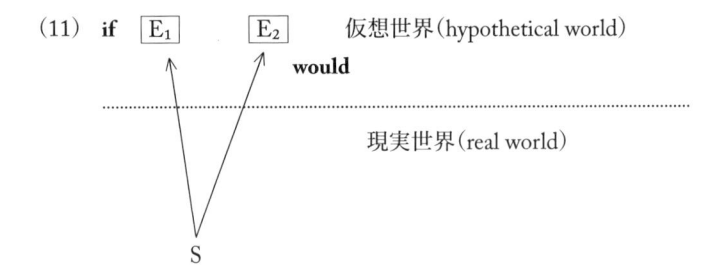

　仮想条件文(ひいては、仮想構文)の基本的な概念構造とは、以下のようなものであると想定してみよう。

　　(12)　仮想条件文の基本的な概念構造
　　　　　　[If E₁], [... (EM) [WOULD[E₂]]...]
　　　　　　　　↑　　　　　　↑
　　　　　　　　前件　　　　　帰結

　この場合、**E** と **EM** は、それぞれ、事柄と認識的モダリティの標識を示し、**EM** は随意的である。ゼロ (= φ) の場合、その事柄 (= **E₂**) は 100％実現することになる。また、**EM** と仮想標識 would は、それぞれ、主観的、客観的な意味を有している。また、この場合、前件の事柄(= **E₁**)の表示には時制の後転移が適用される。

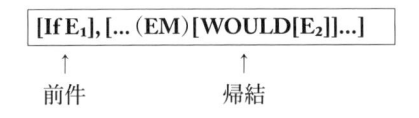

　この概念構造に基づいて、Leech (2004³: 126) の挙げる次の 3 つの例の法助動詞の意味を分析してみよう。

　　(13)　If you got a job in Sydney, you could come to see us more often.
　　　　　(= 'it would be possible for...')
　　(14)　If Holmes were playing, Scotland might win.
　　　　　(= '...it's possible that Scotland would win.')
　　(15)　If you were a real friend, you'd do anything I asked.
　　　　　(= '...you would be willing to...')

　はじめに、(13)の could の場合、その基本的な概念構造は次のようなものであり、

　　(16)　[**If E₁** (= you got a job in Sydney)], [φ [WOULD [**E₂** (= you CAN come to see us more often)]]].

　その概念は以下のように表示される。

(17) (i) [**If** you got a job in Sydney], [you could come to see us more often].
　　　　(**WOULD [CAN] = COULD**（＝できるのに）)
　　(ii) [**If** you got a job in Sydney], [it **would be possible** for you to come to see us more often].
　　(iii) [**If** you got a job in Sydney], [you **would be able** to come to see us more often].

　上の(13)の could は「シドニーで仕事があれば、あなたはもっと私のところに遊びに来ることができるのに」と、力動的モダリティ(＝可能・能力)を仮想世界に位置づけている。このモダリティは客観的である。
　次に、上の(14)の might の場合、その基本的な概念構造は次のようなものであり、

(18)　[**If E₁**（＝ Holmes were playing)], [**MAY** [**WOULD** [**E₂**（＝ Scotland win)]]]. (**MAY[WOULD] = MIGHT**（＝かもしれないのに）)

その概念は以下のように表示される。

(19) (i) [**If** Holmes were playing], [Scotland **might** win].
　　(ii) [**If** Holmes were playing], [**perhaps** Scotland **would** win].
　　(iii) [**If** Holmes were playing], [**it is possible** that Scotland **would** win].

(14)の might は「もしホームズが出場しておればスコットランドは勝つかもしれないのに」と、勝利という仮想的な事柄が生じる可能性があることを述べている。「ホームズが出場している」、「スコットランドが勝つ」という状況そのものは仮想世界の状況である。(40ii)は主観的推量であり、(40iii)は客観的可能性である。
　最後に、上の(15)の would の場合、その基本的な概念構造は次のようなものであり、

(20)　[**If E₁**（＝ you were a real friend)], [φ [**WOULD**[**E₂**（＝ you **WILL** do anything I asked)]]]. (**WOULD[WILL] = WOULD**（＝しようとしてくれるのに）)

その概念は以下のように表示される。

(21) (i) [**If** you were a real friend], [you **would** do anything I asked].
　　(ii) [**If** you were a real friend], [you **would be willing to** do anything I can asked].

(15)の would は「あなたが本当の友人だったら、私が頼むことは何でもしてくれるのに」と、客観的なモダリティ(＝意志)を仮想世界に位置づけている。

　英語の仮想構文において、どのような法助動詞が現れるのかと調べてみよう。例えば、must はこの構文には現れないが、それはなぜであろうか。

参考文献

Aijmer, K. (1972) *Some Aspects of Psychological Predicates in English.* Stockholm: Almqvist & Wiksell.

安藤貞雄(1969)『英語語法研究』研究社.

安藤貞雄(1983)『英語教師の文法研究』大修館書店.

安藤貞雄(1986)『英語の論理・日本語の論理』大修館書店.

安藤貞雄(2005)『現代英文法講義』開拓社.

Austin, J.L. (1962) *How to Do Things with Words.* Oxford: Oxford University Press. (坂本百大(訳) (1978)『言語と行為』大修館書店.)

Battistella, E. (1987) Some Remarks on *Have*-Raising vs. *Have*-Support. *Lingua* 72: pp. 211–224.

Behre, F. (1955) *Meditative-Polemic* Should *in Modern English That-Clauses.* Stockholm: Almqvist & Wiksell.

Binnick, R.I. (1972) *Will* and *Be Going To* II. *CLS* 8, pp. 3–9.

Boyd, J. and J.P.Thorne (1969) The Semantics of Modal Verbs. *Journal of Linguistics* 5: pp. 57–74.

Brennan, V.M. (1993) Root and Epistemic Modal Auxiliary Verbs. Ph.D. Dissertation, University of Massachusetts.

Chalker, S. (1984) *Current English Grammar.* London: Macmillan.

Close, R.A. (1980) Will in *If*-Clauses. In Greenbaum et al. (eds.) *Studies in English Linguistics for Randolph Quirk.* London: Longman.

Coates, J. (1983) *The Semantics of the Modal Auxiliaries.* Croom Helm.

Costa, R. (1972) Sequences of Tenses in *That*-clause. *CLS* 8: pp. 41–51.

Dancygier, B. (1998) *Conditionals and Prediction.* Cambridge: Cambridge University Press.

Dancygier, B. and E. Sweetser (2005) *Mental Spaces in Grammar: Conditonal Constructions.* Cambridge: Cambridge University Press.

Davidsen-Nielsen, N. (1990) *Tense and Mood in English: A Comparison with Danish.* Berlin: Mouton de Gruyter.

Declerck, R. (1991) *A Comprehensive Descriptive Grammar of English.* Kaitakusha. (安井稔(訳) (1994)『現代英文法総論』開拓社.)

Declerck, R. and S.Reed (2001) *Conditionals:A Comprehensive Empirical Analysis.* Berlin: Mouton de Gruyter.

Graver, B. D. (1986³) *Advanced English Practice*. Oxford: Oxford University Press.
Haegeman, L. (1989) Be going to and will: A Pragmatic Account. *Journal of Linguistics* 25: pp. 291–317.
Haegeman, L. and H. Wekker. (1984) The Syntax and Interpretation of Futurate Conditonals in English. *Journal of Linguistics* 20: pp. 45–55.
Halliday, M. (1970) Functional Diversity in Language as Seen from a Consideration of Madality and Mood in English. *Foundations of Language* 6: pp. 322–361.
Hornby, A.S. (1956) *A Guide to Patterns & Usage in English*. Tokyo: Kenkyusha.
Hornstein, N. (1990) *As Time Goes By*. Cambridge, MA.: The MIT Press.
Jacobsson, B. (1979) Modality and the Modals of Necessity MUST and HAVE TO. *English Studies* 60: pp. 296-312.
Jenkins, L. (1972) Modality in English Syntax. Ph. D. Dissertation, MIT.
Jespersen, O. (1949) *A Modern English Grammar* (Part IV). London: Geroge Allen & Unwin Ltd.
Johannesson, N.-L. (1976) T*he English Modal Auxiliaries: A Stratificational Account*. Stockholm: Almqvist & Wilsell International.
柏野健次(2002)『英語助動詞の語法』研究社.
金田一春彦 (1976)「国語動詞の一文類」金田一春彦(編)『日本語動詞のアスペクト』pp. 5–26. 麦書房.
Kiparsky, P. and C. Kiparsky (1970) Fact. In Bierwisch, M. and K.E.Heidolph. (eds.) *Progress in Linguistics*. The Hague: Mouton.
吉良文孝(2010)「未来表現」澤田治美・高見健一(編)『ことばの意味と使用』pp. 161–173. 鳳書房.
国広哲弥(1971)「『意味と英語動詞』(G.N. リーチ著)訳注」大修館書店.
Lakoff, R. (1972) The Pragmatics of Modality. *CLS* 8: pp. 229–246.
Langacker, R.W. (1991) *Foundations of Cognitive Grammar*. Vol.II. Descriptive Application. Stanford, Cal.: Stanford University Press.
LeSourd, P. (1976) Got Insertion. *Linguistic Inquiry* 7: pp. 509–516.
Lyons, J. (1977) *Semantics* II. Cambridge: Cambridge University Press.
McCawley, J.D. (1971) Tense and Time reference in English. In Fillmore, C.J. and D.T. Langendoen (eds.) *Studies in Liguistic Semantics*. New York: Holt, Rinehart &Winston.
McCoard, R. W. (1978) *The English Perfect: Tense-Choice and Pragmatic Inferfences*. Amsterdam: North-Hplland Publishing Company.
Mittwoch, A. (1988) Aspects of English Aspects: On the Interaction of Perfect, Progressive and Durational Phrases. *Linguistics and Philosophy* 11: pp. 203–254.
Murphy, R. (2000²) *Grammar in Use Intermediate*. Cambridge: Cambridge University Press.
長友俊一郎(2010)「条件文」澤田治美・高見健一(編)『ことばの意味と使用』pp. 58–

68. 鳳書房.
中村愛理 (2010)「現在完了形」澤田治美・高見健一 (編)『ことばの意味と使用』pp. 138–148. 鳳書房.
中野弘三 (1993)『英語法助動詞の意味論』英潮社.
Palmer, F.R. (1987²) *The English Verb*. London: Longman.
Palmer, F.R. (1990²) *Modality and the English Modals*. London: Longman.
Palmer, F.R. (2001²) *Mood and Modality*. Cambridge: Cambridge University Press.
Palmer, F.R. (2003) Modality in English: Theoretical, Descriptive and Typological Issues. In R. Facchinetti, M. Krug, and F. Palmer, (eds.) *Modality in Contemporary English*. Berlin: Mouton de Gruyter.
Poutsma, H. (1928) *A Grammar of Late Modern English* (Part 1). Groningen: P. Noordhoff.
Quirk, R., S. Greenbaum, G. Leech, and J. Svartvik (1985) *A Comprehensive Grammar of the English Language*. London: Longman.
Rivière, C. (1981) *Is Should* a Weaker *Must? Journal of Linguistics* 17: pp. 179–195.
Reichenbach, H. (1947) *Elements of Symbolic Logic*. New York: The Macmillan Company.
Salkie, R. (1989) Perfect and Pluperfect: What is the Relationship? *Journal of Linguistics* 25: pp. 1–34.
佐藤健児 (2010)「「自然の成り行き」を表す will be -ing 構文の意味論」『英語語法文法研究』17: pp. 83–98.
澤田治美 (1990)「認識的法助動詞の命題内容条件」国広哲弥教授還暦退官記念論文集編集委員会 (編)『文法と意味の間―国広哲弥教授還暦退官記念論文集』pp. 205–217. くろしお出版.
澤田治美 (1992)「アスペクトから見た時点副詞類の意味と文法」(上／下)『英語青年』138 (1–2): pp. 14–16, 63–65.
澤田治美 (1993)『視点と主観性―日英語助動詞の分析』ひつじ書房.
澤田治美 (1993)「心的態度を表す法助動詞」『言語』22 (10) (1993 年 10 月号): pp. 50–57.
澤田治美 (2001)「認識のパタンと法助動詞の意味解釈 (上／下)」『英語青年』147 (3–4): pp. 185–189, 225–229.
澤田治美 (2006)『モダリティ』開拓社.
澤田治美・高見健一 (編) (2010)『ことばの意味と使用』鳳書房.
澤田治美 (編) (2010)『ひつじ意味論講座１―語・文と文法カテゴリーの意味』ひつじ書房.
Searle, J.R. (1969) *Speech Acts*. Cambridge: Cambridge University Press. (坂本百大・土屋俊 (訳) (1986)『言語行為』勁草書房.)
Searle, J.R. (1979) *Expression and Meaning*. Cambridge: Cambridge University Press. (山田友幸 (訳) (2006)『表現と意味』誠信書房.)
Swan, M. (2005³) *Practical English Usage*. Oxford: Oxford University Press.

Sweetser, E. (1990) *From Etymology to Pragmatics*. Cambridge: Cambridge University Press. (澤田治美(訳)(2000)『認知意味論の展開』東京:研究社出版).

高司正夫(1994)「進行形文の発話行為行為―解説の視点から」『英語青年』139(10)(1994年1月号):p.18.

Thomson, A.J. and A.V.Martinet. (1986[4]) *A Practical English Grammar*. Oxford: Oxford University Press. (江川泰一郎(訳注)(1988)『実例英文法』オックスフォード大学出版局.)

Tottie, G. (1985) The Negation of Epistemic Necessity in Present-day British and American English." *English World-Wide* 6(1): pp. 87–116.

Tregidgo, P.S. (1982) MUST and MAY: Demand and Permission." *Lingua* 56: pp. 75–92.

内田真弓(2010)「進行形」澤田治美・高見健一(編)『ことばの意味と使用』pp. 125–137. 鳳書房.

Vendler, Z. (1967) *Linguistics in Philosophy*. Ithaca: Cornell Univ. Press.

言語学テキスト叢書（原書テキスト編）
Hituzi's Linguistics Textbook Series

【第1巻】 Meaning and the English Verb [Third Edition]

発行	2011 年 5 月 25 日　初版 1 刷
	2023 年 3 月 10 日　　　4 刷
定価	2400 円＋税
著者	Geoffrey Leech
注釈者	澤田治美
発行者	松本功
印刷・製本所	三美印刷株式会社
発行所	株式会社 ひつじ書房
	〒 112-0011 東京都文京区千石 2-1-2 大和ビル 2F
	Tel.03-5319-4916　Fax.03-5319-4917
	郵便振替 00120-8-142852
	toiawase@hituzi.co.jp　https://www.hituzi.co.jp/

ISBN978-4-89476-562-7

造本には充分注意しておりますが、落丁・乱丁などがございましたら、
小社かお買上げ書店にておとりかえいたします。ご意見、ご感想など、
小社までお寄せ下されば幸いです。

●ファンダメンタルシリーズ●

基礎を完結に、過不足なく記述
新しい時代に対応した新しいテキスト

ファンダメンタル英語学 改訂版
中島平三著　定価 1,400 円 + 税

ファンダメンタル英語学演習
中島平三著　定価 1,600 円 + 税

ファンダメンタル英語史
児馬修著　定価 1,500 円 + 税

ファンダメンタル英文法
瀬田幸人著　定価 1,600 円 + 税

ファンダメンタル音声学
今井邦彦著　定価 2,400 円 + 税

ファンダメンタル認知言語学
野村益寛著　定価 1,600 円 + 税

●言語学翻訳叢書●

話し言葉の談話分析

デボラ・カメロン著
林宅男監訳
定価 3,200 円＋税

ことばの裏に隠れているもの
子どもがメタファー・アイロニーに目覚めるとき

エレン・ウィナー著
津田塾大学言語文化研究所読解研究グループ訳
定価 3,200 円＋税

認知と社会の語用論
統合的アプローチを求めて

ジェフ・ヴァーシューレン著　東森勲監訳
五十嵐海理、春木茂宏、大村吉弘、塩田英子、飯田由幸訳
定価 3,500 円＋税

文化と会話スタイル
多文化社会・オーストラリアに見る異文化間コミュニケーション

ヘレン・フィッツジェラルド著　村田泰美監訳
重光由加、大谷麻美、大塚容子訳
定価 2,800 円＋税

●ひつじ意味論講座●

澤田治美編　定価 各3,200円＋税

言語研究において「意味」の解明は究極的な目的の1つである。言語がどのような意味を持つのか、意味はどのように実現されるか、意味はどのようなコミュニケーションをもたらすのか、その発話はどのような事態を呼び起こすのか、その発話は相手にどのような効果を与えるのか、ということは、言語研究の最も重要なテーマである、と言えるだろう。本講座は、言語学の著名な研究者から中堅・若手の研究者までを総結集するとともに、関連分野の研究をも鳥瞰し、21世紀の来たるべき意味研究を提案するものである。本講座が、言語研究を公開するともに、新しい意味論の誕生を促すひとつのきっかけになることができれば幸いである。

第1巻　語・文と文法カテゴリーの意味
国広哲弥／松本曜／阿部泰明／今仁生美／須田義治／鷲尾龍一／菅井三実／影山太郎／久島茂／西山佑司／神崎高明／樋口昌幸

第2巻　構文と意味
山梨正明／大堀壽夫・遠藤智子／加賀信広／高見健一／小野尚之／藤井聖子／澤田治／奥野忠徳／岸本秀樹／吉村公宏／三原健一／李在鎬

第3巻　モダリティⅠ：理論と方法
ナロック・ハイコ／飯田隆／堀江薫／仁田義雄／益岡隆志／安達太郎／近藤泰弘／高山善行／澤田治美／安藤貞雄／和佐敦子／阿部宏／宮下博幸

第4巻　モダリティⅡ：事例研究
柏本吉章／長友俊一郎／吉良文孝／澤田治美／黒滝真理子／宮崎和人／土岐留美江／野田春美／半藤英明／杉村泰／井上優／守屋三千代

第5巻　主観性と主体性
大庭健／澤田治美／池上嘉彦／上原聡／秋元実治／青木博史／本多啓／八木克正／澤田淳／小野正樹／森本順子／滝浦真人

第6巻　意味とコンテクスト
渡辺伸治／久保進／加藤重広／清塚邦彦／東森勲／野本和幸／澤田治美／中本敬子／野田尚史／庵功雄／冨樫純一

第7巻　意味の社会性
山口節郎／亘明志／児玉徳美／堀井令以知／リリアン テルミ ハタノ／クレア・マリィ／影浦峡／北山修／野呂幾久子／堀田秀吾／名嶋義直／東海林祐子／森山卓郎